BEYOND THE NEOLIBERAL CREATIVE CITY

Critique and Alternatives in the Urban Cultural Economy

Robert G. Hollands

BRISTOL
UNIVERSITY
PRESS

First published in Great Britain in 2023 by

Bristol University Press
University of Bristol
1–9 Old Park Hill
Bristol
BS2 8BB
UK
t: +44 (0)117 374 6645
e: bup-info@bristol.ac.uk

Details of international sales and distribution partners are available at bristoluniversitypress.co.uk

© Bristol University Press 2023

British Library Cataloguing in Publication Data
A catalogue record for this book is available from the British Library

ISBN 978-1-5292-3312-4 hardcover
ISBN 978-1-5292-3314-8 ePub
ISBN 978-1-5292-3315-5 ePdf

Cover design: Andrew Corbett
Front cover image: Jose Tlaxcaltecatl / Mi Casa No Es Su Casa
https://www.facebook.com/MiCasaResiste/
Bristol University Press uses environmentally responsible print partners.
Printed and bound in Great Britain by CPI Group (UK) Ltd, Croydon, CR0 4YY

FSC
www.fsc.org
MIX
Paper | Supporting
responsible forestry
FSC® C013604

I would like to dedicate this book to my wife Carole's 'creative present' and my grandson Arlo's 'urban future'.

Contents

List of Figures, Tables and Case Studies

Figures

Tables

Case Studies

About the Author

Robert G. Hollands is Emeritus Professor of Sociology at Newcastle University. He has also been Visiting Professor in Sociology at the University of Auckland, New Zealand and the Institute of Political Economy, Carleton University, Ottawa, Canada. A former graduate of Queen's University, Kingston, Canada (BA-BPHE 1979; MA, 1982), he conducted his PhD at the Centre for Contemporary Cultural Studies, University of Birmingham, UK (1988). In addition to making a major contribution to youth studies (youth transitions and youth cultures), his academic interests include urban sociology, nightlife studies, alternative cultures, smart cities and the egalitarian arts. His book publications include: (with Hart Cantelon, eds) *Leisure, Sport and Working Class Cultures: Theory and History* (1988); *The Long Transition: Class, Culture and Youth Training* (1990); *Friday Night, Saturday Night: Youth Cultural Identification in the Post-Industrial City* (1995); and (with Paul Chatterton) *Changing our Toon: Youth, Nightlife and Urban Change in Newcastle* (2001) and *Urban Nightscapes: Youth Cultures, Pleasure Spaces and Corporate Power* (2003). He has also written over 50 journal articles and book chapters and presented at over 80 conferences in 45 cities and 18 countries around the world.

Preface

At the core of this book is the idea of struggle. Struggle in the sense of 'to contend' or 'fight to achieve something', as well as 'to proceed with some difficulty'. The need to challenge and move beyond the neoliberal creative city requires critique, resistance and the elusive search for alternatives. This involves contesting dominant ideas, using your imagination and struggling for answers.

In the first instance the actual process of finishing this book has been a struggle. Although the bulk of it was written over the last two years, during which time I suffered a heart attack, it has really been 'in the making' since I started teaching urban sociology at Newcastle University over 30 years ago. It also represents a long-standing conundrum for me. I believe that a society based on democratic and egalitarian forms of culture and creativity would produce a far better world than the current one based on greed, commodification and inequality. Yet dominant ideas about creative cities and developing the urban cultural economy in contemporary capitalism seem to be as much as part of the problem as the solution. How one squares a vision of an alternative urban future which brings together culture and creativity with concerns of social justice and sustainability is a giant struggle to say the least! This dilemma is at the heart of what this monograph is all about.

The notion of struggle also makes its mark in other senses in this book. For example, it represents a contested debate within the social sciences as to the value of neoliberalism as an explanatory tool of analyses. Some commentators have suggested the term is too diffuse to have much meaning. Others argue that it is mainly an ideological term of derision. Still others contest its explanatory power in understanding the world around us. This book contends that neoliberalism, understood as 'state-facilitated market rule' (Peck and Theodore, 2019: 245), and as a class project to reshape the world (Harvey, 2007), is indeed a powerful analytical tool especially when applied to cities today. It also provides a coherent explanation as to why the most 'successful' capitalist cities in terms of creativity are also paradoxically the ones characterized by the greatest inequality and social polarization.

Struggling to move beyond the limits of the neoliberal city is also apparent in the book through its concern with resistance and contestation. It is also inherent in the need to discover viable alternatives to the dominant creative city paradigm. This is the case despite a realization that there are limits to artist-led urban cultural movements, 'anti-tourist' struggles and attempts to create alternative nightlife forms. Not to mention the failure of many of these interventions to connect with other urban social movements or wider social and political transformations. However, there are many different forms of opposition to the neoliberal creative city and existing examples of alternative practice to learn from. The COVID-19 pandemic has also called into question how well our culture-based cities are able to meet basic foundational needs like health, security and well-being.

My own struggle to think about and address some of these worldly issues has not been a solitary one. Three reviewers and Emily Watt and Anna Richardson from Bristol University Press (BUP) were incredibly supportive in helping me bring my ideas to fruition. Early on BUP asked if the book was too tied to the Global North both intellectually and content-wise. My response is that the origins of the creative city idea are located in North America and Europe and the bulk of the research on it has been conducted in the West. At the same time, I would argue that the dominant neoliberal creative city paradigm has affected many cities globally, including those in Asia, Africa and Latin America. Where the research sources allow and borrowing on other's studies, I also show how this paradigm has spread to the Global South albeit in different ways and through varied contexts. In doing so, I have learned a lot and overall this thinking process has made this a much stronger book.

I am also grateful to a number of funding bodies that have supported me over the years. In terms of projects relating to this book, first and foremost is the Leverhulme Trust. They provided me with a Major Research Fellowship in 2015–2017 to conduct a project on alternative creative spaces and urban cultural movements, which form parts of Chapters 3 and 4. Thanks to all the alternative creative workers around the globe that I spoke to during this research for their various insights and knowledge. Prior to this, I received Economic and Social Research Council (ESRC) funding for a project on the transformative arts in 2008–2009, which was tremendously productive and the ESRC also funded numerous projects of mine on nightlife in the early and late 1990s which I refer to in this book. Thanks also to all the organizations and individuals who graciously granted permission to reproduce their images in this book, including Jose Tlaxcaltecatl and the activist arts group Mi Casa No Es Su Casa for providing the book cover image.

In terms of thanking individuals who have contributed intellectually to this project, at a general level I have been inspired over the years by the work of David Harvey, Manuel Castells, Margit Mayer and Jamie Peck in particular. At a more personal level I am heavily indebted to both John Vail and Paul Chatterton, whom I have had the pleasure and privilege of working alongside in terms of conducting research and writing. They have both taught me a great deal, not just about ideas but about politics as well. The 'Timber Club' (PHE 79) at Queen's University, Canada, helped me at the start my personal and intellectual journey and are still 'buddies for life' 47 years later. I would like to specifically thank two leading scholars of the creative and cultural economy, Justin O'Connor and Mark Banks, for their own inspiring work and for providing encouragement and constructive comments on the project. In addition, thanks goes to a number of other academics who contributed much to my thinking over the years, including Phil Cohen, Rick Gruneau, Hart Cantelon, Rob Beamish, Will Straw, Anoop Nayak, Richard Collier, Rob Shaw, Andy Pike, Oli Mould, Marie-Avril Berthet and Michaela Pixová. Long-time academic colleagues and friends, Rob MacDonald and Vernon Gayle, deserve a special mention for reading and commenting on various draft chapters of the book. Friends Ian and Liz McSally, Hannah Buchanan-Smith and Jim and Errie Sykes also listened to my periodic ramblings on this topic and provided encouragement. Thanks to Lee Mason for numerous conversations about the creative industries, especially film and media, over the years. The 'Heaton gang', Susie Robertson, Gary Main, Cath Ross and Carole Robinson, also provided support and I was inspired by the intellectual curiosity of my dear friend John 'Mac' McEvoy who passed away suddenly in 2021. Newcastle University colleagues Tracy Shildrick, Ruth McAreavey, Janice McLaughlin and Kyle Grayson all deserve a big round of thanks for believing in me and trusting me to finish this book. The MA students on my Cities, Economies and Cultures course have also made a valuable contribution to my thinking, particularly those in the class of 2020–2021 and 2021–2022.

I would also like to thank my grandson Arlo and son Joe Carr-Hollands for regularly getting me to 'down tools' and go to the park or play with Lego. Both activities were a welcome break from writing. Last but never least, I'd like to thank my wife, Carole Wears, for living with and hearing many of these arguments made here over a 20-odd year period. In addition to her many editing suggestions and 'social event distractions', she has singlehandedly cultivated my belief in the power of culture to transform lives through her own inspirational work in producing theatre. Not only has she helped in my struggle to come to terms with the some of the issues mentioned previously, but she has also spurred me on to finish this book. Wearsy, you are not only my rock, but my sky and ocean as well.

Robert Hollands
Newcastle Upon Tyne, March 2023

Neoliberalism, Creativity and Cities

The development of the creative economy has been heralded as the saviour of the modern city. Urban centres today appear to be more pleasant and vibrant places to live, work and play. What could possibly be wrong with having a strong cultural economy, lots of arts and culture, a vibrant nightlife and a healthy tourism trade? Who doesn't want to live in a creative city? It appears counter-intuitive to argue against urban creativity. In fact, cities not progressing in this direction can be constructed as culturally deficient (Evans, 2017: 315), creatively underdeveloped (Jesus et al, 2020) or simply as 'crap' places to live (Jordison, 2003).

As the World Atlas (2022a) website, 'The World's Most Creative Cities', says: 'When creativity is allowed to blossom, the benefits can be endless. ... As a city's creative sectors grow, so too does its overall economic standing, bringing growth to a variety of industries'. Over the last couple of decades many cities and their urban authorities around the globe have been busy highlighting aspects of their cultural economy through reference to iconic buildings, arts and culture, tourism and nightlife. They have also been jockeying for position in the creativity stakes. As O'Connor (2022: 78) puts it: 'Culture's high-touch, high-care, jobs rich nature has been squeezed into an efficiency-maximising, profit driven, winner-takes-all competitive pyramid model.' It is this competitive and almost entirely positive view of urban development that is encapsulated in the idea of the 'neoliberal creative city'.

Yet underneath this creative 'rat race' lie a series of seemingly intractable urban problems such as widening inequalities, gentrification, job precarity and environmental concerns. Ironically, many of these problematic issues are directly connected to this overwhelming desire of cities to become 'creative hotspots'. The impact of COVID-19 on urban life, and the not so recent climate crisis, have also raised serious questions about how well market economies based on culture and consumption meet basic societal needs in areas like health, welfare, community solidarity, well-being and environmental sustainability.

After decades of enacting urban regeneration strategies based around the cultural economy have the shortcomings of this model finally been exposed (Whiting et al, 2022)? As Oakley and Ward (2018: 15) argue, 'there is no inherently beneficial relationship between culturally led developments and wider social benefits, simply prescribing "more culture" is not an answer'. Even one of the architects of the modern creative city movement, Richard Florida, has recently questioned its viability and has been quoted as saying: 'I found myself confronting the dark side of our urban revival that I had once championed and celebrated' (quoted in Wainwright, 2017; also see Malanga, 2004).

The increasing central role culture plays in cities has generated a significant amount of attention over the last few decades including analyses of the cultural economy and creative industries (see Scott, 2000; Amin and Thrift, 2007; Kong and O'Connor, 2009; Pratt and Jeffcut, 2009; Hesmondhalgh and Baker, 2013; Oakley and O'Connor, 2015; Hutton, 2016; Hesmondhalgh, 2019, among many others). There has been significant discussion on the relative merits (Florida, 2004; 2005; 2014) and shortcomings of the 'dominant' creative city paradigm (see Peck, 2005; Evans, 2009; McGuigan, 2009; Krätke, 2010; Pratt, 2011; Scott, 2014; Mould, 2015; 2018; McRobbie, 2016; Dorling, 2017; Luger, 2017; and Jesus et al, 2020 for starters). And, there has also been some academic coverage of opposition towards creative city policies (for example, NiON, 2010; Kirchberg and Kagan, 2013; Novy and Colomb, 2013; Valli, 2015; Boren and Young, 2017; Serafini et al, 2018; Hollands, 2019). There has, however, been less sustained analysis of the specific relationship between art, culture and neoliberalism (though see Miles, 2015; McGuigan, 2016; Sachs Olsen, 2019; Cudny et al, 2020), and even fewer discussions about how an alternative cultural economy might contribute to a more just and sustainable urban future (though see Banks, 2017a; Oakley and Banks, 2020; O'Connor, 2022).

This book seeks to address this imbalance by focusing on the concept of neoliberalism, particularly how it relates to explaining the limits of the creative city idea and why we need to move beyond it. I define the neoliberal creativity city as *the state-facilitated marketization of creativity and the development of a competitive place-based urban cultural economy*. In terms of critique, I explain the emergence of the capitalist cultural economy through the rise of urban entrepreneurialism (Chapter 2). I also examine the central role creativity plays in reinforcing and adding to social divisions and exclusions in the city (Chapter 7). At the same time the book looks at examples of resistance towards the creative city idea (Chapter 4 and throughout) and explores 'real time' alternatives. Critique and alternatives are explored by looking across different fields within the urban cultural economy like arts and culture (Chapter 3), nightlife (Chapter 5) and tourism (Chapter 6).[1] Each of these fields has been heavily influenced by the state-facilitated marketization and commodification of cities generally (a process known as *neoliberal urbanization*, see Mayer, 2013), yet all retain possibilities of contributing to an alternative urban reality beyond the neoliberal creative city (Chapter 8).

The core argument of the book is not so much 'against creativity' or 'anti' culture. Rather it is about how these concepts have been hijacked within contemporary capitalism (Miles, 2015; Mould, 2018; O'Connor, 2022). It asserts that neoliberal urbanization in general is beset by a series of problems and contradictions that are replicated in the 'dominant creative city paradigm' (Florida, 2004; 2014). While aware of Global North and South differences, as well as national and local variations (Evans, 2017), the neoliberal creative city is characterized generally by *urban image-building, global rankings and attracting the creative class*. There is also a strong emphasis on cultural-led regeneration projects, branded arts, entertainment districts (including nightlife) and high value tourist attractions.

It is suggested that this type of city actually devalues the creative impulses of many independent artists and cultural workers displaced by gentrification and beset by precarious work. It also excludes the working and service classes as 'non-creatives'. In addition, the neoliberal creative city is characterized by corporate property development greed and compliant urban governance, producing social polarization, declining welfare services and environmental unsustainability. Finally, the book argues that we need to explore resistance to this particular type of creative city and encourage alternative visions, practices and policies.

This opening chapter begins with some illustrative examples of cities around the world attempting to brand themselves as creative through reference to various aspects of their cultural economy. It then introduces the concept of neoliberalism and shows how it is closely related to the debate about creativity and urban cultural regeneration. This is followed by a short discussion of the limits of the neoliberal city generally before introducing the book's main themes and chapter contents. It concludes by arguing there is a case for moving beyond the existing neoliberal creative city and considering the possibility of a different urban future.

'Who's your city?': image-building and creative ranking

One of the key features of neoliberal urbanization is global inter-city competition and an obsession with ranking[2] and hierarchy (Smith, 2002). Cities around the world have become highly concerned with branding and marketing themselves. This is not only to lure in global capital, but also to attract creative people, skills, technology and visitors. The internet is packed full of world rankings for cities – from most entrepreneurial, to most creative, to smartest, most vibrant (coolest), and best nightlife and tourist destinations, just to mention a few areas.

Some of these ranking exercises are based on considering a range of economic, social and cultural indicators. Others come across more like popularity contests such as *Time Out*'s 'coolest neighbourhoods in the world' in 2021 (Oliver, 2021). One might expect to find widely divergent ranking lists of even the same phenomenon, which is precisely the case. The point is that many cities actively utilize such exercises to brand and promote themselves in a global competition (Anttiroiko, 2015). I want to utilize some of these recent creative and cultural economy rankings here not so much in terms of measuring their accuracy, but to help guide my choice of the examples discussed in this book. In addition to showing up some of the discrepancies inherent in this 'image-making' exercise, it is also interesting to contrast creative rankings with more socially progressive indicators such as urban liveability, mental health and happiness.

London is a useful place to start with here partly because it is at the top end of, and bridges, some of the city rankings concerned with entrepreneurialism on the one hand and creativity on the other. This general link is pursued in Chapter 2. London is world-renowned as a financial centre and a creative hub with world-class art, culture and nightlife. It is also a global tourist destination and host of mega-events like the 2012 Olympics. Not surprisingly, London recently topped the e-commerce tool company Oberlo's table as the number one city for entrepreneurial success, beating rivals like New York, San Francisco and Sydney (Gould, 2021). At the same time, it also came fourth in two separate surveys of the world's most creative cities (World Atlas, 2022a: inkifi, nd). The latter survey, which used a range of internet tools to produce its creative rating, said, 'with 204 theatres across the city, London is known for its theatre, music, and art scene and is home to 220 art galleries displaying work from some of the most famous artists in the world' (inkifi, nd). The city also housed one of the world's largest concentrations of artist studios in the world in Hackney Wick and Fish Island (Rossen, 2017).

Although not on the same scale as London, Toronto, Canada is an instructive North American creative counterpart. Representing a fifth of the entire Canadian gross domestic product (GDP), the city is home to the famous CN Tower and major league sports franchises like the Raptors (basketball), Maple Leafs (hockey) and Blue Jays (baseball). It also boasts a substantial digital media and film economy, hosting 80 film festivals. These include the acclaimed Toronto International Film Festival, as well as other more experimental festival events (see Figure 1.1). In 2017, it was 'the first Canadian city to be designated a UNESCO Creative City of Media Arts for its leadership in film, music, digital media and forms of cultural expression using technology' (Toronto Creative City, nd). It is also the adopted home

Figure 1.1: 'Brave: The Festival of Risk and Failure 2018' poster, Toronto, Canada

Source: Harbourfront Centre (reproduced with permission)

of the creative city guru Richard Florida whose work is critically discussed in more detail in Chapter 3.

In Europe, following the hosting of the 1992 Olympics, Barcelona has become a burgeoning tourist city with visitor numbers growing from 1.73 million in 1990 to 9.5 million in 2019 (López, 2021). It has also become known as a cultural city, coming only second to Paris in the creative inkifi survey mentioned previously (inkifi, nd; also see Dodd, 2004). Meanwhile former 'underground' cities like Berlin and Amsterdam have now become more mainstream cultural and tourist meccas (Peck, 2011; Novy, 2018). The rebirth of Bilbao as a cultural destination, with the building of its Guggenheim Museum, was so successful that the term the 'Bilbao effect' was coined, encouraging many other cities to seek success through investment in large flagship cultural projects (for example, Hobart's Museum of Old and New Art in Tasmania, see Booth and O'Connor, 2018).

In Scandinavia the highest-ranking creative cities in the inkifi survey are Copenhagen and Stockholm at 27th and 28th respectively (inkifi, nd), although cities like Malmo and Gothenburg are currently pushing for greater cultural recognition. Gothenburg, for instance, 'has undergone a creative resurgence in recent years' and is 'home to exciting bands, cool dance clubs, chic vinyl stores, indie hangouts, cool coffee shops, cutting-edge interior design stores, and more' (May, 2017). Meanwhile, Malmo sees itself as the most alternative creative city type in Sweden, emphasizing its independent artist-run spaces, DIY attitude and affordability (Malmo Tourism, 2018). While Nordic countries and their cities need to be considered slightly differently in terms of their adoption of neoliberal philosophy, it does not mean that that they have not been increasingly affected by this way of thinking (McGlinn, 2018; Stahl, 2022).

Even former post-socialist cities have been transformed into entertainment, cultural and tourist hubs. Prague, in the Czech Republic, drew in over nine million international visitors in 2019 thanks to its plethora of art galleries and theatres (with these two indicators ranking eighth best in the world) (inkifi, nd). The creative label has also been extended to neglected and run-down urban neighbourhoods that were formerly part of East Berlin (Novy, 2018). Friedrichshain, for example, is described as having, 'a creative, vibrant, offbeat energy' and there is even an alternative Berlin Walking Tour (Paige, 2014).

While global cities such as Paris, New York and London still dominate the creative city table rankings (with Paris ranked first and New York ranked sixth in the inkifi survey [inkifi, nd]), they now compete with the likes of many other cultural upstarts. For example, New York now vies with North American centres such as San Francisco and Los Angeles for creative honours. Paris competes culturally and tourism-wise with a host of European centres, including those already mentioned, plus the likes of Istanbul, Rome, Milan and Lisbon, among many others. In the UK, London feels the competitive heat of post-industrial cities like Manchester, Birmingham and Glasgow. For example, in 2019 Glasgow was crowned the UK's top city for culture and creativity by the European Commission based on its 'stellar galleries, fine dining and lashings of live music' (Times Travel, 2022).

Creative urban monikers are not just limited to cities located in the UK, North America or Europe. Various Australian cities have blossomed culturally. For instance, *The City of Melbourne Creative Strategy 2018–2028* document states that the city 'overflows with live music, performances, public talks, festivals and events' (City of Melbourne, 2021). The implementation of creative city policies in Asia is also well established (see Gu et al, 2020), with Luger (2019: 330) arguing that 'Singapore is one Asian city that has been especially receptive to the idea of implementing creativity'. A new cultural plan proposed in 2014 designed to transform Tokyo into a 'cultural museum' (Tamari, 2017) appears to have borne success. According to a study by Adobe, it is home to 12 times more creatives than any other Japanese city (Hough, 2019).

The creativity paradigm has even infiltrated China, albeit through a particularly complex route, which O'Connor and Gu (2020: 6) call 'an impossible conjunction'. For example, Currier (2012) has highlighted the creative branding of the former factory area District 798 in Beijing. This site of 'creative consumption' has been stimulated not only by the influx of artist studios and galleries, but also the development of trendy restaurants, cafes and nightclubs. O'Connor and Gu's (2020) work examines the relationship between real estate, commerce and culture in Shanghai through the creation of 'creative parks' within former industrial zones.

Major cities of the Global South have also championed aspects of their urban cultural economy. In Africa, Dakar, Senegal was listed as one of the top five creative cities in the world in a 2019 BBC list and is known particularly for the Museum of Black Civilizations and the World Festival of Black Arts (Johnson, 2019). Cape Town became the first African World Design Capital in 2014 (Nkula-Wenz, 2019) and it was ranked the ninth most creative city in 2017 (Wood, 2017) (see Figure 1.2).

Meanwhile, Buenos Aires is the highest-ranking Global South creative city in the inkifi (nd) world survey at number 15, while the United Nations Educational, Scientific and Cultural Organization (UNESCO) rates Mexico City as a world-renowned centre of art, highlighting its array of design

Figure 1.2: Cape Town, South Africa: World Design Capital 2014

Source: World Design Organisation website, https://wdo.org/programmes/wdc/past-cities/wdccapetown2014/ (reproduced with permission)

festivals, including the Abierto Mexicano de Diseño (Mexican Open Design), Design Week Mexico and City Mextrópoli (UNESCO Creative Cities Network, ndc). Rio de Janeiro sprang onto the world tourism map by hosting the 2016 Olympics, as well as being a renowned nightlife destination (Gois, 2018). Bogota, Colombia is seen as a new rising creative hotspot by virtue of being the Latin American city with the most foreign investment in the creative industries, pulling in a total of US$464 million between 2005 and 2015 (Trondi, 2019). While there is a debate over how the creativity paradigm is played out in different ways in cities of the Global South,[3] particularly in Latin America (Jesus et al, 2020), Africa (Nkula-Wenz, 2019) and Asia (Gu et al, 2020), it is clearly present in some form or another in many cities there.

It is not just major cities playing the creativity card or trading on their urban cultural economy to promote themselves. Smaller and lesser-known urban centres around the globe are also getting in on the culture and creativity game. The city of Perth has become the 'cultural capital' of Western Australia largely through the global reputation of its fringe festival which has grown to become the third largest in the world in less than a decade (Diss, 2016). Provincetown, Rhode Island, US, having been down near the bottom of Richard Florida's creative city league tables, has similarly engaged in a 'Creative Capital' exercise designed to transform the city and pull its 'creative underclass' up with it (Denmead, 2019). My own adopted post-industrial city of Newcastle upon Tyne has sought to reinvent itself from its manufacturing past through various regeneration projects (Flynn, 2021). This has included the development of its entertainment and nightlife (Chatterton and Hollands, 2001) and more recently culture and tourism. It was rated as the top 'arts capital of the UK' in 2006 (Taylor, 2006) and was, surprisingly, named the number one place to visit in the world in 2018 by *Rough Guides* (Edsor, 2017). The area I live adjacent to, the Ouseburn Valley, was rated the 29th 'coolest neighbourhood' by *Time Out* in 2021 (Oliver, 2021).

A discerning reader will notice that all the images of cities presented so far are entirely positive in nature. This is despite the fact that even the most successful places mentioned face a host of urban problems. Cities today represent themselves as not only centres of economic, technological and social dynamism, but also sell themselves as places of culture and creativity. What sociological explanations are there for this obsession with creative ranking? How might we best understand and conceptualize this reinvention of many former industrial and developing cities through emphasizing their urban cultural economies? To explore this, we need to look in more detail at a broader economic and political philosophy and wider global trend defined as 'neoliberalism'. In the next section I examine its links with current conceptions of creativity and the urban cultural economy.

Neoliberalism, creativity and the cultural economy

While the exact origin and definition of the term neoliberalism is highly contested (see Harvey, 2007), a recent handbook on the subject has stated:

> At a base level we can say that when we make reference to 'neoliberalism', we are generally referring to the new political, economic and social arrangements within society that emphasize market relations, re-tasking the role of the state, and individual responsibility. Most scholars tend to agree that neoliberalism is broadly defined as the extension of competitive markets into all areas of life, including the economy, politics and society. (Springer et al, 2016: ?)

One might add market intrusion into the cultural field to this list as well. Neoliberalism generally is associated with global policies of economic liberalization, including deregulation, free trade, privatization and individual freedom. It has also been linked to austerity politics, particularly following the 2008 economic crash, and reductions in government spending.[4] What distinguishes it from classic 'free market' economics, however, is the changed role of the state, both nationally and locally. The state's primary role within neoliberalism is not so much financial intervention, but rather to facilitate the primacy of 'market mechanisms, relations, discipline and ethos' (Pinson and Morel Journel, 2016: 137). Regarding this, Lorey (2006) argues that neoliberal subjectivities related to precarity, for instance, are introjected into everyday life via the state and normalized through the idea that they are somewhat 'self-chosen' by individuals (also see Lorey, 2015).

Peck and Theodore (2019: 245) refer to neoliberalism as 'an always mutating project of state-facilitated market rule'. Marxist scholar David Harvey (whom I look at in detail in Chapter 2), a long time and prominent critic of these ideas and policies, has characterized neoliberalism as representing the primacy of the capitalist market and as a class-based project (Harvey, 2007). Brown refers to it as 'an unprecedented intimacy between capital … and states' (Brown cited in Shenk, 2015).

Critics of the concept of neoliberalism have argued that it is an over-used phrase and is utilized as a 'catch-all' term to explain too many different economic, political and societal processes (Boas and Gans-Morse, 2009). Other doubters have suggested that it is used largely as a term of derision describing no one person or policy in particular (Magness, 2019). Still others, like Storper (2016) appear to argue that the evidence supporting a shift as to how capitalism operates in the contemporary period is not as strong as many users of the concept seem to suggest. Finally, some argue that it is primarily an Anglo-European concept and does not easily apply to cities of the Global South (Parnell and Robinson, 2012).[5]

In response, while aware that aspects of the term neoliberalism can become somewhat 'hyper-explanatory' (a bit like another classic sociological term like 'community') and used pejoratively, this book rejects much of the criticism that it is inherently imprecise or illusory in nature. Additionally, I am not convinced by arguments that neoliberal tendencies in cities cannot be evidenced.[6] Supporters of the term recognize that it is a multi-faceted concept (Peck and Theodore, 2019) and that one needs to be specific about its changing historical and geographical nature (Brenner and Theodore, 2002). This includes applying it to cities of the Global South. They also suggest a distinction between neoliberalism as an ideology and the application of this idea in policy and reality, a process known as 'actually existing neoliberalism' (Peck et al, 2018). I argue that one can empirically demonstrate that this concept is enacted in capitalist urban development in terms of both philosophy and policy. This book will provide a range of evidence as to the negative effects the neoliberal creative city is having on work precarity, gentrification and social polarization.

The application of neoliberal philosophies and policies to cities is known as *neoliberal urbanization*, a term Mayer (2013) characterizes as the state-facilitated marketization of cities and the commodification of most aspects of daily life and urban space. Brenner and Theodore (2002) argue that this process has occurred in stages over time and applies to many cities globally, though, as suggested, at different speeds and in variegated ways.

There are really five aspects to neoliberal urbanization that need introducing here. First, it involves intense inter-spatial competition between cities through place marketing (Anttiroiko, 2015). A second aspect is the commodification of urban life (Mayer, 2013), with an emphasis on the growing corporatization of cities. The third element of neoliberal urbanization (picked up in Chapter 2) refers to shifts in urban governance towards economic boosterism and regeneration at the expense of the traditional welfare functions of local government (Harvey, 1989a). A fourth element is a widening of social inequalities and polarization in cities (Shi and Dorling, 2020). Finally, a fifth element of neoliberal urbanization is the focus on and valorization of culture and consumption, and an emphasis on creativity (Florida, 2004; 2014). It is this final element which characterizes the neoliberal creative city in particular.

Creativity and the urban cultural economy are of course not the same thing, but both concepts are connected to neoliberalism. Both phenomena have also increasingly been viewed as remedies to the faltering post-industrial economies of the 1980s. A way to reinvent and revive cities, breathing new economic life into them. As Amin and Thrift argue with respect to this 'new' cultural economy:

> Recent years have seen a growth in interest ... in mobilizing urban
> cultural resources for economic revitalization; in making money out of

culture, consumption, and spectacle, all now assumed to be the staples of a knowledge intensive post-industrial economy. ... The urban – more precisely certain types of cities – are being imagined as emblems of a new capitalist era. (Amin and Thrift, 2007: 151)

Hutton (2016) warns that we should not see the development of the cultural economy as a complete break from the past. However, he does argue that the growth of the cultural economy from the 1980s onwards coincides with the onset of neoliberal governance characterized by deregulation in the market economy and the rollback of state provision, tendencies which have continued into this century. This latter period has also seen the rollout of the 'gig economy', zero-hours contracts and fewer benefits for workers (MacDonald and Giazitzoglu, 2019), including those employed in the cultural sector (Hutton, 2016: 22).

In a similar vein, Mould, in his book *Against Creativity* (2018), argues that the recent obsession with the idea of creativity is also closely tied into neoliberal thinking. Mould (2018: 12) says creativity 'is a distinctly neoliberal trait because it feeds the notion that the world and everything in it can be monetised'. Creativity under capitalism, he argues, 'is not creative at all because it only produces more of the same form of society; it merely replicates existing capitalist registers into ever-deeper recesses of socioeconomic life ... capitalism co-opts creativity for its own growth' (Mould, 2018: 29). This marketized notion of creativity is reflected in the UK Department of Culture, Media and Sport's (2001: 5) definition of creative industries as 'those industries which have their origin in individual creativity, skill and talent and which have a potential for wealth and job creation through the generation and exploitation of intellectual property'. This is not to say that creativity cannot take place on the margins of the economy or exist in non-commodified forms within capitalism (see Sholette's [2011] 'dark matter idea' and my discussion of alternative creative spaces [Hollands, 2019] in Chapter 3). The recent obsession with creativity, however, is closely tied with neoliberalism and our entrepreneurial age.

The exact sectors which make up the urban cultural economy are also contentious (Banks and O'Connor, 2009). Amin and Thrift (2007: 143) mention 'the arts, media, tourism, recreation and leisure'. In addition to these sectors, others have emphasized the provision of entertainment in cities as part of an urban creative brand (Hannigan, 1998). The night-time economy (Shaw, 2010), and more specifically nightlife, has become an important marker of urban vitality in the neoliberal creative city (Nofre and Eldridge, 2018). Hutton (2016: 1), meanwhile, says that recent ideas about the cultural economy are dominated by images of 'new media, digital production, cultural tourism and social media', even though he also argues that 'culture pervades every aspect of the city, including issues of identity formation, social organization, production modalities, performance and place'. Culture has always been part of city life historically. So, classic aspects of the cultural sector like galleries, theatres and exhibition spaces, which may be hundreds of years old, but run in quite different ways today, sit cheek by jowl with more contemporary forms of the creative city like new media, television and film, design, digital music, bars, clubs and nightlife (Hutton, 2016: 22). One might also add professional sports here as a significant field of urban cultural economy and neoliberal city identity (Scherer and Davidson, 2011; John and McDonald, 2020), although this is not an area this book deals with. Many of these sectors of the cultural economy have become highly profitable in business terms, not to mention being corporately influenced.

So, while there are some 'fuzzy' boundaries around defining the cultural economy precisely, it is argued here that a number of these fields can best be understood and analysed through the lens of neoliberal urbanization. At the same time, it is important not to limit our discussion of the urban cultural economy to just the arts, but also to include the broader fields of nightlife entertainment and cultural tourism. Despite relying on different sets of literature, and raising some specific problems and issues, all of the fields mentioned here are united by some common neoliberal features. They include an obsession with inter-city rankings (that is, which is the best creative, arts, nightlife or tourist city?), the marketization of cities based around these different aspects of the cultural economy and widening urban inequalities. By looking beyond the positive, almost utopian, emphasis many cities place on creativity and their cultural economies, we can begin to problematize some of these celebratory urban images.

Limits of the neoliberal city

Even though individual chapters will go into much more critical detail in each of the fields already mentioned, let us briefly introduce some of the downsides of the general neoliberal city form. For instance, concomitant with the neoliberal obsession with ranking, what happens to all those cities which do not 'make the grade' in this global spatial competition? In this model, like capitalism in general, there are a few winners and many losers. What are the consequences for former industrial localities who have not been able to utilize culture to recover from manufacturing and economic decline? And how are cities that end up at the bottom of creativity league table supposed to pull themselves up by their own 'bootstraps'? What about those places that have neither the infrastructure nor resources to develop their art and entertainment sectors, or those not in a position to attract the tourist dollar? This is the case not only for certain deindustrialized cities of the West (for the case of Detroit as an 'urban ruin' see Apel (2015) and

Case Study 1.1), but also for poorer cities of the Global South which often come lower down world creative city ranking tables.

Case Study 1.1: Detroit: from Motown to no town and back?

In the post-war period Detroit was a world-renowned centre of innovation in the car industry. Creatively, it was also the home of Motown records. However, with the decline of manufacturing the city became known as a 'rustbelt' region, experiencing high unemployment and plunging house prices. This was caused not only by post-industrialism, but also by 'White flight' out of the urban core and local government mismanagement and bankruptcy (declared in 2013). In 2015, houses in the worst-hit areas of the city were selling for US$1 (with the proviso that buyers had to pay US$2,000–3,000 a year in tax revenue). Fairly recently, Detroit was deemed the city with the lowest population share of creative city jobs in the US (Florida, 2019), having only one-third of the number of the leading city, Washington, DC. However, *Forbes* magazine ironically ranked it the 9th most creative US city, partly because of its affordability for creatives but also because of its strong organic culture (*Detroit Metro Times*, 2014). While experiencing severe urban poverty and crime, parts of the city began to fight back. Numerous community projects and communal gardens (the latter numbering some 1,400 in the city; see Adams, 2019), have sprung up to feed people and provide social solidarity.

Equally important are the negative consequences produced by even so-called 'successful' neoliberal cities. Part of the argument of this book is that the very success of places in reinventing and promoting themselves lends itself to creating several serious urban problems. One issue here is the 'serial reproduction' of cities – that is, in their quest to climb up the rankings they all adopt a similar development model and form of regeneration. For example, the rush to develop spectacular waterfront areas, bid for large-scale mega-events, develop arts and culture districts and encourage conventional tourism infrastructure tend to make all cities alike. It also eventually results in them losing any competitive advantage or unique features they may have once had. A second, and related, aspect here is that the 'over-marketing' of cities can result in the reality of daily urban life becoming divorced from the brand (Gottdiener, 2001). Some commentators have referred to this phenomenon as urban 'Disneyfication' (Zhang et al, 2021).

A final negative consequence of neoliberal cities is that they create spurious inequalities not only through the economy but also through consumption and the process of gentrification (Lees et al, 2013). These distinctions increase urban social polarization and precarity (Lorey, 2015; Slater, 2021). Widening gaps appear not just between the richest and poorest, but divisions also occur between creative workers and the service and working classes. A major study of US cities experiencing growth found that the 'rich are getting even richer than we thought and the poor are getting even poorer than we thought' (Heinrich Mora et al, 2021: 181). Divisions within the creative sector are represented by terms like the 'artistic precariat' (Bain and McLean, 2013) and the 'creative underclass' (Denmead, 2019), while service workers and the working classes are deemed 'non-creatives'.

To illustrate the effect of some of these negative processes, let us return critically to some of the 'successful' cases discussed earlier. For example, despite London's high entrepreneurial and cultural ranking it is obvious to anyone that the city experiences deep-seated urban problems. Issues include unhelpful real estate speculation, astronomical house prices and rents, a dearth of social housing and extensive gentrification. So much so that a recent book on the city is subtitled *How London was Captured by the Super-Rich* (Atkinson, 2021). Culture-wise, the city has an extensive 'artistic precariat' and people on zero-hours contracts. The legacy of mega-events like the 2012 London Olympics has been less about urban regeneration and more about the displacement of independent artists and local businesses, as the case of Hackney Wick and Fish Island, mentioned early, demonstrate (see Raco and Tunny, 2010; Furseth, 2020). Finally, it is a city riven with pockets of severe poverty and significant social polarization between the rich and poor. Despite being one of the wealthiest cities in Europe, of the 290 OECD regions covered, London has the third highest Gini coefficient (0.58) (a measure of income inequality),[7] only behind Corsica and Brussels (Norman, 2021). The East London Borough of Waltham Forest tops the world tables with a score of 0.75, beating Johannesburg, South Africa (World Atlas, 2022b).

Like London, the city of Toronto also suffers from rocketing house prices, significant gentrification and social polarization. A recent article entitled 'What are the most pressing problems facing Toronto?' reveals that despite its creativity boom it is the 'income inequality capital of Canada' (*Toronto Star*, 2020). Major problems identified here include inclusivity, equality, affordable housing and culture, not to mention mental and physical health issues.

European cultural meccas such as Barcelona have also suffered from rising house prices brought on by the rise of Airbnb and cheap flights resulting in strong anti-tourist sentiments (Novy and Colomb, 2018). Cities like Prague have been considering alternative tourism strategies in the past few years due to citizen discontent (Pixová and Sládek, 2018). Research by a coalition of cultural workers in the city of Berlin found that its brand as a 'world leading art city' is questionable, with most artists unable to make a living doing their art in the city (Haben und Brauchen, 2012). Furthermore, the incorporation of alternative neighbourhoods in the city as tourist spaces has resulted in anti-tourism protests and calls for both rent control and restrictions on Airbnb (O'Sullivan, 2019).

Elsewhere in the world, Melbourne mentions feeling the pressure from other creative cities (City of Melbourne, 2021). Its world ranking in terms of liveability in 2021 (winner in 2013) tumbled to ninth due largely to its failure to deal effectively with COVID-19. In terms of entertainment, Newcastle upon Tyne not only found aspects of its party city image problematic (Hollands, 2016b), but had to slash its arts and culture budget to zero in March 2013 due to national government cuts. Finally, in the Global South, Mexico City, despite its creative design credentials, has suffered three decades of neoliberal governance resulting in polarized income distribution, falling wages, increased precarious jobs, poorer health and violent criminal disorder (Laurell, 2015). Numerous cities in Latin America have been ravaged by the impact of neoliberalism in terms of increased poverty rates, precarity and inequality (Banks and Serafini, 2020). Even a 'successful' nightlife and tourist city such as Rio de Janeiro, for example, is a highly polarized urban centre experiencing problems of violence and safety (Gois, 2018).

So, everything is far from rosy in the neoliberal creative city. First, the cultural economy had to survive the impact of the 2008 financial crisis and subsequent austerity response. While there is some evidence to suggest that certain creative industries weathered the storm better than others (United Nations, 2010), the logic of this type of city has been further exposed more recently by the COVID-19 pandemic. The fragility of urban economies based on arts, entertainment, hospitality, tourism and nightlife was clear to see during this time. The impact of COVID-19 resulted, however briefly, in a critique of consumption-based cities and the need for more urban services to foster community, mutual support and good mental/physical health. As Paul Chatterton (2020) argued during the first lockdown, COVID-19 literally thrust us into a real-time laboratory of a sustainable urban future. Yet, some suggest that in the realm of art and culture especially, we may have missed the opportunity to fundamentally rethink their role in a post-pandemic economy (O'Connor, 2020).

While one might argue that cities are slowly returning to normal (whatever that is) amidst the different COVID-19 variant outbreaks, Chatterton's (2020) point remains valid, particularly in terms of thinking about cities and environmental sustainability. Despite, the rhetoric of COP26 in Glasgow in November 2021, can we really think seriously of reviving car culture and the consumptive city? Urban areas produce 75 per cent of the world's carbon and iconic capitalist buildings like the Trump Tower in New York City, for example, exceed acceptable pollution levels. Is now not the time to reassess the cultural economy in terms of its own environmental sustainability (Oakley and Banks, 2020)?

Figure 1.3: Auckland, New Zealand: the most liveable city in 2021

Source: photo by author, 2012

Also, are there not alternative criteria that cities might be judged upon besides them being either entrepreneurial or creative (Davis, 2021; Townshend, 2022)? For example, very few of the cities looked at earlier were even mentioned in the most 'liveable' cities ranking. Auckland, New Zealand, topped the liveability table in 2021 (which includes indicators like stability, healthcare, culture and environment, education and infrastructure), largely due to the way it dealt with COVID-19 (Economist Intelligence Unit, 2021) (see Figure 1.3). Similarly, highly ranked entrepreneurial and creatively ranked cities like London, Paris and Tokyo were all beaten soundly by cities like Reykjavik (Iceland), Bern (Switzerland) and Helsinki (Finland) as the world's best places for mental well-being due to their robust social security structures, political stability and low pollution levels (Haines, 2021). Liverpool was the only UK city to rank in the top 20 here, and London finished in a lowly 69th position! Similarly, a global academic study of cities and happiness was dominated by Nordic and Scandinavian cites like Helsinki, Aarhus, Copenhagen, Bergen, Oslo and Stockholm, all located in countries with lower wealth disparities (De Neve and Krekel, 2020).

The shortcomings of neoliberal urbanization and the limits it imposes on the creative city require both analyses and critique as well as the search for alternatives. The next section provides a wider context for critically considering neoliberal creative cities, including a discussion of the book's main themes, followed by an outline of its chapter contents.

Book themes

The key themes that run through the book are: the need for a critical urban studies approach; attention to historical periodization; a concern with the relationship between the global and the local; spatial changes in cities; urban social divisions and exclusion; and, finally, resistance, opposition and the need for alternatives. I introduce each of these themes briefly in what follows.

One of the initial themes is to locate the book within a wider debate about how we view the neoliberal creative city. Hutton (2016: 26) contrasts more positive views of this transformation, represented by Richard Florida (2004), who saw it largely as a solution to the decline of the post-industrial city, with a more *critical urban studies*, represented by scholars like Jamie Peck (2005) and others (for example, Miles, 2015; Mould, 2015; McGuigan, 2016), *criticizing the neoliberal limits of this urban form*. The analysis adopted here is very much in the latter camp. It is suspicious of the image-making character of this type of city and the way it hides significant urban problems. The role of a critical urban sociology is not to be seduced by rankings, labels and images. Rather, it should seek to critically engage with the complex, and sometimes unintended, effects of the neoliberal creative city.

For instance, while this book asserts that neoliberal urbanization has become dominant over the last 30 years or so, it does not mean that it is a monolithic entity. Rather, it needs to be understood critically as a variegated, complex and contested process (Peck and Theodore, 2019). Neoliberal projects and policies, including creative ones, must be mediated through local needs, goals and values. This is particularly important when thinking about how the creativity paradigm has been adopted in cities in the Global South (Jesus et al, 2020) and China for instance (O'Connor and Gu, 2020), as well as in Scandinavian (Boren and Young, 2017) and post-socialist European cities (Boren and Young, 2016). O'Connor, et al (2020) importantly describe the creative city discourse as 'hegemonic', meaning that while dominant, it is not simply imposed on cities but must be negotiated and struggled over. In other words, we need to be mindful of different national and local contexts and look empirically at how different cities have embraced, adapted and even rejected neoliberal creative strategies in practice.

A second related theme is a *general concern with urban history and periodization, especially regarding thinking about different phases of neoliberal urbanization* (Mayer, 2013). This means looking at the historical past and seeing what role it plays in producing normative versions of the neoliberal creative city. For example, the industrial capitalist city studied by the 'classical tradition' of sociology (the work of Marx, Weber and Durkheim) understood urbanization through the wider context of capitalism, rationality and an increased division of labour. This city threw up a range of social problems including high levels of poverty, ill-health and pollution. Negative representations of cities of the industrial revolution provide a stark contrast to many of the positive images associated with the urban cultural economy. Cities of the Global South, while also being affected by phases of neoliberal urbanization, have a somewhat different history and context here (Connell and Dados, 2014). What is crucial today is that virtually all cities have sought to divest themselves of their industrial or development past by engaging in positive creativity discourses and policies.

Historical periodization is also important in terms of understanding the emergence of the cultural economy as well as exploring resistance towards it. For instance, Chapter 2 captures a key historical moment explaining the origins of the cultural and creative economy in the 1980s through the rise of 'urban entrepreneurialism' (Harvey, 1989a). Additionally, one can contrast the transition from the Fordist capitalist city of the late 1960s and early 1970s to more flexible modes of capital accumulation associated with globalization and neoliberal urbanization from the 1980s onwards. Some writers have distinguished between different phases of neoliberal urbanization. For example, Peck and Tickell (2002) initially differentiated between a 1980s neoliberal 'rollback' politics of deregulation and dismantlement and a 1990s 'rollout' politics of pro-corporate and market-conforming governance. Mayer (2013) has added a further millennial 'consolidation' phase, while Peck and Theodore (2019: 259) more recently talk about a 'roll over' phase of neoliberalism. This is despite the fact that they all recognize that phases sometimes merge, reverse and experience periodic crises.

A third theme of the book is a concern with the *relationship between the global and local*. Chapter 1 has already hinted at the fact that neoliberalism and the shift towards emphasizing the urban cultural economy within capitalist cities are global phenomena. At the same time, we need to look carefully at how particular world regions, countries and cities have adopted, modified, and in some cases resisted, neoliberal urbanization and creative city paradigms. The issue of local autonomy is raised in the first instance in relation to Chapter 2 on urban entrepreneurialism. Harvey's (1989a) work argued that the shift from urban managerialism to entrepreneurialism was an overwhelming global trend and this still appears very much to be the case. Subsequently, however, other writers have challenged the binary nature of this transition (Hall and Hubbard, 1996) and questioned a lack of local agency (Newman, 2014). Still others have highlighted more radical local responses to neoliberalism in the Global North (Russell, 2019; Thompson et al, 2020) and South (Rodríguez, 2021).

A fourth theme that this book is interested in is *how the neoliberal creative city has produced spatial change*. By spatial change I am referring to not only the transformation of buildings, streets, neighbourhoods and downtown areas, but also to what the city looks and feels like.

What is this new creativity identity, what spaces does it produce, and for whom? Brenner and Theodore (2004) note that neoliberal space can be generally characterized by segregation, commodification and exclusiveness. This urban phenomenon is perhaps best represented by the term gentrification. While originally confined to housing and the displacement of traditional neighbourhoods (Glass, 1964), gentrification today has now taken on a much wider meaning. This includes upmarket developments in such diverse areas as entertainment and leisure, retail, arts and culture and nightlife (Chatterton and Hollands, 2003; Brown-Saracino, 2010; Lees et al, 2013). Gentrification and spatial displacement can be exacerbated by the impact of tourism and Airbnb, as well as through the creative economy.

One of the major developments in the neoliberal creative city is the creation of designated cultural quarters and the displacement of traditional neighbourhoods and alternative arts spaces (Pratt, 2018). While these changes may be initiated by the local creative state, the role artists play is somewhat contradictory. The congregation of creative workers in poorer parts of the city (Lloyd, 2006) can often act as a catalyst for real estate developers to move in and gentrify a neighbourhood on the back of its 'creative buzz' (Wilson, 2014; Furseth, 2018). Similarly, the provision of new arts spaces in an area can be utilized as a soft cultural policy to gentrify areas, a process referred to by Pritchard (2018) as 'art washing'. Such creative class infiltration can act to squeeze out working-class residents and so-called 'non-creatives'. Similarly, the creation of corporately owned 'urban nightscapes' (Chatterton and Hollands, 2003) and tourist enclaves (Novy and Colomb, 2018) can also come to dominate cities.

Progressive creatives can also be involved in the creation of *alternative creative spaces*, defined here as arts and cultural organizations that are opposed to the neoliberal city (Hollands, 2019), *nightlife 'counter-spaces'* (Berthet-Meylan, 2022) and *anti-tourism activities* (Novy and Colomb, 2019), thereby involving themselves in anti-gentrification and 'place guarding' struggles like the anti-capitalist art collective Mi Casa No Es Su Casa (Levy, 2019) (see Figure 1.4). The potential of these struggles over space is discussed in detail in Chapters 3, 4, 5 and 6.

A fifth theme is concerned with *how the urban cultural economy has contributed to increased social polarization, precarity and inequality in the neoliberal city*. While the dominant creativity paradigm promised to usher in a new and more harmonious city (Florida, 2004), research shows the most creative places are also the most unequal (Florida, 2014). Not only has the new cultural economy contributed to spatial displacement and gentrification (Wainwright, 2017), it has also produced new social divisions, exclusions and conflicts. For example, Florida's creative class idea creates an unhelpful distinction between them and so-called 'non-creatives' like the service

Figure 1.4: Mi Casa No Es Su Casa's illumination against gentrification, New York City

Source: copyright Jose Tlaxcaltecatl, reproduced with permission

and urban working class. This can result in conflicts between creatives and the service class that provides for them, while the working class in the new cultural economy can be viewed as 'unproductive' and 'troublesome' (Denmead, 2019).

Last, but not least, a sixth key theme of the book concerns *resistance and alternatives to neoliberal urbanization* (Leitner et al, 2007) *and the dominant creative city paradigm* (Mould, 2015). Despite both being dominant for a significant period, this should not imply that there is no opposition or alternatives. Throughout the book there is a concern to explore both resistance to 'late neoliberalism' (Peck and Theodore, 2019) and search for 'alternative ways of doing' the culture economy. These range from exploring more progressive forms of municipalism (Thompson, 2020), through to the fostering of alternative creative spaces (Hollands, 2019), protests against neoliberal nightlife (Berthet and Bjertnes, 2011) and the search for alternative and more sustainable forms of cultural tourism (Guia, 2021). Additionally, 'urban cultural movements', *defined as movements which have creativity and culture at the core of their organization, activities and struggle* (Hollands, 2017b: 1), might also form part of wider political coalitions needed to transform the neoliberal city (see Trans Europe Halles, nd). Key here will be bringing together a debate about the role art and culture can play in fostering a foundational economy (O'Connor, 2022), combining with the search for creative justice (Banks, 2017a) and cultural sustainability (Banks, 2020).

Chapter organization

The aims and themes discussed are reflected in the book organization and chapter contents. Chapter 1 has served as a conceptual introduction looking at some illustrative examples of neoliberal creative cities. It has sought to show how neoliberalism has infiltrated the urban cultural economy and debates about creativity. It has also hinted at some of the shortcomings of neoliberal urbanization generally.

Chapter 2 follows on from this by focusing on the emergence of the cultural economy. It does this through the concept of urban entrepreneurialism developed in the work of David Harvey (1989a). It argues that Harvey's Marxist theory provides a robust basis for explaining the rise of the urban cultural economy. It also provides a useful template for assessing the contradictions inherent in the neoliberal creative city discussed in Chapter 3. In addition to assessing the relevance of Harvey's perspective, the chapter also introduces a discussion of more progressive and alternative forms of local urban development, particularly through the concept of the 'new municipalism' (Thompson, 2020) and 'fearless cities' (Russell, 2019).

Chapters 3 and 4 focus on the field of arts and culture and look at both alternatives and opposition to the neoliberal creative city. The first section of Chapter 3 looks at the dominant notion of the creative city through the work of Richard Florida and critiques some of the weaknesses and contradictions of this popular urban moniker. The second part of the chapter re-examines the urban creativity debate with respect to my own empirical and historical work on alternative creative spaces (Hollands, 2019). Here there is a focus on explaining how such spaces have emerged, how they are organized and how they can be sustained within the dominant neoliberal order.

Chapter 4 follows on by exploring the potential alternative creative spaces have in forming broader urban cultural movements necessary to challenge the negative impact of the dominant neoliberal creative city. It does this by first providing some important background to thinking about urban collective action, through the work of Manuel Castells (1983) and his classic concept of 'urban social movements'. Second, it develops the related concept of 'urban cultural movements' and explores the possibilities (and pitfalls) anti-creative struggles have when trying to make links with wider movements.

Chapters 5 and 6 look at two additional fields of the urban cultural economy through their focus on nightlife and tourism respectively as part of the urban creative brand. Chapter 5 focuses on an analysis of nightlife in the neoliberal city. In addition to revealing that mainstream nightlife spaces continue to be characterized by corporate ownership, segregation, control and exclusion (Hollands, 2016b), the chapter also explores resistance and opposition to them (Hollands et al, 2017; Berthet-Meylan, 2022).

Chapter 6 similarly examines tourism within the neoliberal city, outlining its characteristics and shortcomings. It also focuses on some examples of 'tourism contestation' and explores alternative forms of tourism in terms of justice and sustainability.

Chapter 7 looks at the impact the neoliberal creative city has wrought in terms of social polarization, division and exclusion (Gerhard et al, 2017). First, it analyses more generally how neoliberal urbanization creates increased social polarization between rich and poor. Second, it discusses social divisions between the creative class and other non-creatives, before turning to analyse divisions within the creative class itself, including the idea of the 'artistic precariat' and the 'creative underclass'. Third, it explores how poorer working-class groups excluded from the neoliberal creative city are labelled and stigmatized. Finally, the chapter considers how cities might begin to rethink and tackle socio-spatial polarization, creative divisions and exclusions.

Chapter 8 brings together critiques of the neoliberal creative city with the need for envisioning an alternative urban future. The first part of the chapter returns to discuss the main limits of creative neoliberal urbanization and teases out some of the main features of alternative practice in different fields of the cultural economy. In seeking to move beyond the neoliberal creative city it discusses the need to reset art and culture within the foundational economy (O'Connor, 2022), seek creative and urban justice (Marcuse, 2009a; Fainstein, 2010; Banks, 2017a) and achieve cultural, social and environmental sustainability in cities (Chatterton, 2019; Oakley and Banks, 2020). A final section will confront not only what should be done to begin to move beyond the neoliberal creative city, but also how we might think about achieving this. In doing so it discusses obstacles as well as opportunities.

To conclude this chapter, I have suggested that there is a strong argument for moving beyond both neoliberalism and the dominant creative city idea. Neither of these linked paradigms are inevitable or natural. Indeed, it has been suggested that both are in crisis and change is sorely needed. As this book argues, underneath the normative glow of creativity lie hidden problems of work precarity, poverty, social polarization and environmental concerns.

To paraphrase two separate authors, while both neoliberalism and the creative city ideas are supposedly 'dead', they still appear dominant and effecting (Smith, 2008; Luger, 2017). The maintenance of power, privilege and wealth inequalities is supported by powerful vested interests. When and under what conditions might cities begin to cast off their creative brand mantle and start to build a strong foundational economy (Foundational Economy Collective, 2018) benefiting all citizens? We need a broad collection of people, organizations and movements to think imaginatively about a range of strategies here (Joy and Vogel, 2021; Vail, 2022). From developing convincing critiques of the neoliberal city to creating new and credible narratives about a decommodified, just and sustainable urban future.

There is no blueprint for the future or an easy road map to follow here. Achieving such a feat will take all of our collective brainpower, political will and practical knowledge. Multiple levels of change are needed, from small acts of resistance, through to community and local initiatives, to city action and inter-city cooperation. As Harvey (2012: 112) argues, an alternative to capitalism will not come from 'on high' but rather from multiple local urban spaces 'conjoining into a broader movement'.

Neoliberalism has been around for more than 40 years now, and we have been living with the corrosive effect of creative city policies for at least two decades. So, things are not easily changed. Yet, we would be doing the next generation a disservice if we are still trying to patch up the same flawed system in 20 years' time. And while the COVID-19 crisis has given us an excuse to at least try and press the 'reset button', it is more likely that the path of social transformation beyond neoliberalism and the dominant creative city will be long and tortuous rather than straightforward. This book is a humble attempt to lay some groundwork. It will be a monumental collective effort to continue to construct a path that completes this epic journey.

2

Urban Entrepreneurialism: The Emergence of the Cultural Economy

This chapter forms an important theoretical backdrop for explaining why contemporary neoliberal cities have shifted their accumulation regimes towards developing their cultural economies. It illuminates how many of the main problems created by urban entrepreneurialism end up getting reproduced in the creative city (Florida, 2004; 2014). The chapter draws primarily on the Marxist work of David Harvey. It argues that Harvey's (1989a) analyses of the shift from urban managerialism to entrepreneurialism provides a powerful explanation for the emergence of the capitalist urban cultural economy. It also provides a useful template for critiquing the limits of the neoliberal creative city (see Chapter 3).

The chapter begins with a summary of Harvey's general work on understanding the neoliberal city and looks at how he utilizes Marx's theory of capitalist accumulation for understanding urban development. It then turns more specifically to his notion of urban entrepreneurialism. Particularly relevant are governance strategies for developing the 'spatial division of consumption' in cities – namely the idea of producing urban advantage though enabling the cultural and creative economy. In addition to analysing the features and contradictions of the entrepreneurial city and providing some varied case study examples, the chapter also assesses the value of Harvey's position. In doing so it explores the degree to which we can envisage thinking beyond entrepreneurial models. Examples of this include considering 'green entrepreneurialism' (Ersoy and Larner, 2020), participatory alternatives afforded through what has been called the 'new municipalism' (Thompson, 2020) and a discussion of the 'Fearless Cities Network' (Barcelona En Comú, 2019; Russell, 2019).

David Harvey: capital accumulation and urban development

David Harvey is a hugely respected and well-cited human geographer who is known for his substantial Marxist work on the political economy of cities. He has been writing about the city for over 50 years now. One of his early books was called *Social Justice in the City* (1973) and exemplifies one of Harvey's lifetime concerns. Over the course of his academic career, Harvey has written a spate of books on capitalism and the city (Harvey, 1985a; 1985b; 1989c; 1996, among others), including various works on political resistance to this urban form (Harvey, 2000; 2012). He also wrote a short, but key, book on the history of neoliberalism (Harvey, 2007) and a masterful critique of postmodernism (Harvey, 1989b). However, it is of one of Harvey's (1989a) most famous articles 'From managerialism to entrepreneurialism: The transformation in urban governance in late capitalism', that is referred to most specifically in this chapter. It is this particular analysis, it is argued, that helps explain the rise of the modern urban cultural economy. Additionally, Harvey's critique of the limits of urban entrepreneurialism also helps frames some of the 'displaced' contradictions of the neoliberal creative city idea discussed in Chapter 3. First, though, this section introduces his general theory of the relationship between capital and urban development.

If we were to characterize Harvey's work generally, to quote Smith (1984: 125), his approach can best be described as 'the most systematic attempt to relate the theory of accumulation to the specific geography of capitalism'. Not only does he use Marx's ideas, but he elaborates and extends them, bringing them into the 21st century. Harvey also gives Marx's idea a specific focus by explaining capitalist transformations in the urban environment.

There are really three elements to Harvey's basic argument about capitalist cities. First, Harvey (1985b) asserts that the city is a 'built' not a 'natural environment'. Why is this important? Partly this is to critique explanations of urban capitalism as a 'natural competition' like the metaphorical ecological theories of the Chicago School, for instance (Park, 2013). Instead, Harvey (1985b) talks about the city as a 'built environment' because he wants to emphasize that it is made by and for capitalism. The city is never a neutral phenomenon. Its essence is to function for the benefit of the capitalist system and hence it reflects the interests of powerful groups such as urban financiers, corporate property developers, and building and technology companies.

Second, Harvey's approach links urban change directly to economic transformations. The following quote from Pile (1998: 8) neatly sums up this approach: '[A] city is built on the circulation and use of capital. ... It matters then how the money circulates between and within cities, where money accumulates, where people decide to invest it and how they chose to spend it'. Harvey's (1989b) work provides a strong critique of urban approaches that ignore the impact of the economy, especially the workings of capitalist economic principles and tendencies.

The third part of Harvey's (1989a) argument, is that the fortunes of cities are both created by and destroyed by the contradictions of capitalism. What does he mean by this? Harvey's emphasis on the flows of money around the world suggests that when capital moves into cities, they become prosperous. Successful cities develop their urban infrastructure. They look more vibrant. But capital can also easily flow out of cities, Harvey (1989b) argues, even successful ones, resulting in all sorts of problems. Harvey's position always goes back to Marx's notion of the limits and contradictions of capitalism (Harvey, 2018) where every success contains its own seeds of destruction.

The core of Harvey's arguments lies in Marxist theory, so it is important to introduce a few basic ideas here. The first is Marx's theory of capital accumulation. In *Capital* volume 1, Marx (1977) argues that capitalism is a dynamic economic system. To function, capitalism can't stand still – it always needs to change, and more importantly, expand. The logic of capital is 'accumulation for accumulation sake' and 'production for production sake' (Marx, 1977: 558), rather than catering for human need. The idea that capitalism is a dynamic and constantly expanding economic system means in some sense that Marx is the 'godfather' of more recent theories of globalization and critiques of neoliberalism (also see Harvey, 2007).

At the same time, Marx (1977) also argues that capitalism as an economic system is beset by a series of contradictions. One of the problems has to do with its very success. In other words, sometimes surplus capital accumulated cannot be employed efficiently or fast enough. In a word, while the circulation of capital is 'limitless' (Marx, 1977: 150), there are often obstacles to invest this excess capital.

A second contradiction of the capitalist system is the intractable conflict between capital and labour (Marx and Engels, 1981). To make capital, capitalists have to extract as much 'surplus value' from labour as they can (Marx, 1977). There is a systemic tendency to suppress wages. Having done this, the very people who are required to consume commodities within the economy have less to spend, thereby causing a problem of under-consumption. Marxists also talk about capitalism being prone to a 'falling rate of profit' (Moseley, 1991: 1). Part of this has to do with the fact that technological innovations within capitalism soon became dispersed so that any early competitive advantage is nullified.

A final contradiction is capitalism's tendency towards conglomeration and domination by very few capitalists. Marx said in *Capital* volume 1 that 'one capitalist always kills many' (Marx, 1977: 714). One of the features of modern capitalism is a concentration of capital with the rise of the multinational corporation, for instance. This becomes important when we talk about the entrepreneurial city because, in essence, what Harvey (1989a) is concerned with here is not small local entrepreneurs but the operation of global corporate capital.

These and other contradictions within capitalism as an economic system are well-known and have resulted in periodic crises. Not only the 1930s economic depression, but also the 1970s oil crisis, the Global South 'debt crisis' of the 1980s, and the financial crash of 2008. One might also argue that the COVID-19 pandemic was not only a health crisis, but an economic one, showing up real weaknesses in capitalist economies. Finally, one of the biggest problems of capitalism is raised by the environmental movement. If capitalism must ceaselessly expand in order to function, this does not sit well with the fact that we have finite resources in the world. There is a fundamental contradiction between capitalism, urbanism and ecological sustainability principles that simply cannot be resolved (Dawson, 2019).

To sum up, Harvey takes Marx's assertions about the contradictions of capital and applies it to the city. Fundamentally, he does this by looking at changing regimes of capital accumulation and how surplus capital can be employed in investing in the urban infrastructure. Harvey utilizes parts of this framework in his most famous article on 'From managerialism to entrepreneurialism' (Harvey, 1989a) discussed in the next section.

From urban managerialism to the entrepreneurial city

Harvey (1989a) begins his article by talking about a colloquium held in New Orleans in 1985 which brought together academics, businessmen and policy makers from eight large cities from seven advanced capitalist countries. He notes that the colloquium came to a strong consensus and that was that urban governments had to become much more innovative and entrepreneurial in their orientation. Harvey (1989a: 4) says, 'in recent years in particular, there seems to be a general consensus emerging through the advanced capitalist world that positive benefits are to be had by cities taking an entrepreneurial stance to economic development'. What is remarkable about this phenomenon, Harvey argues, is that this consensus seems to hold across national boundaries and even across political parties and ideologies.[1]

The quotation from Harvey in the previous paragraph sums up his overall argument. The task of urban governance has become largely focused on what he calls luring mobile production, financial and consumption flows into its spaces. But first, as a precursor, we need to explain his idea about changing modes of capital accumulation. In terms of this, Harvey (1989b) compares what he calls 'Fordist accumulation' with 'flexible accumulation'. There are several dimensions in which he talks about this transformation.

For example, Fordist capitalist accumulation centred around manufacturing in the industrial city which continued until the early 1970s

(Harvey, 1989b). Capital was largely accumulated on a national level. The method of production was described as Fordism with an emphasis on 'mass production' and the standardization of goods. If we think of the post-war period, we can see that Western capital accumulation occurred through the mass production and consumption of commodities like white goods, automobiles, TVs and so on (Harvey, 1985b). In fact, Harvey links urban development, particularly the process of suburbanization, specifically to the creation of automobile culture (Emanuele, 2017). However, there were limits to this mode of production, some due to its own success. Fordist production was 'successful' in that it was able to mass-produce items and ensure mass distribution. Everyone was able to own a television, refrigerator and car, even though consumption was still stratified. Harvey (1989b) theorized that the Fordist mode of capital accumulation had reached its limit by the 1970s.

As such, it had to figure out a way to move beyond the limits of Fordist accumulation by adopting a more flexible form (Harvey, 1989b). It did this in a number of ways. First, capital became more global, moving away from national economies. This move also helped overcome the 'labour problem' by lowering wages through outsourcing production. Second, rather than industrial production, flexible accumulation is more characterized by the information economy, the creation of 'brands' and the addition of 'symbolic value' on goods.

For example, take the case of Nike, the number one clothing brand in the world with a value of over US$30 billion. During Fordist accumulation capitalism produced a limited number of types of running shoes. With flexible accumulation, running shoes become a brand and gain additional profit through their symbolic value, that is, by being Nike running shoes. People were prepared to pay more for the brand. Profit levels were assured not just through adding brand value but also through the outsourcing of production to cities of the Global South (in Nike's case to China, Vietnam, Indonesia and Thailand) and developing a global market. Flexible accumulation is also characterized by niche and flexible production methods producing an array of different models that constantly need updating by the consumer.

The second development within Harvey's theory has to do with the relationship between capital accumulation and urban restructuring. One of the arguments he makes is that the city itself is a useful vehicle to solve the contradiction of capital 'over-accumulation'. Harvey (1985b) suggests that 'underemployed capital' can be invested in the urban infrastructure to temporarily solve the problem of surplus capital. Excess capital might be invested in buying up land in cities. It might be put into property or office space development, services or technologies, or it might also be invested in lifestyle and consumption amenities. While this would seem to be good thing for cities, Harvey (1989a) argues that such speculative investment of capital in the urban infrastructure carries no guarantee of a return on investment.

Mobile multinational companies try and overcome the fact that there are no guaranteed investments by looking around the world at cities where they can get the best deal. They look at what labour costs are in a particular city. They ask, what are local tax rates? How much does land cost? Capital, Harvey (1989b) argues, is much more mobile in an era of flexible accumulation. It can literally move around the globe in seconds. He uses the term 'spatial fix' to suggest that corporate capital today can partly offset the problem of how to guarantee investment by calculating these costs and being highly mobile geographically (Harvey, 2001).

Harvey likens this notion to the anthropological idea of the 'cargo cult', where remote tribes would lay out symbols in the ground in the belief that they would bring a passing plane down to earth (Schouten, 2008). Cities become like tribes, trying to pull down and lure in this mobile capital. To cite Harvey (1989a: 5): 'The task of urban governance is, in short, to lure highly mobile flexible production, financial, and consumption flows into its space.' They might do this by building large office blocks in anticipation of attracting a big global finance company to relocate. Cities can offer multinational companies cheap land or reduced tax rates. They might build a big airport in anticipation of increasing tourism or bid to hold the Olympic Games like Rio de Janeiro did in 2016 or Beijing did in 2020. One of Harvey's favourite examples, in the US, is that a city might build a big sports stadium to attract investment for a professional sports franchise (Harvey, 1989a).

Harvey (1989a) further argues that this phenomenon can sometimes involve a coalition of property developers, investment bankers, multinational corporations, city councils and even trade unions. It is interesting to think about the way in which the idea of a 'coalition' helps to sell the notion that luring capital to town will benefit everyone equally. That it will be good for employment prospects or that the building of facilities and infrastructure will be used equally by the whole population. But that is not the reason why this process is happening, Harvey argues. It is occurring in order to aid capital accumulation. The worldwide shift we have witnessed in the past 40 years towards more entrepreneurial forms of urban governance reflects a transformation of the traditional functions of local government. They have moved away from their administrative and welfare function to one almost wholly oriented to assisting the capital accumulation process. This role of the local state is essentially to facilitate capital accumulation in cities (Peck and Theodore, 2019).

Harvey (1989a) is careful to argue that this is not a completely monolithic process and cities can pursue different combinations of strategies here. Looking at the case of Durban, South Africa, Martel and Sutherland (2018: 397) argue that it is important to consider 'localised knowledge production processes and the actors and power embedded in them, which result in particular urban development outcomes in cities'. Harvey (1989a), in fact, outlines four different strategies local governments can take. One is cities may engage in aiding industrial production to locate to their city or their region directly. One of the best examples of this would be the city of Sunderland bringing Nissan to northeast England. The background to this move is that the city council gave Nissan cheap land. It also did not require the company to pay full local taxes for a number of years. The council also emphasized that there was plenty of reasonably priced and skilled labour in the region (see Garrahan and Stewart, 1992). So local governments may subsidize multinational companies to come to their region and reward them for staying.

A second strategy is that cities may attempt to encourage the movement of financial services or attract informational capital into their orbit. While Shanghai, London and New York are world-renowned for their financial services, many cities have sought to develop this side of their economy with varying degrees of success (Immergluck, 2001). Others have tried to focus on the knowledge economy side to draw in global investment. Universities may get drawn into this strategy, with business schools developing links to information technology firms. Perhaps the most famous moniker to develop out of this strategy is the idea of the 'smart city', a concept which encapsulates a strong entrepreneurial (Hollands, 2008) and corporate dimension (Hollands, 2015).

A third strategy is a straightforward redistribution one, where cities bid for a contract to bring a large corporate or state employer to their area. Often there may be a political motive here, where contracts for siting such a company in a particular area become part of a political payback.

Finally, and most importantly, for the discussion here (and for the book as a whole), is that cities may choose to develop what Harvey (1989a) calls their 'spatial division of consumption'. This is a focus on providing premier services around tourism, heritage, entertainment, culture and leisure as an urban draw. Harvey traces the origins of different aspects of the urban cultural economy like the development of consumer attractions (Hannigan, 1998), cultural innovation in the arts (Miles, 2015) or the 'festivalisation' of cities (McGuigan, 2016) as different ways to attract capital and people to a city. Even those cities which struggle to attract capital, like post-industrial ones, could retreat to their industrial heritage in order to sell themselves, Harvey argued. Many of the features Harvey discussed have become central elements of the urban cultural economy (Hutton, 2016). Ironically, he foresaw these cultural regeneration strategies prior to the so-called 'creativity turn' (Florida, 2004). Harvey's general critique of urban entrepreneurialism as a regeneration strategy is therefore a useful forerunner to identifying similar shortcomings in the neoliberal creative city discussed in Chapter 3.

Features of the entrepreneurial city

What are the general features of urban entrepreneurialism or what others have called the entrepreneurial city (Jessop, 1997)? First, it is essentially a 'business city', one that functions primarily for capital and profit. Importantly, while many pro-business city proponents emphasize the role of small local entrepreneurs, urban entrepreneurialism is, Harvey (1989a) argues, all about meeting the needs of global corporate capital. An example of this would be the city of Songdo in South Korea. Songdo has been described as a purpose built, technologically advanced, capitalist business park (see Case Study 2.1).

Case Study 2.1: Entrepreneurial urbanism and the making of Songdo City, South Korea

One of the most well-developed examples of corporate business involvement in moulding an urban environment is the coming together of the giant information technology corporation Cisco and the US property development company Gale International, in the creation of Songdo City, South Korea. Songdo is a US$40 billion urban development the size of Boston built on a man-made island in the Yellow Sea. Cisco, which technologically kitted out the city, says on its website that it is 'the ultimate lifestyle and work experience' (Hollands, 2015: 63). Although it is designed to be a certified Green City, producing only about one-third of greenhouse gases of a traditional urban conurbation, there are many criticisms of the project. The first one, from Harvey's perspective, is that Songdo is not so much a city as a giant business park. It was literally created within a free economic zone designed to lure in multinational companies to do business in South Korea and win back foreign investment lost to China and others over past years (Shin, 2016). As Shin (2016: 2) argues, 'Songdo has come to cater exclusively for the needs of domestic and global investors as well as the rich who have financial resources to grab upmarket real estate properties'. Developers have also benefited from huge subsidies provided by the municipal government in the form of cheap reclaimed land (Shin, 2015).

A second characteristic of the entrepreneurial city is a shift in the *raison d'être* of city governments from their administrative and managerial function, to one almost wholly focused on urban branding and 'economic boosterism'. This results inevitably, Harvey (1989a) says, in a decline of urban governance concern with maintaining the welfare functions of the local state. This has been exacerbated in the UK by shifts in local funding structures, inability to raise local income and austerity cuts (Atkins and Hoddinott, 2022).

Similarly, in Prado-Trigo's (2017: 132) study of the transition to urban entrepreneurialism in Machala, Ecuador, he notes that 'funds that could have been spent on housing and education have been cut back' and redirected towards enhancing investment opportunities and 'shantytowns had no basic services, in contrast with the regenerated areas'.

Additionally, the local state's involvement in large-scale projects through the moniker 'public–private partnerships' often results in shunting public resources away from providing basic services to the majority of people that live in cities (Jessop, 1997). So, while entrepreneurial cities may have excellent convention centres, big airports, luxury hotels and good telecommunications, they are also likely to have poor local services. Local transport, education and basic youth and adult services may be underfunded because urban resources have shifted from the welfare side of things to entrepreneurial projects designed to subsidize business relocation (see the Newcastle upon Tyne example in the next section).

A further side effect of this redistribution of resources is increased polarization and gentrification in entrepreneurial cities. This is often reflected in a drastic rise in house prices which is often heralded as a positive trend in this type of urban development model. It is no coincidence that London was voted the most entrepreneurial city in the world in 2020 and that it has experienced some of the highest house price increases around the globe in recent years – making it a city largely for the rich (Atkinson, 2021). Along with this is the gentrification of previously accessible neighbourhoods, with a shift to upmarket wine bars, restaurants, leisure and entertainment. At the same time, Harvey (1989a) draws attention to how urban entrepreneurialism not only exacerbates the problems of the urban poor but also attempts to hide the latter social group from view.

Urban entrepreneurialism in 'ordinary cities'

'World cities' like New York and London have always been seen as entrepreneurial centres historically and they remain so today (see Table 2.1). What is more interesting, according to Harvey's theory, is how many 'ordinary cities' over the last three decades have embraced this urban development model. In his article he mentions unlikely post-industrial examples like Gateshead, Halifax, Liverpool and Sheffield in the UK and Baltimore in the US (Harvey, 1989a). In a recent poll of the UK's most entrepreneurial city, Manchester and, perhaps more surprisingly, Leicester came ahead of London based on business starts per head of population (Instant Offices, 2021). Recent applications of Harvey's urban entrepreneurialism perspective have also occurred in less well-known Chinese cities like Kunshan and Lijiang (Chien and Wu, 2011; Su, 2015). In this section we look at how urban entrepreneurialism applies to three

Table 2.1: Top ten cities for entrepreneurial success worldwide, 2021

1. London
2. New York
3. San Francisco
4. Sydney
5. Melbourne
6. Los Angeles
7. Singapore
8. Boston
9. Berlin
10. Chicago

Source: *Business Traveller* (2021)

ordinary cities located in three different parts of the world – Edmonton, Canada; Newcastle upon Tyne, England; and the small city of Machala, Ecuador in Latin America (see Case Study 2.2).

With a population of just over one million, Edmonton is the fifth largest city in Canada. A major economic centre in the province of Alberta, particularly concerning the oil and gas industry, Edmonton is a governmental (home to the Provincial Legislature), educational (University of Alberta) and cultural centre. In terms of urban development and entrepreneurialism, the city was an important centre of financial capital for a time in 1970s and 1980s, resulting in a spate of office tower building in the centre (Harvey's [1989a] 'build it and they will come' idea). In the 1990s this sector declined, making way for retail, cultural and tourism development. The city is home to North America's second largest mall, and is known as 'Canada's Festival City', with the Edmonton International Fringe Festival being the largest fringe theatre festival in North America. It also has a number of professional sports teams (including the National Hockey League team the Edmonton Oilers; see Scherer and Davidson [2011]) and tourism numbers were up prior to the COVID-19 pandemic with 3.3 million overnight visits in 2017 (Morris, 2017).

Fifteen years ago, when I was conducting some research into smart cities, I looked at the main web page of the city of Edmonton. One of the interesting things I found (Hollands, 2008) was that when you looked at the list of criteria the city used to describe itself, 60 per cent of the features it mentioned could be categorized as 'business friendly'. The role of local government was said to provide a 'strong pro-business environment … reasonable taxes … and low cost to do business' (Hollands, 2008: 308). Providing good international transportation links and an exceptional arts and entertainment scene were also mentioned. All of this sounded very much like Harvey's entrepreneurial city.

What, if anything, has changed over the past couple of decades? A recent promotional video on YouTube, entitled 'Edmonton, a City Well Built' (City of Edmonton, 2012), highlights another wave of urban development backed by the city authorities and provincial and national government funds and loans designed to reinvigorate the city once again. What is interesting about the clip is how such infrastructural development is promoted as benefiting everyone in the city as opposed to largely boosting business and real estate development (Jones et al, 2019). Additionally, it says little about the need for social housing and welfare services for the urban poor. The Edmonton region has one in ten in poverty with the data showing that 53 per cent of this group are women, 11 per cent Aboriginal and 42 per cent visible minorities (End Poverty Edmonton, 2019). Harvey's perspective would question how many of these mega-developments in the city relate to the less well-off and the provision of basic services and support.

The second example comes from my own city of Newcastle upon Tyne (population: 300,820 in 2019; with a metro area population of 818,000 so comparable with Edmonton). Harvey's (1989a: 9) article mentions the city in a passage about 'thirteen ailing cities in Britain'. Hence, it is useful to look briefly at Newcastle's transformation over the last 40 years and highlight some of the major changes it has gone through. Known historically for its industrial past, particularly around coal and shipbuilding, in the 1960s employment rates and wages for skilled work were good and the city provided decent social housing (Robinson, 1988). Tourism and the development of the city's cultural economy were in their infancy. Twenty years on, Newcastle was on its knees economically due to a decline in manufacturing and the neoliberal politics of Thatcherism. The city was hardest hit in 1981, losing 10 per cent of its jobs in a single year (Robinson, 1994: 12). Recovery was slow, with service and public sector jobs not matching the losses in manufacturing for many years. Also, Newcastle was not as successful as some UK cities in luring multinational capital, head offices and financial services to the region (Robinson, 1988).

In terms of retail, Newcastle saw the further development of the shopping centre Eldon Square (Flynn, 2021) but has never been able to attract the likes of Harvey Nichols. It also suffered from out-of-town shopping with the building of the Metro Centre Mall by the entrepreneur John Hall. The Quayside area, once the haunt of early artist collectives (Hollands and Vail, 2015), began to gentrify in the millennium with the building of the Baltic art gallery and Sage music centre and the construction of the Millennium Bridge. Retail and the night-time economy were developed (Shaw, 2015) and nightlife also began to gentrify on the Quayside (Chatterton and Hollands, 2001). However, the party city moniker soon gave way to the 'arty city' with

Figure 2.1: Newcastle-Gateshead's creative and cultural corridor on the Quayside

Source: photo by author, 2022

the establishment of Newcastle-Gateshead's cultural corridor (see Figure 2.1). The city began to pursue mega-projects such as the European capital of culture bid 2008, where it came second to Liverpool. Despite its growing reputation in art and culture, the city experienced a 100 per cent cut in its culture budget in 2013. Undeterred, Newcastle curated another large event, the Great Exhibition of the North, held in 2019. Since this time, arts and culture and tourism have been hit financially by the COVID-19 pandemic.

Newcastle was also named the most entrepreneurial city in the UK in 2018 based on a survey which found that 55.8 per cent of people living in the area would consider starting their own business (Manning, 2018). However, in another survey which looked at actual business start-ups as a percentage of the population, the city comes a distant 11th in the UK (Instant Offices, 2021). Additionally, Newcastle City Council faces significant cuts, having to save over £40 million on top of the £305 million it has had to save since 2010 (Newcastle City Council, nda: 2). Latest budget figures show that while the council has allocated £100,000 to help address food poverty this is only around 0.06 per cent of its budget and major savings will have to be made in adult and social care (Newcastle City Council, ndb: 7). This is despite the fact that the city has become relatively more deprived between 2015 and 2019, moving from the second most deprived quartile, into the most deprived quartile (Ministry of Housing, Communities & Local Government,

2019). So, while Newcastle appears culturally vibrant, the city clearly has some serious urban problems to address.

Case Study 2.2: Latin America and urban entrepreneurialism: Machala, Ecuador

Harvey's urban entrepreneurialism concept remains relevant today, spreading to middle-sized cities in North America and Europe (as already discussed) as well as in cities of the Global South. Prada-Trigo (2017) provides an informative case study from the small city of Machala, Ecuador (population approximately 250,000). The city is in coastal southwestern Ecuador near the border with Peru and it is the capital of the province of El Oro. Prada-Trigo (2017) highlights the transition as moving from 'chaotic urban managerialism' in the 1970s characterized by rapid growth, a lack of services and urban disorder, to an entrepreneurial model in the 1990s. This transformation included the disappearance of public space and the historical identity of the city in favour of generic architecture situated around a series of shopping centres, gated housing communities and international franchises (for example, McDonald's). His study reveals the 'symbolic reconquest' of downtown areas by the middle class and neoliberal projects related to security, business investment, real estate and tourism. This contrasts with a lack of concern with urban problems like a lack of services, affordable housing and few public green areas. Opportunities for investment took priority over citizens' quality of life with a 'dual city' developing. Prada-Trigo's (2017: 124) main conclusion is that urban entrepreneurialism in this case has 'generated "islands of investment" attractive to foreign capital without resolving such long-standing problems as poverty, inequality, underemployment, and scarcity'.

These varied examples clearly demonstrate that Harvey's urban entrepreneurial perspective is applicable to less prominent cities in three very different parts of the world. It also hints at some of the contradictions this type of economic development model poses for cities around the globe.

Contradictions of urban entrepreneurialism

Previously we looked at Harvey's use of Marx in explaining some of the central contradictions of capitalist economic development. Harvey's application of these ideas is grounded in the notion that these contradictions are displaced geographically into the city. Furthermore, with the subsequent founding of the creative city paradigm, I argue that the contradictions of urban entrepreneurialism are yet further displaced into the cultural economy realm. Next, I discuss three central contradictions as a backdrop for understanding the limits of the neoliberal creative city in Chapter 3.

The first contradiction of urban entrepreneurialism is related to how the over-accumulation problem is solved by the spatial fix and the global movement of capital. The contradiction of too much surplus capital is solved by displacing it geographically, creating a worldwide competition for global capital (Harvey, 1989a). Cities, particularly post-industrial ones, have to 'play the game' as 'luring in capital' appears to be the only way to regenerate themselves. However, being in such a competition holds no guarantees. Mobile capital can just as easily flow out of a city as it flows in. This is as much the case for the attraction of human and creative capital (Florida, 2004) as it is for production or finance capital, as we shall see in Chapter 3.

The second problem faced by urban entrepreneurialism is related to the contradiction created by the loss of competitive advantage. This again is expressed geographically in cities as 'serial reproduction'. In the race to develop aspects of their 'spatial division of consumption' all entrepreneurial cities begin to look curiously alike (Harvey, 1989a). For example, every city seeks to develop its waterfront, build luxury flats, pursue mega cultural events and create a gentrified nightlife/restaurant culture. Every city government develops a tourism strategy and bills itself as 'business friendly'. While initially these developments may create a competitive advantage in terms of attracting global or human capital, this is quickly lost when all cities begin to pursue similar initiatives.

The third contradiction of urban entrepreneurialism is that those cities that are most 'successful' in attracting capital or developing their consumptive and cultural amenities are also the ones that produce the most inequality and social polarization (Harvey, 1989a). The attraction of multinational capital benefits property developers, builder and financiers. Luxury flats and high-end art and culture cater for rich locals and wealthy tourists. The working and urban poor classes are left with a diminished welfare state and support structure. 'Attraction-oriented' approaches carry risks, for instance in reinforcing economic inequities within cities. Anttiroiko (2015: 247) suggests that lifting 'development processes away from grassroots level realities … may cause problems in the long run by bringing destructive elements to local economy, creating exclusive enclaves to a city, and relying on risky large-scale investments'. Rising house prices, gentrification and high rates of polarization between the super-rich and the poor characterize the entrepreneurial city, just as they now do so in the neoliberal creative city (see Chapter 7).

Assessing Harvey's perspective

In terms of assessing Harvey's analyses, I want to begin by briefly outlining some general weaknesses before looking at its strengths. I've taken this route partly because all perspectives have omissions and shortcomings, but also because some of the criticisms made against him might be rebutted. The main issue is does Harvey's approach have explanatory power and resonance and does it provide a useful basis for developing a critique of the urban cultural economy today? Can modifications of Harvey's urban entrepreneurialism idea also be used to help us think about alternatives to neoliberal urbanization and the dominant creative city paradigm in particular?

Some writers suggest that Harvey's Marxist argument is theoretically abstract and that he does not provide adequate empirical verification of urban entrepreneurialism as a process (Wood, 1998). A linked point is that his approach suffers from a well-known weakness of Marxism – economic reductionism. Are cities only just about class inequalities and changing modes of capital accumulation? What about explaining the relationship between urban space and gender, for instance (Massey, 1991)? A final criticism is that Harvey's urban entrepreneurialism concept is largely developed in conjunction with Western, post-industrial cities.

While there are valid criticisms of Harvey's work, particularly around an absence of other inequalities and processes that make up urban life, there are also points of rebuttal. Regarding the first critique of abstraction, one line of defence would be to argue that his aim is to provide an overarching theory. Harvey's theory is a comprehensive one designed to explain global urban processes. The argument that Harvey himself has not provided enough empirical verification is neither here nor there. There has been plenty of application of Harvey's ideas over the years (McLeod, 2002; Schouten, 2008; Thompson et al, 2020). The sign of a good theory is that it is used and modified by others. Finally, regarding the last point about urban entrepreneurialism being a Western-centric concept, there are numerous case studies using the concept in Asia (Su, 2015; Song et al, 2020), Latin America (López Morales, 2009; Prada-Trigo, 2017) and Africa (Cornelissen, 2017; Martel and Sutherland, 2018). Harvey himself provides plenty of discussion of Global South cities in his later work (see Harvey, 2007; 2012).

More specific questions surrounding Harvey's urban entrepreneurialism thesis concern the rather deterministic and binary nature of this governance transition (Hall and Hubbard, 1996; Peck, 2014). Others stress a lack of agency in how the local state might differentially respond to what is essentially the rise of urban neoliberalism (Newman, 2014). Pike et al's (2019) research on the 'financialization' of urban infrastructure in the UK has demonstrated that entrepreneurial and managerial approaches can co-exist. They also suggest that Harvey does not pay enough attention to the impact of national policy and initiatives on the local. However, rather than tearing down Harvey's approach, much of this discussion is about building on and modifying aspects of his approach. For example, Brenner and Theodore (2002) have emphasized the way the local state may be involved in both reproducing and reworking neoliberalism through its own policy strategies and agendas. Newman (2014) also talks about the mediation of neoliberal projects in line with local needs, goals and values. These approaches represent a dialogue with Harvey rather than a thoroughgoing critique.

One trajectory of urban entrepreneurial theory has been developed by Phelps and Miao (2019). This approach emphasizes a variety of overlapping yet qualitatively different forms of innovation which local governments can engage in. They discuss variations like new urban managerialism, urban diplomacy, urban intrapreneurialism and urban speculation as typologies here. As Harvey (1989a) had already argued that there were different urban entrepreneurial strategies adopted by cities within his own approach, this does not really form a full-blown critique. Additionally, perspectives emphasizing more autonomy by the local state (Newman, 2014) are somewhat countered by evidence of continuing constraints and complicity foisted on many city governments following austerity (see Peck, 2012). A final line of work here is whether more progressive forms of urban entrepreneurialism can be created.

Progressive urban entrepreneurialism?

Can urban entrepreneurialism ever be made more progressive, inclusive or sustainable or is this a contradiction in terms? In their article about the 2015 Bristol Green Capital case, Ersoy and Larner (2020) argue that such an alternative form is possible. They say: 'We argue that rather than reiterating narratives of urban entrepreneurialism as dominated by narrow economic agendas and being socially exclusionary, this form of urban entrepreneurialism encourages us to look at cities as places that can be coproduced in context-sensitive ways by multiple entities' (Ersoy and Larner, 2020: 791). Their article, they claim, draws attention to what they call an emergent form of urban entrepreneurialism that privileges environmentalism, social inclusion and grassroots creativity.

Their case study concerns Bristol's success in winning the European Green Capital Award, which came out of a European Union initiative to 'reward cities leading the way in environmentally friendly urban living' (Ersoy and Larner, 2020: 797). The initiative included a wide range of evaluation areas such as climate change; local transport; nature and biodiversity; ambient air; waste production and energy performance, among others. While the authors admit that Bristol's initial aim was to give the city a higher profile in Europe, there was always a strong emphasis on collaboration and partnership with diverse organizations across the city. They argue that this form of urban entrepreneurialism was significantly different from growth coalitions and the domination of private developers pursuing high-end market growth.

The question is, however, is this really an example of urban entrepreneurialism or is it something different? For instance, it does not really fit Harvey's

(1989a: 8) definition of 'a public–private partnership focusing on investment and economic development with the speculative construction of place'. Instead, this competition grew out of an initiative taken by 15 European cities designed to reward places leading the way in environmentally friendly urban living. Another criticism is that environmentalism is a relatively safe issue for involving a wide range of urban constituents to debate and come to some consensus over. Could we say that the same level of consultation and participation would happen if the city was developing a new business strategy, for instance?

Rather than calling this an alternative form of urban entrepreneurialism, some might simply refer to the Bristol Green Capital case as an example of a more progressive municipal policy approach. This is where the local state sets out to create a democratic partnership between itself, civil society, commerce and the academy (Chatterton, 2019: 117). A more sceptical view might see such an exercise as a form of 'green branding' (Andersson and James, 2018) which 'can subsequently be used to market the green city internationally as an attractive place to visit and in which to live, work or do business' (North and Nurse, 2014: 1). Finally, it should be mentioned that this is a single-issue project in one city. What is perhaps more interesting is where a network of local states can begin to create alternatives together and challenge urban entrepreneurialism models on a larger scale.

The 'new municipalism' and 'Fearless Cities Network'

Another way of thinking about alternatives to urban entrepreneurialism is the idea of municipalism. This concerns looking more closely into the relative power cities have over political and economic governance. At the one end of this spectrum are pragmatic responses to neoliberal austerity by local governments creatively utilizing or financializing their assets. This approach has been labelled 'financialised city statecraft' by some thinkers (Pike et al, 2019). In their discussion of UK City Deals, O'Brien and Pike (2019: 1448) discover a 'mixing of new entrepreneurial and enduring managerialist forms' and emphasize the important role national state policy and initiatives play in financing urban infrastructure. The managerial side of financialization means that local assets or resources, usually land, can be used to create alternative revenue streams for funding essential services. However, O'Brien and Pike (2019) do admit that such schemes can also be used by the national state to discipline and control localities.

At the other end of the spectrum, Thompson et al (2020) say scholars associated with the Foundational Economy Collective (Foundational Economy Collective, 2018) have offered the 'grounded city' as an alternative to the entrepreneurial 'competitive city' (Engelen et al, 2017). Here the city is grounded in its locale and is seen as a space of collective civic provision which meets social needs. As Thompson et al argue:

> The grounded city approach departs from this to re-socialise development as a three pronged Polanyian countermovement: pursuing public–common partnerships (see Milburn and Russell, 2018) rather than public–private partnerships; spending public funds on foundational services and investing at risk in the social and foundational economy rather than in profitable land speculation; and focusing more on tackling socio-spatial inequalities and economic injustices within a particular municipal jurisdiction as opposed to place marketing. (Thompson et al, 2020: 1176)

A UK example of this type of approach can be found in the unlikely case of the city of Preston in Lancashire. Fed up with competing for global multinational capital, Chakrabortty (2018) suggests that the city has adopted a form of 'guerrilla localism', while Hanna et al (2018) talk about it as a new model of 'community wealth building'. Amidst drastic national cuts, Preston has sought to make the economy work for everyone through encouraging local spending. Chakrabortty (2018) says it 'keeps its money as close to home as possible so that, amid historically drastic cuts, the amount spent locally has gone up' with six local bodies spending £111 million in Preston in 2017 as opposed £38 million in 2013. Instead of global capital leaking out of the city, it is using its new-found resources to further encourage urban development such as establishing two new worker co-ops and revamping the city's covered market (Chakrabortty, 2018).

Another 'supra' example of this approach designed to utilize the municipality as a strategic site for developing a transformative and prefigurative politics is the Fearless Cities Network. Made up of 50 municipal organizations from 19 countries located on every continent, the network is a mixture of European, North America and Global South[2] urban organizations. The network describes themselves as 'a movement known by many names, from Fearless (or Rebel) Cities, to Cities of Change, Indy Towns, neomunicipalismo, democratic confederalism, communalism and our own preferred term, municipalism' (Barcelona en Comú, 2019: 7). It was spearheaded by the election of the social movement Barcelona en Comú (Barcelona in Common) in 2015 (Burgen, 2016), whose philosophy is grounded in participatory democracy in conjunction with developing civil society. Its urban approach is encapsulated in the phase 'If we're able to imagine a different city, we'll have the power to transform it' (Barcelona en Comú, 2016).

A jointly produced book entitled *Fearless Cities: A Guide to the Global Municipalist Movement* (Barcelona en Comú, 2019) reveals a concern with issues such as feminization of the city, political participation, the urban

Figure 2.2: Fearless Cities Network summit, 'Cities Without Fear', Rosario, Argentina, 2022

Source: Ciudad Futura (reproduced with permission)

commons, public space, climate, re-municipalizing basic services, housing, gentrification and tourism, among others, in combating some of the pernicious effects of neoliberal urbanization. The network also holds an annual summit which in 2022 was in Latin America (see Figure 2.2).

Russell (2019: 991) describes the Fearless City Network as 'an emerging global social movement of citizen platforms aiming to democratically transform local government and urban economies'. He argues that it represents a radical break with post-democracy and neoliberal austerity. One of its prominent spokespersons, Ada Colau (2019: 145), mayor of Barcelona, says '[a]s a consequence of the brutal neoliberalism that has managed to take hold of the global economic system, we live in a world in which inequalities and injustice are increasing at an alarming rate'. Another prominent member of the network, Debbie Bookchin (2019), highlights the strengths of municipalism as a tool of social and political transformation.

The Fearless City Network is viewed as an attempt to both challenge neoliberal globalization and avoid the 'local trap' (see Purcell and Brown, 2005).[3] It attempts to do this by 'adopting the "municipal" as a strategic entry point for developing broader practices and theories of transformative social change' (Russell, 2019: 991). It represents a good example of what Harvey (2012: 112) calls 'multiple local spaces – urban spaces in particular – conjoining into a broader movement' (Harvey, 2012: 112), necessary to begin to challenge neoliberal urbanization. We will return to a further discussion of the network and the exemplary case of Barcelona en Comú in the final chapter of the book.

In conclusion, this chapter has argued that Harvey's approach does provide a robust explanation for the development of the urban cultural economy. It also prefigures many of the shortcomings of the neoliberal creative city paradigm discussed in the next chapter. Additionally, political ideas such as the 'new municipalism' and 'fearless cities' also provides a basis for thinking about anticreative city struggles and alternatives in the urban cultural economy. Interestingly, the book produced by the Fearless City Network does not contain a chapter on culture and creativity. Similarly, O'Connor (2022) has recently argued that art and culture are largely absent from discussions about the foundational economy (Foundational Economy Collective, 2018), despite his view that they should be central to the debate. Ironically, we return to Harvey himself to highlight the importance that struggling over the 'cultural commons' might have in effecting wider social and political transformation: 'The problem for oppositional movements is to speak to this widespread appropriation of their cultural commons and the use of the validation of particularity, uniqueness, authenticity, culture and aesthetic meaning in new ways that open up new possibilities and alternatives'. (Harvey, 2012: 114) The creative variant of urban entrepreneurialism is the neoliberal creative city. Alternatives and opposition to it exist in the form of 'alterative creative spaces' and 'urban cultural movements'. Their potential as well as limitations are the subject of the next two chapters.

3

Critiquing the Neoliberal Creative City: But Long Live Alternative Creative Spaces!

In Chapter 2 it was argued that Harvey's (1989a) analyses of urban entrepreneurialism provides a sound basis for explaining the emergence of the neoliberal cultural economy. His critique of the entrepreneurial city also prefigures many of the shortcomings of the dominant creative paradigm. Follow on from Harvey, Peck (2005: 764) takes particular aim at the ideas of Richard Florida (2004) when he argues that '[c]reative-city strategies are predicated on, and designed for this neoliberalised terrain'. More recently, Mould (2018) also suggests that Florida's creative city model is conceived within a neoliberal framework producing gentrification and social inequalities. In an earlier work, he offers up an alternative version of creative practice in cities through his notion of 'urban subversion' (Mould, 2015).

Following these arguments, this chapter is organized into two main parts. The first part focuses on a critique of the neoliberal creative city, defined here as *the state-facilitated marketization of the creative economy*. It concentrates on the work of Florida for two reasons. First, although his approach has been heavily criticized previously it best represents the dominant neoliberal creative city approach. Second, Florida's schema has been highly influential worldwide both in its conceptual reach as well as in terms of urban policy. Rather than rescuing cities, Florida's creative paradigm has contributed to a new neoliberal 'urban crisis' and growing inequalities (Dorling, 2017). Should we ditch the idea of creativity altogether or are there existing alternative artistic practices that might inform a new urban vision? The second part of the chapter contributes to the urban creativity debate through my own research on 'alternative creative spaces' defined here as *art and cultural spaces which are oppositional to the neoliberal creativity paradigm* (Hollands, 2019).

The popularity and origins of the creative city

The popularity of the creative city idea is beyond debate. It is one of the most pervasive global paradigms of urban regeneration of the last 20 years. As Miles (2013) says, '[c]ulturally-led urban redevelopment became the norm throughout Europe during the 1990s', while Malanga (2004: 36) talked about the creativity paradigm 'sweeping urban America'. Mould (2015: 2) suggests the term creative city is 'now firmly entrenched in the parlance of urban politics'. Cities deemed as creative cover the globe from the US and Canada, to Europe, Australia, Latin America, Africa and Asia, including China.

Chapter 1, for instance, mentioned well-known North American examples like New York, Toronto, San Francisco and Los Angeles, while in Europe cities like Paris, Amsterdam, Barcelona, Berlin, Bilbao, Istanbul, Rome, Milan, Lisbon and Prague were also cited. In the UK, London is often held up as the most creative city, challenged by others like Manchester, Birmingham and Glasgow.

Further afield, Australian cities like Melbourne are often spoken about through the creative lens, while in Asia, besides well-established global cities like Tokyo, Singapore, Shanghai and Beijing, lesser-known examples like Bandung, Bonifacio and Seoul are also mentioned in the creativity stakes (Gu et al, 2020). The UNESCO Creative Cities Network website says the African city of Dakar 'intends to make culture, creativity and innovation the driving forces of local development' (UNESCO Creative Cities Network, ndb). It is estimated that the creative industries contribute US$1 billion gross value added and provide approximately 27,760 jobs in Cape Town, SA (UNESCO Creative Cities Network, nda). The World Atlas (2017) has also produced a list of the 11 most creative cities in South America, topped by Buenos Aires, followed by other cities like Belem, Curitiba, Santos and Salvador in Brazil, Montevideo in Uruguay, Duran in Ecuador and Medellin, Bogota and Popayan in Colombia. Forty-five cities in the region are currently included on UNESCO's Creative Cities Network list, representing over 20 countries (Seminario, 2020).

Finally, Peck (2005) in his critical assessment of the creative city paradigm has cited other less well-known North American cities keen to adopt a creative mantle such as Providence, Rhode Island, Green Bay, Wisconsin and Memphis, Tennessee. Elsewhere, smaller regional cities such as Perth (Australia), Newcastle upon Tyne (UK) and George Town (Malaysia), among many others, have also sought to link themselves to creative and cultural regeneration as part of their urban identity. The list here is virtually endless.

With so many cities clambering to be heard in the 'creativity marketplace', it is hardly surprising that comparisons are made and rankings established. Chapter 1 discussed this phenomenon in relation to a number of different

Table 3.1: World's most creative cities in 2016 and 2017

2017	2016
1. New York	1. Tokyo
2. Berlin	2. New York
3. Copenhagen	3. Paris
4. Barcelona	4. London
5. Melbourne	5. Los Angeles
6. Amsterdam	6. San Francisco
7. Portland	7. Berlin
8. Manchester	8. Others
9. Cape Town	
10. Dublin	

Source: McCarthy (2016) and Wood (2017)

surveys, including the World Atlas' (2022a) 'World's Most Creative Cities' and the inkifi (nd) ranking. One of the most interesting things about these surveys is that they represent a neoliberal inter-spatial competition, allowing city authorities to utilize such creative rankings for branding purposes (Tamari, 2017; Cudny et al, 2020).

A second notable phenomenon is the degree to which different surveys throw up inconsistent rankings. For example, Table 3.1 cites two earlier surveys (just one year apart from each other) of the world's most creative cities. What is interesting about comparing these is a lack of cross-over between the two lists. Only New York and Berlin are found on both. Tokyo tops one table but does not even feature in the top ten on the other one. Thirteen other cities are on one list but not on the other.

While some of these discrepancies may come down to how each survey was conducted and what indices are used to produce the rankings, it also raises a bigger set of questions. Even if we could all agree on common criteria, can we really measure urban creativity? Why do cities need to not only measure their own creativity but also feel compelled to compare themselves with others? The answer lies with a dominant belief that creativity not only fuels wider economic growth (Florida, 2004; World Atlas, 2022a), but also that the 'creative label' can also be actively utilized in the 'marketization' of cities (Anttiroiko, 2015; Evans, 2017).

Previously, it was argued that the emergence of the cultural economy had its origins in one particular strategy adopted within urban entrepreneurialism. Namely, that cities saw an opportunity to revitalize their flagging capitalist economies by investing in what Harvey (1989a) called 'the spatial division of consumption'. While he did not use the term creative city then, as its

46

discourse was not fully formed, there are numerous examples within Harvey's (1989a) schema that relate closely to the neoliberal development of the urban cultural economy. For instance, he talked about how post-industrial city authorities could invest in cultural infrastructure, encourage tourism or use their heritage to reinvent themselves. Miles (2013) characterizes the dominant creative city idea as 'the insertion of new art museums in post-industrial zones, the designation of cultural quarters, and the adoption of city branding strategies based on reductive images of the city as a cultural site'. The creative city idea was, from its very inception, steeped in a neoliberal context of market competition and shift towards new capitalist modes of accumulation (Peck, 2005). This transformational strategy, however, has only served to displace urban capitalist contradictions into the creative sphere, raising the legitimate question of *who is the creative city actually for?*

The origins of creativity itself, of course, pre-date the notion of the creative city, which is a more recent phenomenon. Creativity is a much older and radial historical idea going back to discussions in traditional philosophy (Mould, 2018). For example, Marx (1977) in *Capital* volume 1 says that what distinguishes human production from that of animals and insects is the creative mind rather than instinct. He used this notion of creativity to critique the notion of alienating work under capitalism. Marx's idea is part of a historic 'artistic critique' of industrial capitalism, where creative work is contrasted with the drudgery of industrial production as in the work of Ruskin for instance (Ryan, 2018). Ironically, it is now being argued that this artistic critique has been turned in on itself, with creative work itself acting as a legitimation tool of modern capitalism (Boltanski and Chiapello, 2017).

The contemporary idea of the creative city, however, is understood as having two primary versions. Miles (2013) argues that one is Charles Landry's European model, which is discussed only briefly here.[1] The other is Richard Florida's popular North American based perspective, though both his and Landry's ideas have been applied more globally.

Landry's approach is outlined in his book, *The Creative City* (2000), although Landry and Bianchini (1995) also produced a short Demos book on the creative city earlier. Landry's (2000) perspective differs from Florida's in that he focuses particularly on art projects rather than creative professionals in calculating the degree of urban creativity. In other words, Landry places much more emphasis on the cultural organization of creativity rather than on the notion of a 'creative class' (Miles, 2013). Landry's ideas have been influential in their reach, especially in the UK and Europe more generally, but they have also been transferred to other cities of the Global South (Nkula-Wenz, 2019).

A second perspective on the creative city comes from the writings of Richard Florida and can be traced back to his most famous book, *The Rise of the Creative Class* (2004) first published in 2002 (and revisited in Florida, 2014). Here he develops this notion of the creative class and how they are transforming work, leisure and community. Later, Florida (2003a; 2005) more directly goes on to talk about the impact of the creative class on cities, including his book *Who's Your City?* (Florida, 2008). Finally, Florida's (2018) most recent book, *The New Urban Crisis*, is worth mentioning, as it searches for solutions to urban problems that, some argue, are of his own making (Dorling, 2017).

Although Florida has recently played down his impact on the way creative cities have developed, particularly with respect to the process of gentrification (Wainwright, 2017), Peck (2005) convincingly argues that his ideas have been adopted widely in North America and Europe partly through his extensive touring of cities worldwide. Mould (2015) also refers to his model as the 'dominant CC paradigm'. Florida's work has also been influential in Latin America (see Creative Class Group, 2016) and in certain parts of Asia (Luger, 2019). However, it is important to be aware of the limits of his creativity schema for cities of the Global South (Nkula-Wenz, 2019; Jesus et al, 2020; Kaymas, 2020). We begin here by outlining Florida's general creative city model before going on to critique its inherent neoliberal tendencies.

Florida's creative city model

In order to contextualize Florida's creative city idea, it is instructive to contrast his approach to Harvey's urban entrepreneurialism approach in Chapter 2. Distinct from Harvey's (1989a) critical Marxist perspective, which basically looked at urban development through the flows of global capital and the attempt by cities to capture it, Florida's approach very much emphasizes the human capital side of this equation, with a 'creative twist'. He says:

> From my perspective, creative people power regional economic growth. And these people prefer places that are innovative, diverse and tolerant. My theory thus differs from the human capital theory in two respects. Number one, it identifies the type of human capital, creative people, as being the key to economic growth. And two, it identifies the underlying factors that shape the location decision of these people instead of merely saying that regions are blessed with certain endowments of them. (Florida, 2003a: 8)

Florida defines the creative class as '[p]eople who engage in creative problem solving, drawing on complex bodies of knowledge to solve specific problems' (Florida, 2002: 4). The distinguishing characteristic of the creative class is that its members engage in work whose function is to create 'meaningful new forms' (Florida, 2003a: 8). Florida (2004) estimated that 38 million Americans could be considered members of this class (around 30 per cent of the workforce). Over the last 20 years this has allegedly increased by a further 10 per cent so the creative class today make up over 40 per cent of the US workforce, encompassing some 150 million workers worldwide (Florida and Pedigo, 2017: 1). This figure alone underlies the importance Florida gives to the creative class in transforming cities and driving economic growth.

What are the main components of Florida's thesis? To begin, he divides the creative class into two main groups. The first one is what he calls the 'super creative core', which he defines as including 'scientists and engineers, university professors, poets and novelists, artists, entertainers, actors, designers and architects, as well as the "thought leadership" of modern society' (Florida, 2003a: 8). Essentially, this super creative core produce things and create forms and designs that can be used more broadly. The examples that Florida gives are about designing a product that can be made, sold and used. One might think of an inventor or an engineer here, or an academic or a policy person coming up with a new theory or strategy. Or someone who composes music that can be performed again and again.

Beyond this core group, Florida (2003a: 8) also talks about another sector which makes up the creative class called 'creative professionals'. This group works in a wide range of knowledge-based occupations in the high-tech sector, financial services, the legal and healthcare professions, and business management. These people have a high degree of education and engage in problem-solving and creative thinking.

In researching the creative class, largely via focus groups, Florida (2003a; 2004) suggests that these types of people seek out cities that have other creatives already there, have good creative amenities, and are attracted to locations that value diversity and tolerance. He also emphasizes that this group is attracted to the idea of weak ties and anonymity (Florida, 2002; 2004). This creative group are seeking diversity and locations in which they can develop loose networks of social capital. Florida (2004) believes that the job of city authorities is to attract this creative class, thereby powering economic development.

Importantly, Florida also creates an index to measure creativity which he uses to produce creative city rankings. This 'creativity index' is driven by what he calls the three T's – technology, talent and tolerance. Table 3.2 suggests some of the criteria that Florida adopts to measure each of these indictors. For example, the technology index is measured by the number of high-tech firms and high-tech money in an area, the level of innovation and the number of patents in a particular city. In terms of talent, he measures this quite straightforwardly by looking at the percentage of the population with degrees. Finally, his tolerance index is driven by levels of immigration and diversity in cities as well as their percentage of gay population. Florida finds a significant correlation between high levels of creativity and a higher percentage of gay people in cities. He also finds a strong link between

Table 3.2: Richard Florida's creativity index

Creative index	Measurement
Technology	High technology index/firms and finance, innovation index/patent growth
Talent	Percentage with bachelor's degrees+
Tolerance	Melting pot index/bohemian index (artists)/gay index

Source: Florida (2004)

creativity and the number of artists within the city, which he refers to as the bohemian index.

Whatever one thinks of the validity of Florida's indictors, the main point to be drawn here is that his index has contributed directly to the *neoliberal ranking and marketization of creativity between cities*. As Peck (2005) notes, Florida himself has made a career of going to different cities around the world, talking about his creativity index and advising urban governments about how to best attract this creative class. While much of this self-promotion has been in North America and Europe, we have already noted Florida's influence in Asia (Luger, 2019) and Latin America (Creative Class Group, 2016). This has helped to not only popularize the model but has also forged a strong link between his ideas and creative regeneration strategies and policies (Evans, 2009). As such, Florida's model has become the dominant and most well-known version of urban creativity, influencing a significant number of cities around the world, albeit in different ways (Evans, 2017).

Critiquing the dominant creative city paradigm

While critiques of Florida's creative class and creative city model are plentiful (Peck, 2005; Evans, 2009; McGuigan, 2009; Krätke, 2010; Pratt, 2011; Scott, 2014; Mould, 2015; 2018, among many others), rather than reproduce them all this section focuses on weaknesses related to its association with neoliberal thinking. No one has provided more of a thoroughgoing critique of Florida from the point of view of the limits of neoliberalism than Jamie Peck (2005). Peck argues:

> For all their performative display of liberal cultural innovation, creativity strategies barely disrupt extant urban-policy orthodoxies, based on interlocal competition, place marketing, property- and market-led development, gentrification and normalized socio-spatial inequality. More than this, these increasingly prevalent strategies extend and

recodify entrenched tendencies in neoliberal urban politics, seductively repackaging them in the soft-focus terms of cultural policy. (Peck, 2005: abstract)

What is essentially argued here that Florida's creative city paradigm is shot through with neoliberal ideas of global ranking, not to mention fuelling dubious urban 'image-making' practices. Furthermore, even 'successful' creative cities produce increased gentrification and social polarization (see Chapter 7 for more detail). Peck (2005) also argues that creative city policies and strategies function to make neoliberalism more palatable and hide underlying problems created by this political ideology. In terms of critiquing Florida, let us unpack some of his ideas in more detail.

First, let us start with some basic definitional and measurement issues surrounding the notion of the 'creative class'. One criticism is that Florida's expansive definition seriously over-estimates the size of this grouping. Regarding this, while the most recent calculation takes the creative class to over 40 per cent of the workforce in the US (Florida and Pedigo, 2017), other analyses of the US, Canada and the UK suggest that the percentage of workers actually employed in the 'creative industries' is only around 10 per cent of the jobs total (Nathan et al, 2016: 5). Research on the creative class in the Global South also suggests that a lack of investment in education and training (see Alexandri and Raharja, 2020) has meant that this group may be smaller (Jesus et al, 2020). It might be argued that Florida's over-calculation affords the creative class too much importance, particularly in terms of justifying urban policy prescriptions designed to attract them.

The second definitional issue concerns who is including in the creative class. Numerous scholars suggest that Florida's schema pulls together occupational groupings that do not necessarily belong together. For example, Whiting et al (2022) argue that his creative class contains a significant percentage of 'professional, managerial and scientific' workers who do not actually work in the creative industries. Similarly, they argue that it groups together creative workers that have very different economic, cultural and political 'life worlds' into a single class (Scott, 2014). Are we really to believe that a well-paid, secure and influential policy academic like Florida himself shares the same class position as an unemployed artist? Class, by definition, implies a similar economic position, not to mention having a common set of political values. Florida's homogeneous creative class idea hides significant social divisions and polarizations within the class itself.

A third critique concerns several contradictions related to Florida's neoliberal approach to the creative city, particularly in terms of how we encourage its growth. For example, he argues that cities will become more creative and economically prosperous by providing an urban infrastructure that will attract higher numbers of the creative class. But is creativity in cities simply just about numbers? Furthermore, in a similar fashion to Harvey's (1989a) argument that urban entrepreneurialism creates few winners and many losers, Florida's creative city competition to attract more of the creative class is also doomed to fail. Additionally, what happens to those cities that do not have the resources to attract creatives, like Middlesbrough in the UK for example (see Case Study 3.1)? Where does this leave cities of the Global South, unable to provide as many creative amenities or attract sufficient numbers of creative workers (Nkula-Wenz, 2019: 587–588)? Finally, what happens in even the most 'successful' creative cities when they become 'overrun' with members of this class, thereby producing an unbalanced economy between them and a so-called 'non-creative' service and working class?

Case Study 3.1: Middlesbrough's disadvantaged bid for creativity

Like Detroit (discussed in Chapter 1), the UK town of Middlesbrough used to be an industrial powerhouse. In the 1970s and 1980s, its manufacturing industries of steel, chemical and engineering came under severe attack and it became known as one of the most deindustrialized locales in the UK (Byrne, 1999: 93). The neighbourhood of East Kelby, studied by MacDonald and Marsh (2005), is, in turn, one of the most deprived areas of one of the poorest towns in England. Initially low-paid and part-time service employment ('poor work') unsuccessfully tried to fill the gap created by the loss of manual jobs. More recently, the city has emphasized its creative credentials in a bid to revitalize itself. A recent headline states: 'Once known for steelmaking and chemical factories, Middlesbrough wants to reinvent itself, and is looking to arts and culture to help', exemplified by the Tees Valley bid to run for the UK City of Culture in 2025 (Youngs, 2019). In March 2022 another headline read: '£5m boost to make Middlesbrough "the most creative town in the UK"' (Dodd, 2022), reporting that a bid led by the Middlesbrough Cultural Partnership and Middlesbrough Council from the Cultural Development Fund had been successful. Recently there has also been talk about the creation of a cultural quarter in the city (Charles, 2021). Despite all this potential development, and the fact that the town, like Detroit, has a vibrant independent cultural scene (Twizell, 2020), Middlesbrough has failed four times to gain city status seen as necessary to drive urban regeneration (BBC News, 2022). Additionally, it only came 59th in 2022 in a list of the most creative UK cities and towns (Startupgeeks, 2022).

The most powerful criticism of Florida's model is that it is embedded within a neoliberal creative competitive ranking system. This ironically

Figure 3.1: Grayson Perry's artwork 'Gentrification'

Source: Grayson Perry (reproduced with permission)

effects more 'successful' creative cities as much as it does 'creative failures'. Successful creative cities may begin to believe their own hype and city governments may forget how they became creative in the first place. Additionally, they might begin to side-line key service workers in favour of creatives or decrease the provision of basic services to the urban poor. Florida himself has warned of this in relation to his adopted creative city of Toronto (Wainwright, 2017). The creative city moniker drives up the cost of real estate and house prices in addition to creating gentrification and furthering urban social division.

There are a number of aspects to this 'neoliberal creative destruction'. One is in relation to changes to the urban landscape through the process of 'creative gentrification'. Regarding spatial urban change, Grayson Perry's artwork 'Gentrification' (see Perry, 2014 and Figure 3.1) illustrates this rather insidious process perfectly. First, there is the development and take-over of older working-class industrial buildings by groups of artists and activists. Community-led and cooperative arts spaces are then transformed into more 'official' creativity hubs which are then used in urban marketing campaigns. These, in turn, are then transformed into expensive high-rise flats. Finally, the area eventually loses its creative vibe altogether when artists themselves cannot afford to live there and move out. The very thing that made it creative in the beginning is displaced by capitalist real estate greed and gentrified housing development. While Florida denies that his creative class model directly produced gentrification (Wainwright, 2017), his approach has provided the academic logic behind many such regeneration developments (Evans, 2009).

A good example of this process in real life is the case of Hackney Wick and Fish Island, London, mentioned in Chapter 1. In 2008, it had one of the highest concentrations of artist studios in the world, with around 600 spaces. One artist described its early energy as 'DIY and anarchism' and 'making something out of nothing' (quoted in Furseth, 2018). With the 2012 Olympics, gentrification went into overdrive and with land values rocketing some artists began to leave the area, unable to afford rents (Rossen, 2017). Artist studios are also being torn down to make room for mixed-use developments with flats and shops. Those that have stayed have fought to negotiate the future of the area (Furseth, 2020: 4), though there are significant power differentials between artists, activists and developers.

A second, and related, part of this process concerns how the creative class contributes to urban social division, precarity and polarization. The argument here is that it 'maps onto' existing divisions and exclusions within the neoliberal city, hiding, extending and creating new social inequalities (Gerhard et al, 2017) (see Chapter 7 for an extended discussion).

I end this critique section by making two qualifying points about Florida's popular neoliberal creative city paradigm. First, although I have made several general criticisms of his perspective, it is important to remember that 'while the Floridian creative city may be a meta-brand, the way in which its dominant discourses have been received and shaped, including resistances to it, vary according to historical period and place' (Hollands, 2019: 733). In order to provide a more nuanced analysis, it is important to explore the way in which creative paradigms have been adopted, modified and indeed resisted in different cities and international contexts. Another additional factor here concerns which decade the creative city discourse arrived in a given city in relation to the historical phases of neoliberal urbanization (see Hollands, 2019 for a discussion comparing Amsterdam, Berlin and Milan). Finally, it is important to consider the way in which Florida's theory and influence is mediated in other geographical contexts, such as in Case Study 3.2 from the Global South.

Case Study 3.2: Renegotiating 'creative cityness': the case of Cape Town

In her fascinating study of creative city-making in Cape Town, Nkula-Wenz (2019: 581) seeks to understand 'how the creative city paradigm is being grounded, renegotiated and put into practice in so-called "Southern" cities'. She does this by carefully focusing on the complex and situated expression of 'creative cityness' within the context of this globalizing urban economy. Nkula-Wenz (2019) finds that early attempts to adopt the creativity paradigm in Cape Town were disjointed and short-lived due to the competing demands of a post-apartheid city. Rather than being influenced directly by Florida's (2004) idea that cities need to invest in high-level urban amenities to attract creative talent, Cape Town instead followed the UK model of folding arts and culture into creative public–private partnerships and encouraging creative clusters (Nkula-Wenz, 2019: 587–588). This shift towards a more market-oriented and entrepreneurial strategy, Nkula-Wenz argues, was enabled when the city successfully bid for the title of World Design Capital in 2014, which became the 'discursive glue' needed for the creative label to finally stick. Ironically, this accolade had a two-pronged and somewhat contradictory effect. On the one hand, becoming the 'first African design city' propelled the city into the global neoliberal creative rankings, where it was listed as ninth in 2017, the same year that it joined the UNESCO Creative Cities Network. On the other hand, Nkula-Wenz (2019: 589–593) draws attention to the bid's centrepiece of 'designing for development' rather than just meeting the consumption needs of 'first world desires'. This more progressive element of the bid led to a coming together of the Cape Town Design Network and the Social Justice Coalition to offer their services and lobby city authorities to come up with a solution to inadequate refuse removal in informal settlements. Interestingly, this particular linkage between creative design and social justice concerns speaks as much to the idea of urban social movements discussed in Chapter 4 as it does to the link between neoliberalism and creativity.

The final point of this section concerns the future of the creative city idea and the need for alternative examples of creative praxis. This idea is represented bluntly in a quote from Jason Luger (2017) when he says: 'The creative city is dead, even if still dominant', while a recent article on it is entitled 'Creative City R.I.P.?' (Whiting et al, 2022). Luger here is hinting that while the creative city paradigm is still influential, perhaps its star is now fading. The urban cultural economy has also been hit by the 2008 financial crash and the COVID-19 pandemic, which have made some question its future role in cities. Rather than returning to 'business as usual', these crises can provide us with the opportunity to rethink what a non-neoliberal form of creativity might look like. Also, what role the alternative cultural sector might play in cities in the future (O'Connor, 2022). To begin to consider this, we need to move away from the creative class idea and city rankings and look more closely at the history of alternative art and cultural groups, spaces and practices. They provide a glimpse of a future alternative creativity.

Alternative creative spaces

Florida's creative class approach does not really consider the possibility that a healthy array of alternative creative spaces might act as a different or even better proxy of urban creativity. This part of the chapter focuses precisely on this issue. Of course, artist-led alternative spaces and arts activism have existed in some form or another in the West since the 1960s at least (Dickinson, 1999; Tickner, 2008; Bryan-Wilson, 2009), pre-dating the ascendance of both neoliberal thought and Florida's creative class idea. In more recent decades such spaces have been affected by different phases of neoliberal urbanization (Mayer, 2013) and creative city policies (Hollands, 2019). Examples of these affects include the emergence of anti-squatting legislation in many cities (Dadusc and Dee, 2015), and the incorporation of alternative arts models into mainstream creative city regeneration schemes (Anders, 2011) (see Case Study 3.3).

Case Study 3.3: Amsterdam: can it be both alternative and creative?

Amsterdam has been ranked as high as the fourth most creative city in the world according to Global Cities. This ranking is based partly on the fact that supposedly 46 per cent of the workforce is employed in creative occupations (Gowling, 2013). Known historically for its unique brand 'mash up' of alternative (squatting), liberal (coffee houses) and seedy (red-light district), Peck (2011: 465) notes that the urban economy spluttered in the 1970s–1980s, until a property boom in the 1990s began to transform the city. In the late 1990s, the city embarked on a reformist *broedplaatsen* (or 'breeding spaces') policy, designed to dissuade politically motivated squatting concerned with gentrification, displacement and property development. It did this by encouraging and financing the formation of cultural spaces in particular (Draaisma, 2016). While the result has been the survival of some alternative arts spaces (Keizer, 2014), others have argued that it has meant a weakening of radical urban social movements in the city (Owens, 2008). This is evidenced by the demonization of squatting which was made illegal in 2010 (Dadusc and Dee, 2015). While Amsterdam continues to trade on its reputation as an 'alternative city' (see Uitermark, 2011), the current booming property market, the dominant creativity paradigm and increased gentrification are rapidly taking their toll on its historic moniker (Dalakoglou, 2018).

The main aim of this section and the subsequent chapter (Chapter 4) is to focus on the role alternative creative spaces and their possible formation into wider urban cultural movements might play in challenging the 'unsustainable' neoliberal creative city (Kirchberg and Kagan, 2013). It suggests that such spaces are critical contributors to urban creativity (Shaw, 2005; 2013) and a different urban future. Contemporary alternative creative spaces, however, face not only the problem of incorporation into neoliberal city strategies, but they also incur obstacles in connecting to wider political struggles in these uncertain times (Mayer, 2013).

This section, and the second section of Chapter 4, are both based on my own research project conducted during a Leverhulme Major Research Fellowship (2015–2017). It draws on interviews with 57 creative workers, representing 30 alternative creative spaces from the 1960s to the present. These artists (made up of 42 per cent women and 58 per cent men, aged from their early 20s to mid-70s) were all associated with an alternative space, group or movement, and included those working within sculpture, glass and ceramics, installation art, DJs, theatre and performing artists, photography, film, video and TV, as well as those acting as coordinators or members running alternative studios or galleries. The study was conducted in 17 cities in 11 countries in North America, Europe and Australia, though I seek to supplement this bias with a short case study from the Global South.

The research project asked four main questions:

1. Under what conditions do alternative creative spaces emerge and how are they affected by different phases of neoliberal urbanization?
2. What is alternative about their creative ethos and organization?
3. What kind of challenges to the neoliberal city do these spaces pose?
4. How do they sustain themselves without being incorporated into the dominant creative city paradigm?

Defining what is meant by alternative is not a straightforward task. It is also historically contingent. Today, within consumer capitalism, 'cool hunting' and the appropriation of anti-aesthetic cultures into the market can result in the alternative becoming yet another commodified niche brand (Heath and Potter, 2006). Williams' (1977) work on 'emergent cultures' reminds us of the important distinction between 'alternative as different' and 'alternative as oppositional'. As such, this book purposely chooses to retain the term alternative partly to reclaim the more oppositional and autonomous side of such creative spaces. Additionally, while concepts such as 'Do It Yourself (DIY)', 'grassroots' and 'independent' are suggestive of something different about a creative space, they are all rather subjective in terms of describing alternative organizational structures or political philosophies.

A definition of alternative space comes from Pixová's (2012: 1) work. She defines it as 'alternative to hegemonic commercial use and predominantly used for non-profit youth culture activities, alternative subcultures, and artists'. St John (2000: 6–7) sees alternative culture as 'a diverse network of discourse and practice oppositional to perceived deficiencies in the parent culture, which is the system of values, beliefs and practices hegemonic under modernity'. More specifically, alternative creative spaces looked at by Hollands (2017b) focus specifically on *art and cultural spaces that challenge the neoliberal creative city paradigm in some form or another*. There are, of course, other kinds of alterative spaces like social centres, political squats and so forth, which is why the term 'creative' is inserted in the definition here.

Despite historical, national and city variation, I argue that these alterative creative spaces are characterized by certain core features, including: having a collective rather than an individualist orientation; motivated by a creative rather than monetary ethos; a desire to remain autonomous (despite some having state support); engaging in different practices of artistic production; having a use rather than a market exchange approach to space; favouring a gift economy of solidarity and sharing; having a local place-based identity; and, finally, expressing some form of urban dissent and activism (Hollands, 2019).

Theorizing alternative creative spaces

To understand the impact alternative creative spaces have on the urban fabric, we need to remind ourselves about some of the profound transformations cities have undergone over the past three or four decades. Neoliberal urbanization refers to the increasing marketization of our cities (Mayer, 2013). Additionally, Harvey's (1989a) related concept of 'urban entrepreneurialism' and the changed role of the local state is also relevant. As this book has already argued, as part of these general transformations, we have seen a shift in the economic base of cities towards culture and the creative industries (Pratt, 2011), including the development of a dominant creative city paradigm (Florida, 2004).

With these changes the role of artists in the city also becomes transformed. Initially, it might appear that this group might benefit from the shift towards the creative and cultural economy. Yet, as we have seen from the critique of Florida, the fact is that only sections of the creative class benefit from such developments. Many artists, musicians and actors suffer from precarious employment, increased housing/studio prices, gentrification and displacement from neighbourhoods as they become cool and trendy (Bain, 2003). While it is true that the 'arts in entrepreneurial times' (Sholette, 2011) can breed individualist solutions and incorporation into neoliberal culture branding schemes (McLean, 2014b), it can also result in the creation of new types of alternative creative spaces and wider anti-creative city activities and movements (Novy and Colomb, 2013).

Several different thinkers are useful in thinking about the emergence of alterative creative spaces and resistance to neoliberal urbanization. One of the most significant attempts to theorize the hidden critical potential of contemporary alternative artistic production can be found in the work of Gregory Sholette through his concept of 'dark matter'. Sholette (2011: 1) defines creative dark matter as 'the bulk of artistic activity produced in our post-industrial society, which includes a wide range of makeshift amateur, informal, unofficial, autonomous, activist, non-institutional, self-organized practices'. He also talks about the proliferation of creative workers in the contemporary period and their subsequent disaffection expressed as what he calls the 'revenge of the artistic surplus'. Mould's (2015) work shows how the dominant Floridian creative city paradigm results in a series of contradictions which ultimately undermines its own success, thereby producing resistance and opposition. He goes on to discuss the role artists might play in subverting the contemporary neoliberal city. Finally, Harvey's 'art of rent' thesis argues that the capitalist need to commodify all aspects of urban culture, including the work of artists, can 'often produce widespread alienation and resentment amongst cultural producers' (Harvey, 2012: 110).

All of this is useful for thinking about the potential of alternative creative spaces to challenge the current neoliberal creative paradigm. However, it is Mayer's (2013) historical work that is particularly instructive for helping to explain the evolution of alternative creative spaces in relation to different phases of neoliberal urbanization. For instance, Mayer (2013: 5–6) mentions a pre-neoliberal urbanization phase characterized by struggles against state and capital in the late 1960s and early 1970s Western Fordist context. These took the form of early squats and autonomous cultural centres. This is followed by her application of Peck and Tickell's (2002) 'roll back' and 'roll out' phases of neoliberalism. These phases are represented by the 1980s rollback politics of deregulation and dismantlement and the 1990s rollout politics of pro-corporate and market-conforming governance. While the rollback stage was met with some opposition, including a renewed squatting movement in Europe particularly, Mayer (2013: 8) argues that institutional change meant that during the rollout phase, alternative spaces found themselves relying on alliances with the local state rather than being in opposition to it.

Mayer (2013: 8) adds a current period of neoliberal consolidation from 2000 onwards, which is represented by increasing cooperation with the local state to legitimize such spaces. Peck and Theodore's (2019) more recent discussion of the direction of travel of neoliberalism shows that while it is still dominant it has always been an unstable ideology. This was particularly the case around the 2008 financial crisis and following the COVID-19 pandemic. One can discern a further rise of alternative spaces and anti-creative city movements occurring around these crisis points (d'Ovidio and Rodríguez Morató, 2017). Using my own research findings, the remainder of this chapter looks at alternative creative spaces in terms of their conditions of emergence, their changing ethos and organizational form, and their resistance towards and incorporation in neoliberal creative city strategies.

Conditions of emergence of alternative creative spaces

A key historical factor for understanding the emergence of alternative creative spaces concerns the wider political opportunity and mobilization context (Tilly, 2004). The first wave of alterative arts spaces came about in Western Fordist capitalist cities of the 1960s. As Mayer (2013: 7) suggests, due to Fordist capitalist contradictions many cities at this time 'developed progressive alternative projects of their own, generating a vibrant infrastructure of community and youth and cultural centers, alternative and feminist collectives, autonomous media and a host of other self-managed projects'. An interview with one UK creative worker from the 1960s makes clear the political opportunity context for how their theatre collective came about with reference to the events of May 1968: "We started in the late 60s after the cultural revolution in France, basically where it was clear that art could have a very direct role in what was a potentially revolutionary situation" (interviewee 31, male, London, 1960s theatre collective). The UK student movement (Steadman-Jones, 1969) and protests in various arts schools (Tickner, 2008) also gave rise to numerous alternative arts organizations and spaces (see Dickinson, 1999).

In the US context, the creation of alternative arts groups came out of similar political ruptures in American political life. These emerged from wider countercultural shifts and the activities of "the women's movement, anti-Vietnam protests and the struggle for civil rights" (interviewee 50, male, New York/Toronto, 1960s artist collective). Many of these arts groups tackled class, race and gender inequalities in the cultural field (Bryan-Wilson, 2009). Alternative creative spaces formed in this period were radical in their philosophies and organization. They were also autonomous from the capitalist marketplace and were often in direct conflict with the state.

Dramatic economic and political change in Eastern Europe 20 years on created opportunities for a second wave of alternative creative spaces in cities like Berlin and Prague as these two quotes testify:

> 'Yeah, the situation was that after the fall of the wall in Berlin there kind of opened up this other half of the city in terms of living and art space.' (Interviewee 10, female, Berlin, 1990s art house squat)

'[W]e grew up in an era when there was an atmosphere in the air that everything is possible.' (Interviewee 52, male, Prague, guerrilla artist collective, established 2003)

Political opportunity in the first case arose out of the collapse of the Berlin Wall in 1989. This resulted in a rather unique chance for artists to experiment with and reconfigure city space (Steglich, 2016). In the case of Prague, the mobilization of this guerrilla arts collective was forged in the wake of the 1989 'Velvet Revolution'.

Elsewhere in Western Europe, the pro-corporate, rollout phase of neoliberal urbanization in the 1990s (Mayer, 2013) led to a lack of 'non-commercial' space in many cities. This resulted in a growing resistance through squatting, including arts-based ones, as this artist explained: "But so this squat experience became something very important so okay we can build our own studios ... so everyone was coming there to smoke joints, to listen to music, to do art" (interviewee 22, male, Geneva, 1990s artist collective). Many of these European alternative spaces were framed through a 'right to the city' idea (Mitchell, 2003; Marcuse, 2009b; Harvey, 2012), which can be traced back to the work of Lefebvre (1996), taking on a collective organizational structure and alternative politics. There was also, perhaps because of artistic self-preservation, the beginnings of an uneasy cooperation with the local state (Uitermark, 2004; Pattaroni, 2020).

In the contemporary period, alternative creative spaces have increasingly been shaped by what some artists describe as a crisis of "late capitalism" (interviewee 53, male, Montreal, alternative fringe, established 2004). This included resistance against national and local state responses to dealing with the aftermath of the 2008 global economic crash and subsequent austerity. When asked why their alternative creative space was formed during this period, one creative worker from Milan suggested: "One was the quite evident crisis of the traditional institutional form of our production and cultural spaces ... especially Milan that this creative industry was very connected also with the plan of the city and the processes of gentrification" (interviewee 34, male, Milan, artist-run squat, established 2012). In some Latin American countries, like Argentina for instance, 'there is currently a growing promotion of the creative economy on behalf of the state, which coexists with other "popular" and alternative cultural economies', emphasizing more local, horizontally organized, post-extractivist approaches (Banks and Serafini, 2020: 22).

In some cases, these issues have resulted in a renewed DIY spirit among alternative artists. This has been due to significant cuts in budgets for the independent arts sector, disagreement with current cultural policy and frustration over a lack of affordable creative space. However, to survive at all, many progressive artists have had cooperate with the local state to obtain artist-led spaces as the following quotes suggest:

'There were no studios and there was four of us that wanted to work with the council and a regeneration strategy was in place, there was regeneration officer, there was an economic development department … and we were able to negotiate our building with a peppercorn lease which is unthinkable now.' (Interviewee 40, female, Newcastle, contemporary not-for-profit arts studio)

'[I]t was a way to bring people back into a downtown that was kind of experiencing a little bit of a slump because of the construction … we had the landlords showing our [temporary] spaces to prospective buyers because they're like it doesn't look like it's been empty for six years.' (Interviewee 23, female, Kingston, Canada, fringe festival director)

Ironically, city regeneration and cultural incubator schemes promoted by the local state have been some of the main facilitators of alternative temporary spaces in recent times (Draaisma, 2016; Coffield et al, 2019). Reliance on these has implications not only for resistance against the neoliberal creative city but also has had an impact on the ethos of contemporary alterative creative spaces.

Changing alternative philosophies and organizational forms

Emanating largely from the wider context of liberation, left and anti-capitalist politics of the Fordist city, many of the alternative arts groups forming in the late 1960s and early 1970s framed themselves around ideologies of social change, collectivism and egalitarianism. Autonomy and independence were also key features of many of these spaces. There was a strong sense of egalitarianism within many of the radical arts groups formed at this time, with a collective and cooperative structure being the dominant organizational model (Hollands and Vail, 2012; Sandoval, 2016).

The spirit of collectivism has persisted in the formation of numerous alternative creative spaces in Europe and North America in the 1980s and early 1990s. Part of this reaction was created by the rollback and rollout phases of neoliberal urbanization (Mayer, 2013) and partly to do with issues of autonomy (see Case Study 3.4 on KuLe, for instance). In the European context, cultural politics in cities like Berlin, Amsterdam and Geneva were closely tied up with anarchist ideas and with the practice of combining squatting in the city with artistic collaboration, as the following quotation suggests: "We wanted to combine art and life … politically we were very interested in anarchy" (interviewee 11, female, Berlin, early 1990s art house squat). Interviews with several alternative creative spaces in North America at this time, located in cities like New York, Toronto and Montreal, also revealed the alignment of artistic practice with trade unionism, feminism and community politics to combat the impact of neoliberal politics.

Case Study 3.4: KuLe (Berlin): just about surviving neoliberal urbanization?

KuLe (derived from 'Kunst & Leiben' or 'Art and Life') originated out of tumultuous political change in Europe symbolized by the fall of the Berlin Wall and came into being when 10 Auguststrasse in the Mitte district of the city was squatted in July 1990 (Brezborn and Weismann, 2016). Inspired by both anarchist and feminist ideas, it has been described as an 'art house' (von Falkenhausen, 2016: 13), rather than as a utopian commune or an explicitly political squat. KuLe's specific evolution as an alternative creative space over the next decade was largely spared from the impact of neoliberal creative city strategies, as Berlin's property and tourism boom happened slightly later than many Western European cities (Colomb, 2011). It was also sustained in these early years by its collective structures and its many collaborations with other artists, neighbours and the wider squatting community (Brezborn and Weismann, 2016). However, when the city finally became recognized as 'cool', neoliberalism arrived with a vengeance. For example, transformations in their local neighbourhood over the last couple of decades means the art house is now literally floating as 'an island in a boutique district' (Koch, 2016: 143). The combined effect of gentrification, property development and anti-squat legislation in Berlin has led to the closure of numerous well-established arts collectives near KuLe over the years (like Tacheles), diminishing its support structure. Like many spaces of their era, they have found it harder in recent years to cultivate networks with other local artist groups in the city in the context of trying to maintain their own building space and artistic practice.

The commitment to collectivism and egalitarian decision making were apparent in the formation of some recent alternative creative spaces I researched. There were also examples of different usages of the collectivist label in the contemporary period. In talking about the new generation of artists calling themselves collectives or artist-led, one creative worker hypothesized that "what they're interested in is not the collective, but as they would see it, being independent" (interviewee 14, Birmingham, 1990s media arts collaborative space). Some contemporary artist groups may indeed have very different ideas of what it means to be called 'artist-led': "when we say artist-led, I think it's not such a literal interpretation of the term. It's not that we have artists who are the directors, who are the members of the staff who are doing the accounts who are, you know who are installing all the exhibitions" (interviewee 41, female, Newcastle, contemporary artist-led space).

Today, alternative creative spaces encompass many different types of political philosophies and organizational structures beyond the egalitarian art squats and collectives of the 1960s. They include community interest companies, charities, partnerships, volunteer-led, social or cultural enterprises, and not-for-profit companies. This is not to argue that such different forms cannot be understood as potentially resistant to aspects of the neoliberal creative city, only that the capacity to challenge it may become more difficult to engage in.

Artistic interventions against neoliberalism

Alternative creative spaces, by definition, should seek to challenge neoliberal urbanization. This includes opposing the dominant creative city paradigm based on a growth model, gentrified space and commodified culture (Kirchberg and Kagan, 2013). It is inevitable that artistic urban interventions can adopt a variety of forms ranging from direct action through to more everyday forms of dissonance (Boren and Young, 2017). These might include actions like occupations, squatting, marches and protests, artwork on the outside of a building (see Figure 3.2), to more subtle pranks, stunts and everyday resistance.

In the post-Fordist capitalist city such interventions often occurred through artistic collaborations with disadvantaged communities around an important political issue of the day, as the quote here reveals: "And it began as street

Figure 3.2: 'How Long is Now', Tacheles, Berlin

Source: photo by author, 2016

theatre and it got involved very directly with the London Rent Strikes, there were massive rent strikes in '69, 70s in London, and we wrote a play with the tenants so that the relationship you had with your audience was there organically" (interviewee 31, male, London, 1960s theatre collective).

Artistic urban interventions in the contemporary period are still possible and can also be collective in orientation (Pruijt, 2004). Here, one creative worker talks about the impact of organizing an alternative arts fair in the centre of his city in 2015 to challenge preconceptions of this sector: "Yeah, but I think we need much better communication and also be more present to change the image we have and the image that the right wing is spreading about what is this alternative space. And I think what we did in June by organizing this big event" (interviewee 18, male, Geneva, artist residency, established 2012).

Communication by alternative creative spaces in the form of 'culture jamming' is also a resistant strategy used today against the neoliberal creative city. For example, the Montreal based Infringement group have used what they call "social media techniques of disruption" (interviewee 53, male, Montreal, alternative fringe, established 2004) for years against what they see as the corporate tendencies of the official St Ambrose Fringe Festival. The anti-capitalist New York-based collective Mi Casa Resiste manages to use its art and direct action to challenge gentrification and displacement in its community, thereby engaging in 'place-guarding' and political issues beyond the arts (Levy, 2019).

Creative artistic stunts, guerrilla branding and mockumentary have also been engaged in by different spaces. More direct action like protesting and squatting are more difficult today, however. As one artist remarked: "[S]ome of the work that we did back then I just don't know if we could do it now, like it would be so problematic" (interviewee 43, female, Perth Australia, 1990s tactical media arts group). Stricter legislation against squatting (Dadusc and Dee, 2015) and political protest generally means that while artistic intervention against the neoliberal city is not impossible, it is certainly more challenging.

While alternative creative spaces and artistic resistance have been around in Western urban cities since at least the 1960s, they also exist, albeit in slightly different forms, in the Global South. Spaces critical of the creative city paradigm are perhaps more recent in some Global South cities simply because the paradigm may have been adopted slightly later there (Nkula-Wenz, 2019). They may also operate in different circumstances and contexts. For example, see Luger's (2019) research on discontent against the creativity paradigm in the 'soft' authoritarian state in Singapore (discussed in Chapter 4), Shin's (2020) study of alternative arts spaces fighting against hyper-gentrification in Seoul or Habibi's (2020) research on creative disruption carried out in Malaysia (see Case Study 3.5).

Case Study 3.5: Disrupting the creative city in George Town, Malaysia

Habibi (2020) provides a thought-provoking study of disruptive tactics by several creative collectives located within a space known as Hin's Bus Depot in George Town, a city in Penang Island, Malaysia. George Town went from being a colonial settlement to a manufacturing and holiday resort in the 1970s. It later embraced the creative city paradigm completely with an emphasis on cultural heritage and global tourism. Habibi (2020: 115) argues that state-led 'creative' strategies were followed by other initiatives from commercial organizations in the form of 'city branding, economic advancement, and global tourism'. Urban development focused on spectacular, design-led retail and entertainment zones in the contemporary city. However, this had the effect of neglecting local identities and cultural practices, leading to resentment and resistance. Several creative collectives have been housed in Hin's Bus Depot in George Town since 2014 and this space shares some of the same characteristics as Western alternative creative spaces. They include being less market-oriented, possessing collaborative and non-hierarchical working practices, defending organic community spaces and having political concerns about social inequality. These groups also expressed critical views about official mega-events and festivals as well as bemoaning city cultural authorities' lack of appreciation of local artists.

Alternative sustainability and neoliberal incorporation

When one of the founding members of a long-standing 1970s UK film collective still operating today was asked what its greatest achievement was, his response was simply 'survival' (Vail and Hollands, 2013: 542). Historically, the conditions for sustaining alternative creative spaces over long periods of time included a high commitment to the values of autonomy and collectivism. These value structures were also used to provide emotional and physical support for the artists involved. For example, a founding member of the long-standing art house KuLe in Berlin (see Case Study 3.4) cited the existence of a wider collective support structure as critical to the long-term maintenance of their space and identity in this quote: 'We were living in a large community [of other squats] with a strong sense of identity and the feeling of happiness that came from knowing that moments can be created in which it worked' (Brezborn and Weismann, 2016: 49).

The chances of survival for more recently formed alternative creative spaces are diminished under the consolidation phase of neoliberal urbanization characterized by corporate property development, hyper-gentrification and 'over-regulation'. One respondent blamed the lack of spaces on the fact that "the owners of the buildings are using them for the rents" (interviewee 3, male, Barcelona, academic–activist). This is especially the case in cities where there has been a boom in the rental and tourist market. Another cultural worker mentioned how the local state used the threat of closure to discipline the alternative creative space she worked in: "[I]t was starting to be like really you know, kind of sterilization of the building and putting some control inside which was really frightening. ... But they do this kind of threat with the closing" (interviewee 21, female, Geneva, 1990s non-profit cultural centre). While some contemporary alternative creative spaces have successfully adopted strategies to maintain their collective structures and autonomy (Keizer, 2014; Bain and Landau, 2018), the main threat has been incorporation into neoliberal creative city strategies.

In the current neoliberal consolidation phase (Mayer, 2013), many alternative creative spaces felt that they had little choice but to move into official state-recognized programmes or succumb to mainstream creative city legitimation. This was clearly the case in Amsterdam when squatting was discouraged from the millennium and then made illegal in 2010. Artist spaces had to decide whether to close or become state-subsidized breeding hubs (*broedplaatsen*), as explained by one interviewee:

'[B]ut of course, it's also a way of surviving especially in this period with this booming property market. What can you do, you can resist and then you go down proud but still nothing survives or just find another way to keep on going. And a lot of people eventually choose for the last option.' (Interviewee 2, male, Amsterdam, 1970s ex-squatter, now a *broedplaatsen* advisor)

This situation meant that compromises had to be made, with some alternative creative spaces and groups becoming complicit in local creative state branding policies and schemes (see Bader and Scharenberg, 2010; Anders, 2011; Luger, 2019). As I have argued elsewhere, '[i]ronically, in recent years, the neo-liberal creative state has even begun to reach out to the alternative creative sector, in order to increase urban vibrancy and authenticity' (Hollands, 2019: 735). The contradictions entailed in this incorporation process (Citroni, 2017) are summed up perfectly by this creative worker:

'It is impossible to ask for the authorities to create spaces of freedom. We have to create because they don't know how to do it. But my idea is that everywhere, even avant-garde ways of doing things, is being reused by this system to transform itself. ... I'm not sure there are really alternative cultural spaces anymore.' (Interviewee 22, male, Geneva, mid-1990s artist collective)

There are examples where alternative creative spaces have been able to sustain themselves long-term without totally compromising (Pruijt, 2004; Hollands,

Figure 3.3: OT301, Amsterdam: remaining committed to its squatting history

Source: photo by author, 2016 (wall message reproduced with permission)

2019). For example, in the late 1990s, artistic squatters pushed back against the policy of squat clearances in Amsterdam by raising the need for creative space (Jansen, 2014: 249). This resistance provided the opportunity context for the emergence of OT301, a former film academy, which was squatted on 14 November 1999, by a group of artists who called themselves EHBK (Eerste Hulp Bij Kunst or 'First Aid for Art'). While remaining a squat in practice for the next two years, OT301 very quickly entered into a series of negotiations with city authorities and district municipalities, signing a letter of intent to become a 'breeding space' (Jansen, 2014: 256). Despite various organizational changes, OT301 has insisted on holding firm to a collective philosophy (Jansen, 2014: 261) and the group bought the building in 2006. While owning a building can be seen as 'selling out' by the wider squatting movement, OT301 remains committed to its collectivist roots (see Figure 3.3) and opposition to neoliberal creative city strategies.

To conclude, this chapter has focused in on some of the key problems, contradictions and criticisms of Florida's neoliberal creative city paradigm. Rather than accept his analyses and creativity index, it has been suggested that perhaps we should gauge the health of the alternative creative sector as a better indicator of urban creativity. The key question is how do we sustain existing alternative creative groups and spaces and encourage new ones under the present conditions wrought by 'late actually existing neoliberalism' (Peck and Theodore, 2019)? One of the ways is for local governments to jettison dominant creative city strategies and put into place new ideas to support an alternative creative space infrastructure. This might include creating policies and laws designed to provide council buildings at cheap rates; differential licensing and regulatory requirements for independents; and aiding alternative creative space networks (Artist-led Research Group, 2019; Coffield et al, 2019). A more comprehensive strategy might be to explore under what circumstances individual artist-led spaces can begin to act in concert as more collective urban cultural movements. This is the main subject of Chapter 4.

4

Urban Cultural Movements and Anti-Creative Struggles

Within the last decade or so, there has been a global resurgence of artist-led struggles around neoliberal urban space (Serafini et al, 2018). While organized anti-creative city movements have tended to be more prominent in Europe (NiON, 2010; Kirchberg and Kagan, 2013; Novy and Colomb, 2013; d'Ovidio and Rodríguez Morató, 2017; Romeiro, 2017; Sanchez Belando, 2017, among others), resistance also exists in countries like the US (Grodach, 2017), Canada (McLean, 2014b; King, 2016), Australia (Shaw, 2014) and in cities of the Global South (Luger, 2019; De Beukelaer, 2021; Martin-Iverson, 2021).

For example, 2011–2012 saw the growth of a range of cultural occupations across Italy, including the creation of an imaginary 'People's Center for Art' in a 31-storey skyscraper in Milan by a movement known as MACAO (d'Ovidio and Cossu, 2017). Their focus on guerrilla branding tactics and self-organized cultural production has resulted in a broader cultural experiment in creative democracy in the city (Valli, 2015). Luger's (2019: 330) research on Singapore also reveals how the current 'arts generation' is 'striking back, against the state, in the form of critical expression' despite facing creative incorporation and 'authoritarian boundaries'. In 2016, the Infringement movement staged their own alternative gathering in Montreal in protest against the World Fringe Congress's increasingly corporate approach to fringe (Montreal Infringement Festival, 2016) (see Figure 4.1). Meanwhile, in Berlin in 2012, Haben und Brauchen ('to have and to need'), a movement of alternative cultural workers, challenged conventional arts policy in the city by producing a powerful manifesto (Haben und Brauchen, 2012).

These varied examples feed into the notion of opposition towards the dominant neoliberal creative city paradigm and represent what I, and others, refer to as 'urban cultural movements' (Novy and Colomb, 2013; Valli, 2015; Hollands, 2019). I define these as *movements that have creativity or culture at the*

Figure 4.1: Infringement World Congress poster, Montreal, Canada, November 2016

Source: Montreal Infringement, http://infringemontreal.org/archived-pages/2016-festival/montreal-infringement-festival-2016/ (reproduced with permission)

core of their principles, activity and struggle against the neoliberal city. This chapter builds upon critiques of Florida's creative city paradigm and the discussion of the potential of alternative creative spaces developed in Chapter 3. It is concerned to explore how activist artists and groups can work collectively and liaise with other urban social movements to envisage an alternative urban future. As Miles argues:

The creative city is not a socially coherent but – in contrast to the modernist city of public well-being – a socially divisive city, in which culture as the arts is privileged over culture as the articulation of shared values in everyday life. The 2008 financial services crisis has interrupted this trajectory, however, providing an opportunity to re-assess the idea of a creative city and the values implicit in it. Alternatives emerge in direct action – notably Occupy in 2011–12 – and activist art. Could there be a post-creative city? Could the creative imagination of diverse urban groups lead to new socio-political as well as cultural formations? That might be another urban revolution. (Miles, 2013)

To address the questions Miles (2013) raises, this chapter is divided into two sections. The first section provides some background on urban collective action by introducing the work of Manuel Castells and his concept of 'urban social movements'. The second section develops the related concept of urban cultural movements. In doing so, it looks at some case study examples of creative resistance from Milan, Singapore and Berlin. It explores the potential of anti-creative struggles as well as the pitfalls urban cultural movements face in making links with wider social and political contestations in the neoliberal city.

Castells and urban social movement theory

To contextualize a discussion about the potential alternative creative spaces have in forming cultural movements, it is useful to introduce Castells' classic idea of urban social movements. While he is perhaps most well-known for his work around the network and information society (Castells, 1996; 1997; 1998), previously Castells was also a very influential figure in the field of urban sociology (Castells, 1968; 1977; 1978). Politically he was involved in the student cultural struggles in Paris in May 1968 and was heavily influenced by 'new social movements' ideas (Touraine, 1971). This section of the chapter focuses briefly on Castells' early work in urban sociology in the 1960s and 1970s, before turning to his later empirical work on urban social movements (Castells, 1983).

Castells was a key thinker in Marxist urban sociology in the late 1960s and 1970s. In a similar vein to Harvey (1989a), Castells was trying to argue that the 'urban effect' was really a result of capitalism rather than other forces like ecology (Chicago School), community power or urban culture (Saunders, 1981). Castells' (1968) early work suggested that it is the structures of capitalism, not urbanism, that produces city life. Essentially, he was arguing against the idea of a specifically urban sociology. Ironically his sophisticated theoretical interventions (Castells, 1977; 1978) had the reverse effect of reviving, rather than diminishing, the status of the sub-discipline.

Where Castells (1977; 1978) differs from Harvey's (1989a) work is his focus not on production and the movement of capital around the world and into cities, but his emphases on the 'reproduction of labour power'. The concept refers to the conditions necessary for workers to continue to work each day. He also gives credence to the contradictions of capitalism and particularly centres in on some of the tensions as to how labour power gets reproduced. What Castells (1977) argues is that the reproduction of labour power requires state intervention around the provision of services – what he calls 'collective consumption'. Capitalism ideally does not want to provide such services. For example, it does not want to be responsible for providing adequate housing, proper education and training, or transport systems to get workers to work. And yet, labour power requires all these things for capitalism to function properly. State intervention, Castells (1978) argues, is necessary to complete this circuit. However, struggles to obtain such service provision by the urban population creates expectations of their continuance. One of the ways in which this struggle is enacted is through what Castells calls 'urban social movements'.

Earlier on in his work Castells (1977) talked about the positive link between urban social movements and left organizations and political parties. However, it is his later work, *The City and the Grassroots*, written in 1983, which empirically looks at such movements in detail. In his classic study of urban social movements, Castells (1983: 305) defines the concept as 'urban oriented mobilizations that influence structural social change and transforms the urban meanings'. In this latter work he shifts his political position regarding the link between urban social movements and political parties. Here, Castells suggests urban social movements may be more effective if they are not so closely associated with political parties. If independent, they form 'non-institutionalized' forms of political action which are less amenable to corruption or co-optation by the state.

There are three aspects to understanding Castells' (1983) urban social movements. First, he suggests that they are characterized by struggles for improved 'collective consumption'. These are protests for the provision of public housing, increased transport and other urban services (which might include art and culture). Second, Castells suggests that such movements are also the struggle for community communication and this includes three aspects – the fight for place or territory, local culture and identity. And, third, he argues that urban social movements are also a struggle for 'political self-determination' against the local state. Non-institutionalized political action is about enacting decentralized and participatory forms of democracy.

Castells (1983) looks at a range of urban social movements, including historical ones. For example, he examines cases like the Paris Commune of 1871 and the Glasgow Rent Strikes of 1915. He also looks at more contemporary examples like the Madrid Citizens' Movement of the 1970s, which Castells sees as the most 'ideal type' of urban social movement in his research. For instance, he sees it as successful in fighting for collective consumption in terms of it suggesting a programme funding public housing and other urban facilities. It also had a strong sense of identity, being a self-conscious movement fighting for particular kinds of outcomes. Finally, it represented a non-institutionalized and cooperative approach to the city which sought to democratize Spain from within. Castells suggests, however, that the movement was eventually crushed by wider party politics, including parties of the left.

Castells' (1983) work is also applicable to urban struggles in the Global South, particularly Latin America, as he provides an early analysis of studies of squatter movements there. Summarizing his approach, Schönwälder (2002: 24) says Castells' principal argument is that squatter settlements are largely dependent on state policies and are open to manipulation and changing political ideologies. Hence, they are relatively unstable as an urban social movement.

Perhaps Castell's most well-known case studies of an urban social movement is the 1970s San Francisco gay movement. This trajectory of the movement is represented most graphically in the film *Milk* (2008) about the gay activist turned politician, Harvey Milk. In Castells' assessment this movement succeeded in challenging local political structures. They also developed a strong urban and spatial identity, but perhaps fell short in terms of fighting successfully for collective consumption. In this sense, urban social movements from Castells' (1983) point of view, are sometimes referred to as 'local utopias' intended to change the urban meaning. They raise questions like who is the city for, what is the city for, and how can we envisage new uses for the city? Due to being spatially rooted, these local utopias can be limited. Yet they can also act as the forerunner for larger political movements for social change, like the fight for gay rights for example.

Castells' (1996; 1997; 1998) later focus on the rise of the network and information society took him away from urban sociology and cities, while his book *Networks of Outrage and Hope* (2012) brought him back to the role social media plays in social movements. This more 'non-spatial' type of approach is perhaps less relevant to an understanding of urban cultural movements in cities even though social media can be used successfully in some anti-creative struggles (see Cossu and Francesca Murru, 2018). Before turning to a discussion of such movements, the next section considers the usefulness of Castells' work.

Critiquing Castells

In terms of assessing Castells' work, one can divide critiques into two phases. First, his early theoretical work around the urban question (Castells, 1968;

1977; 1978). Second, his later thinking on urban social movements in *The City and the Grassroots* (1983) and movements in the network society (Castells, 2012).

With respect to his early writings, it is clear that Castells (1977; 1978) develops quite an abstract theoretical approach which is dogged by overly structuralist thinking (Saunders, 1981). Like many Marxists of his day, he also adopts a position akin to what some people would call 'epistemological privileging'. In other words, Castells assumes his argument is automatically more comprehensive and explanatory than other theories, without empirically testing them. While he may be justified in critiquing previous urban sociology perspectives like the Chicago School's urban ecology theory (Park, 2013), its weaknesses should not imply that Castell's own approach has no shortcomings, for instance, its structural determinism (Althusser, 1971).

One might also argue that Castells' (1977) notion of collective consumption is somewhat time-specific. The notion that urban groups automatically resist any attempt to roll back the public provision of urban services is belied by the 'successful' introduction of austerity politics of the 1980s and following the 2008 financial crash. Urban social movements in the late 1960s and early 1970s clearly rebelled against the Fordist local and national state and were against urban police repression. By the millennium many of them are starting to liaise with local authorities in order to cushion the worst effects of global neoliberal urbanization (Mayer, 2013). In other words, resistance strategies of urban movements in the contemporary period may have shifted away from those used in the 1970s. Castells' early theories then may appear somewhat dated.

As mentioned, Castells' theory of urban social movements is geographically applicable to cities of the Global South. But there are still some issues here due largely to Castells changing his position about the relationship such movements have with political parties. Schönwälder (2002) highlights three issues in relation to understanding urban popular movements in Latin America in particular. First, he suggests that Castells' early Marxist position led him to downplay the significance of urban social and political change taking place at a level below system transformation (Schönwälder, 2002: 12). Second, the class composition of squatter movements in many Latin America cities were often a mixture of the working and non-working class (urban poor), different ethnic groups, as well as small-scale traders and street entrepreneurs. This made the formation of a singular collective identity movement harder to achieve (Schönwälder, 2002: 16-17). Finally, Castells' (1983) later assertion that autonomy from the state was a characteristic of a successful urban social movement was less applicable to some urban struggles in Latin America, as often regimes were semi-authoritarian (Schönwälder, 2002: 14).

Other Marxist perspectives, like Harvey's (1989a) urban entrepreneurialism approach, can also be used to criticize Castells. For example, it might be said that Castells plays down the massive impact the global productive economy has had on cities in favour of his focus on the reproduction of labour power. In contrast to Harvey's consistent politics, one of the other criticisms made towards Castells is his 'about face' in changing various aspect of his approach. While part of the explanation is his understandable movement away from the strictures of the Communist Party and from Marxist structuralism to a more empirical approach, it does cause inconsistencies in his work.

Finally, even Castells' more empirically based approach in *The City and the Grassroots* (1983) comes in for some criticism. For example, Mayer (2006) suggests that he is more concerned with the formal characteristics of urban social movements in judging their effectiveness, rather than with discussing the wider context behind them or how and why they emerged. Regarding his later work (Castells, 2012), others have argued that Castells' concern with the network society means that his approach loses an emphasis on space, place and territory which are necessary for understanding what is happening with particular cities (Fuchs, 2012).

Modern urban social and cultural movements

Despite these weaknesses, Castells' original ideas provide a useful backdrop to how we might begin to rethink contemporary urban social and cultural movements. Neoliberal urbanization as discussed by Mayer (2013) is characterized by a number of urban features which developed subsequently to Castells' more Fordist analyses. For example, increased corporatization and globalization of the economy; 'mega' gentrification in cities; the movement towards entrepreneurial governance and branding strategies; and of course the development of the urban cultural economy and the creative city idea.

Mayer's (2013) adoption of a phase model of neoliberal urbanization discussed in Chapter 3 is a useful way of advancing Castells' ideas about urban social movements today. For example, she contrasts resistance strategies in the 1970s Fordist city (Castells' model) with those aimed at opposing the 1980s 'rollback' of the state, the 'rollout' of pro-corporate policies in the 1990s, followed by a consolidation phase (post-2000). Mayer (2013) argues that many urban social movements and community-based struggles today have been subsumed within 'public–private partnerships' with the local state. Therefore, we have seen a shift in modes of resistance from being explicitly 'anti-state' in the late 1960s and early 1970s, to more conciliatory models developed from the millennium onwards. Not only does Mayer develop a more nuanced historical model here, but her approach is also cognizant of how the concerns and character of urban social movements have changed.

Mayer's (2013) work suggests that in the contemporary period urban social movements appear to be coalescing primarily around two struggles – one a renewed set of anti-austerity protests and the other a set of anti-creative city struggles, or what I would call urban cultural movements (Hollands, 2019). Neoliberal urbanization has paradoxically resulted in both increased social polarization (see Chapter 7) and social incorporation. As Mayer explains:

> On the one hand, neo liberalism has led to intense and intensifying social fragmentation. This has exacerbated polarization and displacement, while the recent austerity cuts have been hitting not only the already disadvantaged but increasingly youth, students and more segments of the middle class. On the other hand, it has also allowed concessions and offerings to those movement groups that may be usefully absorbed into city marketing and locational politics that municipalities everywhere are now tailoring to attract investors, creative professionals and tourists. (Mayer, 2013: 10–11)

One of the problems identified by Mayer (2013) here is a tendency towards what might be called 'creative incorporation'. For example, De Beukelaer (2021) talks about the Bandung Creative City Forum as a civil society organization instrumental in helping to form its urban creative strategies. While some might see such an organization as an example of an 'alternative creative city from below' with its development of ten progressive principals (including inclusivity, human rights, sustainable environment, and so on), others might construe this as neoliberal incorporation (Martin-Iverson, 2021: 121–122). Also problematic is that Mayer (2013) suggests that anti-creative city and anti-austerity struggles are not easily joined up. One of the reasons behind this is anti-creative city movements today may have different goals, organizational forms and ways of protesting than that of wider social movements (Novy and Colomb, 2013). There may also be differences between movements that use the language of social justice and those that use the language of creativity.

Mayer's (2013) advancements on Castells' previous model of urban social movements does not mean that some elements of his approach cannot be retained. We may need to rethink other aspects when looking more closely at how cultural movements have evolved under neoliberal urbanization. Similarly, it is important to keep in mind some of the key differences in *when and how* neoliberalism and the creativity paradigm came to cities of the Global South (Connell and Dados, 2014; Jesus et al, 2020), as Mayer's (2013) own analyses is largely limited to the first world.

Urban cultural movements and neoliberalism

This section of the chapter focuses specifically on anti-creative struggles and developing the concept of urban cultural movements. Hollands (2017a: 1) defines urban cultural movements as 'city-based movements that have creativity at the core of their principles, activity and struggle'. Valli (2015) argues that these movements are characterized by three main features:

1. they seek to collectively reconfigure urban space;
2. they aim to foster alternative practices of cultural production; and
3. they provide a critique of the existing neoliberal creative city.

In the West, particularly in European counties, the mobilization of cultural workers in opposition to the neoliberal creative city has grown in the last couple of decades (d'Ovidio and Rodríguez Morató, 2017). More recently, anti-creative sentiments have been researched in cities of the Global South, though these struggles take place in different contexts and may have varying characteristics (Luger, 2019; De Beukelaer, 2021; Martin-Iverson, 2021).

While sharing some elements with alternative creative spaces, urban cultural movements, like all movements, usually only come about periodically. When certain events and conditions require them, they rise up, before falling away over time. Their relationship to alternative creative spaces is symbiotic (Hollands, 2019). On the one hand, urban cultural movements require the existence and banding together of alternative creative spaces in order to create and fuel a movement. Similarly, urban cultural movements themselves may result in the birth of new alternative creative spaces. Both alternative creative spaces and urban cultural movements may engage in a variety of forms of opposition to the neoliberal creative city. These were discussed in Chapter 3 and include strikes, protests, occupations, manifestos, marches and the creation of oppositional networks, among other resistant activities like 'culture jamming', mockumentary and art pranks. Movements may also engage in more everyday and mundane forms of resistance like discontent and disagreement with creative policies or state initiatives (Boren and Young, 2017; Luger, 2019).

In order to more fully understand artistic collective action, we need to look at it historically. Notwithstanding earlier avant-garde arts movements, most well-known and researched urban cultural movements like the Situationist International in Paris (McDonough, 2010), the UK Independent Film Movement (Dickinson, 1999) and the Art Workers Coalition in New York City (Bryan-Wilson, 2009) arose in the late 1960s and early 1970s. This was a time of tumultuous economic, social and political change in Western capitalist economies. We can see that these early art movements were created within wider political ruptures and crises within Fordist capitalism. They also came about in the context of the development of a 'critical mass' of alternative creative spaces. The following quotation demonstrates how a single arts collective in New York City formed alliances with another cultural union to form a broader urban cultural movement:

'So, we formed a collective in New York with 13, 14 members. ... Huge protests which we all got involved in ... we were approached by an anti, well it was called the Anti–Imperialist Culture Union. ... So we became involved with them, and that brought in a whole other level of politics.' (Interviewee 50, male, New York/Toronto, 1960s artist collective)

Around the same time, in the UK, one interviewee spoke about how the formation of a number of alternative film collectives in the late 1960s coalesced into the formation of the UK independent film movement (Dickinson, 1999):

'By that time there was something emerging in London that loosely ... well, became the independent film movement. I also worked with a group called Liberation Films who were in North London. I used to edit their films, and they had come out of 1968 but they were very much interested in community arts. ... And things like Cinema Action were going. Cinema Action came directly out of the events of 1968, and the Berwick Street Collective, and by that time the Independent Filmmakers' Association had been formed in London, and so I was a member of that.' (Interviewee 17, male, Edinburgh, now a university film lecturer)

The independent film movement was followed by another cultural network in the UK, known as the Workshop Movement. This movement sought to radically restructure support and practices associated with independent filmmakers and establish an alternative media sector (see Dickinson [1999], as well as Case Study 4.1 on Amber and the Workshop Movement).

Case Study 4.1: Newcastle-based Amber film collective and the Workshop Movement

While the UK independent film movement was a loose conglomeration of radical film groups, the Workshop Movement was a more structured and formalized affair. One of the main catalysts of the movement was the Amber Film Collective which formed in London in the late 1960s at Regent Street polytechnic (Hollands and Vail, 2012), but moved to Newcastle upon Tyne in the early 1970s (Hollands and Vail, 2015). In addition to acting as a focal point of alternative cultural production in the city, Amber was key in stimulating the development of an alternative cultural economy within the British film sector (Vail and Hollands, 2013). In 1982 the Workshop Declaration was agreed by stakeholders including the Association of Cinematograph, Television and Allied Technicians, British Film Institute and Channel 4 (Dickinson, 1999). Under this new code of practice, workshops consisted of groups with four or more full-time members who engaged in non-commercial work on a non-profit basis; where all staff were paid an equal rate determined through union negotiations; where groups retained sole copyright to their artistic work; and where cross-grade practice, enabling filmmakers to take on multiple roles, was affirmed. Channel 4 agreed to provide long-term funding for workshops that was explicitly regionally based and focused on disadvantaged populations. It also showcased their work in a special time slot in their programming schedule (Dickinson, 1999). By the mid-1980s, this network of independent grant-aided workshops constituted the foundation for a distinct alternative media sector and artistic community. Following a failed attempt to extend the cultural model of the workshops to the rest of Europe, Channel 4 ended its franchise funding of the workshops after a decade of support (Vail and Hollands, 2013).

Today, neoliberal ideology, promoting individualism rather than collective action, has taken its toll on the capacity of even independent cultural producers to entertain anything like the Workshop Movement. Consider the following quote from a Newcastle-based filmmaker when asked if she would support an independent film advocacy organization:

'Well, I remember a few years ago they were trying to formalize something, and I'm not sure if they did or not, but to be honest, that's a huge turnoff to me. I don't want to be part of a formal group like that. I think the difficulty I find is when you set up a formal group like that, I think people come in with agendas, and then you're having to battle their agenda, and I don't really want to get into that. I feel it's much easier if there's a common problem that we all share and we can talk about it and maybe sound off for a little bit and then something will come out of it. ... But if a group was formalized, I think then you have to maybe listen to somebody pushing their own agenda, and I think that's the difficulty.' (Interviewee 54, female, Newcastle, independent filmmaker)

There is a recognition here that networking and problem-solving are important in sustaining an alternative sector. It is equally clear from this quote that building cultural movements today faces obstacles. One of the key factors is neoliberal thinking itself which breeds individualist rather than collective solutions to artist problems (Sholette, 2011). Similarly, challenging neoliberal creative city policies in soft-authoritarian states may make the formation of critical urban cultural movements difficult if not almost impossible (Luger, 2019; also see Case Study 4.3 on Singapore). Another related factor is the 'short termism' of many contemporary alternative creative spaces under neoliberalism (Coffield et al, 2019). For instance, one young creative worker ruminated on the effect so-called 'pop up' or 'meanwhile' art spaces have on collective action by saying: "So now like there are these things that kind of pop up and disappear, but there isn't the sense of cooperation between the different spaces … it's more individualist here" (interviewee 47, male, Prague, collective artist studio, established 2015).

Still other creatives blamed the corporate takeover of city space and a diminished number of alternative spaces for the lack of collective action: "Four city centre artist-led spaces have gone in the last while … we're the last one standing" (interviewee 28, male, Leeds, artist-led community and project space, established 2016). These closures were directly connected to the current domination of corporate led property development, mega-gentrification and austerity in the cultural field. Feelings of isolation and powerlessness can also lead to the idea that collective action is not an option. Urban cultural movement building is also hampered by stricter legislation against occupations, squats and political protests.

Another barrier to cooperation and networking across alternative arts groups that was recognized was, ironically, competition between such spaces, as this interviewee argued: "I don't think the alternative sector is organized enough. Perhaps these people get a little protective. I don't know whether there's a sense of competition" (interviewee 40, female, Newcastle, not-for-profit art studio, established 2010). Favouritism and 'divide and rule' tactics were also used by the local state to fragment the alternative sector, thus discouraging anti-creative city movements from forming (Citroni, 2017).

Finally, numerous spokespersons from different alternative creative spaces mentioned the tension between trying to do their art and keeping their place open, while trying to maintain solidarity networks with others. The following quotation talks about the notion of being 'time poor' with regard to building such networks: "It's so hard isn't it because you're just, you're so time poor … do you actually have time to build these bigger networks?" (interviewee 43, female, Perth, Australia, 1990s tactical media arts group).

Case studies of creative city resistance

Despite these various obstacles there are contemporary examples of urban cultural movements and resistances which have arisen in response to the neoliberal creative city. Problems such as property-led displacement, gentrification and work precarity can produce disaffection with creative state policies and lead to collective and organized resistance (Lorey, 2015). One example of such an urban cultural movement is MACAO in Milan (for some background on the city context see Case Study 4.2).

Case Study 4.2: Milan and neoliberal creative precarity

Milan (population 1.35 million; metropolitan area over 3 million) ranks as a 'tier two' city in terms of economic ranking of global cities alongside Hong Kong, San Francisco and Toronto (Abrahamson, 2014: 35). In cultural terms, it has been recognized as a UNESCO creative city of literature and is well-known globally for its fashion and design industries. Despite these positive economic indicators and cultural accolades, Milan, like many Italian cities, suffered badly from the 2008 financial crash, austerity politics and gentrification. Its creative sector, in particular, is fraught with underinvestment, marketization and workplace precarity (Valli, 2015). A lack of local government investment and a philosophy of minimal intervention in arts and culture in the city over the past couple of decades has also bred resistance and resentment among independent artists (d'Ovidio and Cossu, 2017: 8). There had been a strong history of *centri sociali* (autonomous squatted centres) in Milan in the 1970s and 1980s, but many were forced to shut from 2000 onward (d'Ovidio and Cossu, 2017: 9). There were also anti-gentrification struggles in the city in the 1990s (Valli, 2015). In 2011, the formation of a small group of politicized creative workers in the city, calling themselves Lavoratori dell'arte ('Art Workers'), met weekly to discuss precarity in the creative industries. They later become a driving force behind the occupation of Galfi Tower in 2011 and the formation of MACAO (Valli, 2015: 648).

The emergence of the MACAO movement came out of a more general political crisis and debate surrounding the 'urban commons' in Italy (d'Ovidio and Cossu, 2017). There were a number of occupations of art and creative venues in numerous Italian cities, including Rome and Venice (Borchi, 2018), as well as Milan. Milan's urban cultural economy, in particular, was seriously affected by the 2008 global financial crash and ensuing politics of austerity (Hollands, 2019). A particular constellation of factors in the city, such as an acute lack of state investment in art and culture and severe precarity in the creative industries, resulted in an oppositional urban cultural movement (Valli, 2015). As this core member of the movement recalled:

'The mainly public sector were really in crisis in Italy especially, because of the cuts of funding, and also because of, I mean the cultural, of their way to consider cultural production ... on the other part there was in Italy especially in Milan, maybe also in Venice and in Turin in Italy, like the starting point of the power of creative industry. ... But in the end it was quite perceived that there was a lot of bad condition in terms of working condition, very precarious.' (Interviewee 33, male, Milan, MACAO)

The movement officially came into existence on 5 May 2012, when hundreds of people occupied an empty 31-storey skyscraper, Galfi Tower, in the centre of Milan for ten days, envisioning what a 'People's Centre for Arts' would look like (Cossu and Francesca Murru, 2018: 65). Composed of different groups and professions, including creative workers, and characterized by a strong social media presence (Cossu and Francesca Murru, 2018), the MACAO movement was largely horizontal, run by open assemblies guided by the principles of direct action and democracy. It became known particularly for its focus on guerrilla-branding tactics and self-organized cultural production.

Since then, a core group within the movement occupied a temporary space in a formally disused slaughterhouse office. They continued to critically question precarity in the cultural industries while promoting a radically different vision of creative democracy in the city (d'Ovidio and Cossu, 2017). Despite settling in one place, one of the most interesting things about MACAO as an urban cultural movement is that it has always been seen as 'a crossing' (a meeting point of ideas and groups) rather than a space. Since forming, they claim to have worked with hundreds of different artists, political and community groups. They have done this through a combination of using voluntary labour, developing their own 'common currency' and engaging in a networked 'gift economy'. Utilizing this model, MACAO developed a radically new approach to 'doing culture' differently, while questioning the dominant neoliberal creative city paradigm (Valli, 2015).

Interestingly, MACAO, although highly critical of the local creative state, has chosen to work in conjunction with it. They have sought to avoid the isolationist mistakes of social centres of the past by engaging with the state in what they call a 'reinvention of the way we try to cooperate' (Tozzi, 2016). This has taken the form of 'critical participation'. For example, MACAO got involved in the mega-event Expo 2015, by running a survey project designed to expose the poor working conditions at the event. While I return to the example of MACAO later, in Case Study 4.3 I provide another example of creative resistance from the Global South, where a generation of artists are in yet another critical, yet paradoxical, relationship with the state.

Case Study 4.3: State-led creativity and its discontents in Singapore

Luger's (2019) research examines some of the limits and contradictions of generational resistance to state-led creativity policies in the so-called 'soft-authoritarian Asian city' of Singapore. His study is concerned with showing 'how the "creative class" is striking back, against the state, in the form of critical expression – and probes how recipients of arts policy, envisioned as an "arts generation", have been given a platform for critical views at the same time they face authoritarian boundaries' (Luger, 2019: 330). As background, Luger (2019: 331) mentions 'Singapore's unique soft-authoritarian state-society nexus, city-state geography, and particularly robust embrace of art and culture as a state policy imperative'. Although the city-state's concern with art and culture pre-dates the creative city paradigm, with Singapore becoming a global or world city in the late 1980s to early 1990s, it was influenced by both Florida and Landry's thinking in the 'cultural turn' in the early 2000s. Here the state invested heavily in numerous aspects of the urban cultural economy mentioned in Chapter 1, including galleries, museums and spaces of consumption and entertainment, including nightlife.

The section of the creative class that Luger looks at is referred to as the 'arts generation'. This is a cohort of cultural producers and art-policy officials in Singapore who were the initial recipients of its early arts and cultural policies. Many in this group were founders of early independent theatre companies and arts collectives (essentially alterative creative spaces) in the city. Luger (2019: 330) suggests that this cohort is 'vocally critical of the state, state policy, and sympathetic to a variety of activist causes'. In particular, he says they remain sceptical that the city-state wants to foster a truly grassroots arts ecosystem, are concerned with human rights and inequalities and are discontented by economically driven creative policy making. With one foot in the 'critical grassroots' and the other incorporated into the creative city-state bureaucracy, Luger (2019) argues that the 'arts generation' is in danger of falling back on elite notions of art and privilege as it increasing become the 'arts establishment'. Guilty of reaping the benefits of the 'cultural turn', this generation is unsure about the current creative policy of 'art for all', remaining 'somewhat cloistered in elite enclaves' (Luger, 2019: 330–331). Similarly, its relatively privileged and elite position also raises some doubt as to whether creative discontent is transformative or merely incorporative.

A third example of an oppositional urban cultural movement is that of Haben und Brauchen, which translates as 'to have and to need'. This movement was formed in 2011 in Berlin (for city background see Case Study 4.4) by a collection of around 200 artists, designers, creatives and urban activists in reaction to a neoliberal mega-event entitled 'The Competitive Exhibition of Young Art in the City of Berlin'. Rather than argue that the money behind this event needed to be more widely dispersed within the cultural sector, the movement instead conducted research and produced a well-regarded urban manifesto (Haben und Brauchen, 2012). Written by over 40 people, it looked at the problem of the artist in this city as representative of wider urban problems.

The manifesto expressed dissatisfaction with the fact that Berlin appeared to be capitalizing on using artists to culturally brand the city. Instead, the movement put forward the idea that culture, rather than being seen as a commodity, was rather part of the 'urban commons'. As one member said: "[C]ulture is a common good and ... it's not about producing a hip image for the city" (interviewee 8, female, Berlin, Haben und Brauchen). Additionally, the manifesto critiqued the idea that Berlin was a 'world leading art city' on the basis of their research which showed that nearly 80 per cent of artists were unable to make a living doing art. They also questioning the precarity of artistic labour, including the well-known issue of the under- or non-payment of artists.

Case Study 4.4: Berlin: 'capital of cool' or a creative backfire?

Despite its modern reputation as a popular tourist destination and centre for the arts, Berlin (population around 3.5 million), in fact, experienced economic stagnation during most of the 1990s (Novy and Colomb, 2013: 1823–1824). After the fall of the wall it experienced steady growth, then a boom in tourism, aided later by various city marketing strategies in the first decade of the millennium (Colomb, 2011). Berlin is now one of the most popular urban tourism destinations in Europe, just behind London and Paris (Novy, 2018: 53). Additionally, in the 1990s, cheap available spaces also made it a mecca for rave culture and techno music (Bader and Scharenberg, 2010), and a haven for artists and creative workers from all over the world. Of the 7,000 artists living in Berlin, it is estimated that a quarter are not German but have migrated from elsewhere in the world to the city (Rietz-Rakul and Schepens, 2010: 8). By 2008, the cultural industries made up 21 per cent of the city's GDP and in 2010 it was named Europe's 'Capital of Cool' by *Time* magazine (Novy, 2018: 53). However, its very success in tourism and the arts has recently begun to backfire. Rising rents, created through monopoly landlords and Airbnb, have led to anti-tourist and anti-gentrification protests by local neighbourhoods (Novy, 2018) (see also Chapter 6). Similarly, the rapid influx of artists into Berlin has resulted in a lack of studio space and affordable housing, not to mention creating competition for work among artists (Haben und Brauchen, 2012). These factors, not to mention rapid gentrification in various city centre areas, has led to calls for state intervention to restrict monopoly ownership, impose rent freezes and provide more social housing (O'Sullivan, 2019). There have been some legislative changes in some of these areas, though some have been recently overturned (see Chapter 6 for details).

Finally, rather than arguing for more art and culture funding, the manifesto called for a fundamental rethink of how people are best to live and work in the city. In doing so they drew attention to the lack of affordable housing/studio space in the city and also raised the issue of gentrification. As such the manifesto sought not to separate creative workers from other groups in the city but suggested the need to stand together. Work precarity, community, decent and affordable housing and workspace are issues all urban dwellers have in common.

This idea came through in an interview quotation with one of its prominent members, where they suggest that broader solidarity networks are required: "You have to make solidarities with other groups because you by yourself are not only a cultural worker, and the problems arriving are not only from the art scene, it's a much broader problem" (interviewee 9, male, Berlin, Haben und Brauchen). Despite holding this inclusive view, Haben und Brauchen as an urban cultural movement became a victim of its own success. This occurred post-manifesto when it was invited to help inform cultural policy making in the city.

Possibilities and pitfalls

In this final section I want to explore the potential of urban cultural movements to stimulate social change and create alternative 'urban meanings' (to invoke Castells). I then consider some of their shortcomings. Castells (1983) reminds us that 'successful' urban social movements should challenge the capitalist city in terms of the provision of collective consumption, community communication and political autonomy. Valli (2015) similarly argues that urban cultural movements are also about the reappropriation of urban space, the practising of alternative cultural production and providing urban critique.

In the case of MACAO, it is clear that the movement sought to redefine the urban meaning of the existing creative economy of Milan. This was initially accomplished by their occupation of urban space and later through their engagement in creating alternative and collective forms of cultural production. In becoming a permanent space MACAO also forged a strong identity, territory and community representing the entire alternative creator sector. Overall, they challenged the conditions under which artistic labour is reproduced in the neoliberal city and provided a workable alternative.

Regarding their engagement with wider issues of collective consumption, there is also evidence of MACAO's desire to move beyond just the problems of artistic labour. Working with a significant number of community and political groups across the city on a range of issues (for example, see Figure 4.2), Emanuele Braga, a key member of the group, has said: 'We have a real chance to really challenge the rules of governance here' (quoted in Cultural Workers Organize, 2013: 187). The movement has also championed the general idea of a universal basic income and the use of alternative currencies.

On this issue of autonomy, we have seen that while MACAO remains oppositional to the neoliberal creative city, they have continued to engage with the local state through 'critical participation'. Their desire to have a permanent space through possibly purchasing their building a few years ago has recently changed. A Facebook post on their site dated 5 November 2021, stated, for reasons not completely clear, that they were suspending

Figure 4.2: MACAO event on cooperative versus capitalist platforms, Milan, March 2017

Source: photo by author, 2017

activities at their permanent residence. Whether they will continue as a 'crossing' also remains unknown. This demonstrates that even successful urban cultural spaces and movements are made fragile by the changing conditions of neoliberal urbanization.

Similarly, through the production of their manifesto, Haben und Brauchen also successfully challenged the neoliberal creative city paradigm. This was accomplished through raising issues like work precarity, a lack of artistic space and critiquing the state's support of cultural mega-events. Focusing particularly on the issue of work precarity in the arts sector, Haben und Brauchen have also raised general collective consumption issues around a lack of decent social housing, affordable workspace and basic income. Overall, the movement has been sensitive not to make arguments about the 'special role' of art and culture, but rather locate the problems of the artist as that of the ordinary urban dweller.

Despite their potential, what are some of the shortcomings of urban cultural movements? Following Castells, urban cultural movements, like urban social movements, are limited. They are often restricted to changing the 'urban meaning' of culture rather than providing the capacity to enact major structural change in society. Cultural movements are only often temporary reactions which are hard to sustain over long periods of time. Similarly, they can also face a lack of 'critical mass' in terms of the capacity of alternative creative spaces to work together. They can achieve small victories like keeping an alternative space open or stopping a particular type of urban development. They may even produce an alternative development plan.

One example of this is the Gangeviertel area in the centre of Hamburg which has now been turned into artist studios rather than being redeveloped into office blocks (Novy and Colomb, 2013: 1827–1829). Another is the Bandung Creative City Forum's ten principles for a different 'bottom-up' type of creative city (De Beukelaer, 2021). These important victories, however, remain 'local utopias'. These changes are also somewhat limited to the cultural and urban realm rather than effecting broader social, economic and political change.

A second limitation is that urban cultural movements are sometimes viewed as less political than other urban social movements. Regarding the example of MACAO, Valli (2015: 646) has argued that the movement's rhetoric of challenging 'financialization, biocapitalism, precariat' may not easily chime with wider goals of urban equality and justice. A member of the movement supports this claim when they were discussing the support (or lack of it) MACAO got when they moved into their permanent site: "There were moments of, you know, tension because MACAO, as I was telling you, does not really share all the codes of the antagonistic wider social movement" (interviewee 34, male, Milan, MACAO).

Culture-based movements can be viewed by other social movements as exclusive and self-serving. They can be seen as advancing the interests of the arts as a special sphere or, more damningly, labelled as 'self-interested'. This is certainly the case for Luger's (2019) paradoxical 'arts generation' in Singapore who appear stuck in a privileged trap pulling them towards colluding with the creative state. Alternative cultural associations in the West can also be seen as being self-interested and engaging with the local state in order to gain favour. Even progressive community-based place-making strategies by arts groups, Grodach (2017: 89) argues, can struggle with supporting artistic development alongside community development and engendering revitalization in disadvantaged places. For example, Amsterdam Alternative (see Case Study 4.5), an amalgamation of independent cultural spaces in the city, has been viewed by other urban social movements as acting in their own favour rather than in the interests of the neighbourhood. Ivor Schmetz, a member of both the alternative space OT301 and Alternative Amsterdam, admitted: 'Of course there is some hard-core squatters that don't like us anymore, they think we've gone commercial' (quoted in Venus Orbits for Justice, 2015).

Previously I raised the thorny issue of when movements become legitimate and try and obtain their own space. Will organizations that become legitimate and official be able to retain their autonomy and keep their political edge? Even successful urban cultural movements like Haben und Brauchen who reached out to wider constituencies in framing the so-called 'artist problem' can become incorporated into local state cultural policy making. As one original member of the group said: "I mean it's funny because now we have this kind of political power … it's really a question of who are you speaking for?" (interviewee 9, male, Berlin, Haben und Brauchen). Luger (2019) also mentions a similar incorporation of his critical 'arts generation' into positions of power and bureaucracy in Singapore. All these factors affect not only a movement's credibility but can also quickly lead to their dissolution.

Case Study 4.5: Amsterdam Alternative

Another type of urban cultural movement is Amsterdam Alternative, a collection of 17 independent cultural spaces formed in 2015 (now numbering 34 organizations), with the objective of '[p]romoting and representing the interests of Amsterdam's alternative scene' (Amsterdam Alternative, nd). 'Originating with the city's counterculture and free spaces, Amsterdam Alternative stands for collective action and radical political debate, for the sake of a desirable future for the many, not the few' (Amsterdam Alternative, nd). They go on to say:

> We are not looking for a clear cut definition of 'the alternative,' but fight for a future urban culture that is in line with the open, emancipative aspects of Amsterdam's heritage as a free city. We are a platform for political movements and activists looking for effective tools against the city's perpetual devastation by the rich and powerful. (Amsterdam Alternative, nd)

Besides a website and the production of a newspaper outlining stories and news about the sector, the network meets monthly to offer advice and support. According to one central member, there are grander dreams to turn the organization into a cooperative property development platform: "I would like so much to develop Amsterdam Alternative into a bank. … Everybody who sympathizes with the alternative scene donate money to the Amsterdam Alternative funds then whatever, we would start it up and then we would start buying buildings" (interviewee 1, Amsterdam, 1990s art squat/ collectively owned 2006). Despite their radical stance, the group has been accused of self-interest by groups of other 'hard core' squatters.

To conclude, this chapter returns to two main issues. The first one is how to encourage alternative creative spaces to network and organize themselves into an effective urban cultural movement to challenge the neoliberal creative city. Chapter 3 discussed how the local state could foster such groups by providing space and resources. They could also encourage the formation of alternative networks to tackle issues of artistic precarity, oppose neoliberal arts policy and challenge the wider commodification of culture and creativity. But there are barriers here. They include rivalry between such spaces and a lack of time and energy to forge and maintain solidarity networks. Urban cultural movements are difficult to sustain and naturally wax and wane. Finally, there is the problem of networking only within one's own city or region.

An exception to this latter limitation is Trans Europe Halles. It is one of the oldest cultural networks in Europe and has been active in repurposing abandoned buildings for arts, culture and activism since 1983. Based in Sweden, the network has 140 members in 40 different countries across Europe (Trans Europe Halles, nd). In terms of acting as a 'supra' urban cultural movement, Trans Europe Halles has clearly been at the forefront of transforming urban space and encouraging alternative forms of artistic and cultural production. Yet the network is also pragmatic in terms of wanting to influence existing European cultural policy and making alliances with business, public administration and academia (Trans Europe Halles, nd). While this can make it susceptible to incorporation into existing neoliberal creative paradigm, currently the network is working hard to create a new alternative cultural vision based on cooperation, diversity and sustainability (Fukuma, 2022).

The second major issue concerns urban cultural movements' relationship with other urban social and political movements. Some of the most effective cultural movements have been where artists have not separated themselves off from tackling issues of labour market flexibility, gentrification, affordable housing, sustainability, racism, sexism and community decline. Yet, it is also easy for artist-led movements to be perceived as privileged even though many in the alternative creative sector are likely to be similarly disadvantaged in terms of actual income and material resources (Bain and McLean, 2013). Pritchard (2018) has called on alternative artists to resist culture-led regeneration in neighbourhoods through liaising with other urban social movements to 'place guard' against gentrification and displacement. Harrebye (2015) argues that 'creative activism' needs to embrace a radical critique of the whole society and be prepared to be part of a wider network of social movements to effectively challenge the neoliberal capitalist city. Otherwise, urban cultural movements, however important, will remain isolated and be seen as part of the problem rather than forming a central component of the solution.

The real issue is that the 'problems of artists' in the city are shared by the majority of urban dwellers. In this sense, a progressive creative city cannot be achieved solely by a proliferation of alternative creative spaces or even through the activities of urban cultural movements themselves. Rather, it involves making the creativity issue relevant for all urban groups. It also will involve the fight for a more just and sustainable city. We will return to these issues in the final chapter of the book.

5

Neoliberal Nightlife and its Alternatives

Nightlife, defined here as night spaces that provide for social mixing and socializing such as bars, pubs and nightclubs, has become a crucial aspect of the urban cultural economy (Kolioulis, 2018). Financially it is a billion-dollar industry many times over worldwide. Nightlife is also a marker of 'successful' neoliberal urban development, regeneration and creativity (Eldridge and Nofre, 2018: 4–5). Andrew Tuck, host of a radio show called 'The Urbanist', has argued that nightclubs and bars are 'what draws people to cities, they're what make places feel vibrant' (Petrovics and Seijas, 2021: 2). Meanwhile, Florida (2002: 8) has said of his creative class that: 'A vibrant, varied nightlife was viewed by many as another signal that a city "gets it".' In the past few decades, it has been noted that the night has moved from the margins to the centre of urban governance and policy making (Straw, 2018: 226). In short, nightlife has become a central element of the 'neoliberal creative city package'.

This chapter focuses on an analysis of nightlife in the neoliberal city. The development of the '24-hour city' perfectly represents the impulse to maximize urban branding and extend capital accumulation. It also reveals some of the shortcomings of mainstream nightlife spaces characterized by corporate ownership, segregation, control and exclusion (Hollands, 2016b), not to mention raising a host of other regulatory issues (Acuto et al, 2021) and consumption inequalities (Hae, 2012). Similarly, in much the same way that neoliberal urbanization generally has provoked 'contestation', the development of mainstream commercial nightlife spaces has also generated resistance in the formation of creative nightlife alternatives (Chatterton and Hollands, 2003) and 'experimental counter-spaces' (Berthet-Meylan, 2022). In addition to this, the pub and club sector has been hard hit by the pandemic, calling into question the resilience and future of this part of the urban cultural economy.

This chapter discusses some of the main developments within the subfield of what has been called 'nightlife studies' (Eldridge and Nofre, 2018). In doing so, it relates these to some of the key problems of the creative city. This is not to say that neoliberal nightlife has always developed in the same way even in cities of the Global North, let alone how it is played out in the Global South (Nofre, 2020). While focusing on, not to mention updating and expanding, our research on cities in the UK (Chatterton and Hollands, 2003), I also seek to include examples drawn from elsewhere including European and Global South cities (Gois, 2018; Nofre, 2020). Critical to these analyses will be questions surrounding the production of nightlife including globalization and corporatization; contradictions inherent in neoliberal governance and regulation; and consumption inequalities created through gentrification. Additionally, the chapter will examine alternative forms of nightlife, including a case study of 'night protests' in the city of Geneva (Hollands et al, 2017). Finally, the chapter concludes by discussing the impact the pandemic has had on this sector of the urban cultural economy. It asks, can we move beyond neoliberal forms and create more diverse, accessible and sustainable night-time activities in the future?

The rise of neoliberal nightlife

While the existence of different types of night-time activity pre-date both the Fordist and the neoliberal city (Palmer, 2000), what we understand as nightlife today is a more recent phenomenon. The industrial city was the apogee of the separation of work from leisure time and the beginning of the formalized regulation of night spaces (Evans, 2002). In the Western Fordist city in particular, the rational control of leisure, particularly for the working classes, was evidenced in nightlife through licensing restrictions of opening hours (Gofton, 1983). The decline of industrialism however signalled a need to promote new forms of capital accumulation (Harvey, 1989a), including increasing the provision of entertainment and consumption (Hannigan, 1998; Miles and Miles, 2004). The evolution of the modern night-time economy more broadly represented a golden opportunity for cities to extend capital accumulation and profit-making (Shaw, 2018). The development of nightlife particularly has become economically as well as symbolically important.

Nightlife has become a significant sector of the urban cultural economy, worth around US$3,000 billion, servicing some 15.3 billion clients worldwide (Johnson, 2020). In the UK, it is said to be the fifth-biggest industry with annual revenues of £66 billion (Masud, 2019). Places around the world vie for the title of best nightlife destination including cities like Las Vegas, Paris, Buenos Aires, Amsterdam, Ibiza, Rome and Berlin (Papadopolous, 2019; Picaud, 2019). The success of cities like Barcelona, following the 1992 Olympic Games, Berlin and Amsterdam as cities of alternative culture and even developing post-socialist cities like Prague and Budapest, have all benefited from having a lively bar and club scene to boost their status as growing creative destinations. Nightlife has also become a significant marker of urban success and regeneration for many post-industrial cities struggling to reinvent themselves (Eldridge and Nofre, 2018: 5). Aspects like club-culture are closely intertwined with debates about creativity in cities (Hossfeld Etyang et al, 2020) and nightlife forms an important component of cultural tourism (Sequera and Nofre, 2018). Hutton (2016: 51), in his discussion of the World Cities Culture Report suggests that one measure of urban vitality might include the number of nightclubs, discos and dance clubs a city has.

This is not to argue that nightlife has developed in cities around the world in exactly the same way. Just as neoliberal urbanization and the creative paradigm have developed in different city contexts and taken divergent pathways, so has the night-time economy. Nofre (2020: 130), for instance, challenges the consensus that the origins of the modern night-time leisure economy lie exclusively with attempts to revitalize various UK post-industrial cities, citing other nightlife developments in New York, Madrid, Lisbon, Ibiza and Berlin. Eldridge and Nofre (2018: 5, 7) also mention this Anglo-centric approach and their book provides welcome examples of other nightlife transformations and contexts.

Nofre (2020: 130) goes on to suggest that we should begin to recognize the input of research on nightlife from peripheral European and Global South cities, including the Americas (Gois, 2018) and Asia (Farrer, 2018). He cites Yeo et al (2016: 383), who say that 'these Asian cities espouse cultural distinctive urban practices, revealing space-time geographies that are markedly different from nightlife experience in the West'. Nofre (2020: 132) also notes that Western capitalist contexts can make the understanding of nocturnal activities in countries like Africa or Asia difficult. This is where Anglo-centric concepts like 'youth', 'time' and 'safety' may have different contextual meanings.

Despite these differences, Nofre (2020: 132) calls for a continuing dialogue between Western and Global South discourses on nightlife research. This is partly because nightlife differences exist not only between cities in the Global North and South, but also in cities in the UK, Europe and the US. For instance, researchers have long noted the difference between the alcohol-centred nature of UK nightlife and the more relaxed, less restricted and family oriented night-time economy in Europe. At the same time, the very success of cultural and tourist economies in European cities like Barcelona, Berlin and Lisbon have led to increasing concerns about vandalism, violence and excessive alcohol consumption there (Eldridge and Nofre, 2018). Furthermore, while the idea of the 24-hour city would appear to be the 'apex' of neoliberal nightlife consumption, some researchers have noted that this expansion has been more limited than we think, with some

Western cities even restricting opening hours (Wolifson, 2018). Research on non-Western and non-alcohol-based cities (Amid, 2018) can also help us to think beyond the consumption-based forms of neoliberal nightlife characterizing the Global North.

A final reason for continuing a dialogue here concerns similarities rather than differences between the Global North and South. There is evidence that nightlife in many cities around the world is currently experiencing increased neoliberal 'market rationality', regulatory policies of segregation and exclusion, and more gentrified consumption (Eldridge and Nofre, 2018). Nightlife is also increasingly tied to creative city developments (Kolioulis, 2018) and neoliberal tourism regimes (Sequera and Nofre, 2018). It is these aspects of neoliberal nightlife that many cities have in common, albeit they are often expressed in different forms and exist in different contexts.

In this chapter, I begin by revisiting my own research on nightlife in three UK cities which represents a 'classic' Anglophone study (Eldridge and Nofre, 2018: 7). I use the work here as a 'take-off point' to structure my discussion of more recent developments in neoliberal nightlife, while also seeking to update the analyses and expand it to include other European and Global South examples.

Revisiting *Urban Nightscapes*

The book *Urban Nightscapes: Youth Cultures, Pleasure Spaces and Corporate Power* (Chatterton and Hollands, 2003) was the product of a £123,000 ESRC-funded nightlife study which occurred between 2000 and 2002. In addition to following up the changing nightlife scene in the city of Newcastle upon Tyne (Hollands, 1995; Chatterton and Hollands, 2001), the study strategically included a wealthier (although somewhat more alternative) southern city, Bristol, along with Leeds, a more prosperous northern city known for its financial service economy (Chatterton and Hollands, 2004). We also conducted limited research in some other UK cities (Edinburgh, Manchester and Liverpool) and a small amount of comparative research on nightlife in Barcelona and a few North American (Canadian) cities.

In addition to studying nightlife in three contrasting cities, we interviewed nightlife producers (owners and managers of premises), regulators (police, bouncers, relevant city council officials) as well as a wide range of different nightlife consumers. This latter group ranged from white-collar professionals, students, working-class youth, gay and lesbian revellers, as well as producers and consumers of alternative nightlife spaces. Interviews were supplemented with participant observation methods accompanying different types of revellers on nights out. The study also involved a complete survey of nightlife provision. Every bar and club in the three cities were visited and categorized in terms of ownership, location and style of premises.

The general approach of *Urban Nightscapes* (Chatterton and Hollands, 2003: xi) was summed up as 'an outlook which combines the study of political-economic forces, and in particular a concern about the increasing power of corporate and global capital in our daily lives, with critical ethnographies sensitive to the nuances of locality, agency and political resistance'. Urban nightlife, we argued, was increasingly becoming 'McDonaldized' with big brands taking over our cities, leaving consumers with an increasingly standardized experience and a lack of alternative creative provision.

We also suggested that nightlife is best understood through three dimensions (production, regulation and consumption) which help to produce three different types of nightlife spaces (mainstream, residual and alternative). In terms of production, what we revealed was the domination of corporate and branded mainstream nightlife spaces. Regarding regulation, our research focused in on the neoliberal state contradiction of 'selling the city' via the vibrancy of its nightlife while having to deal with the many social problems created by this sector of the economy. The argument around neoliberal nightlife consumption was that it had become increasingly segmented and gentrified. Finally, we were interested in the decline of traditional community-based pubs and the squeezing of alternative spaces to the margins of the city. The next three sections highlight these main aspects of neoliberal nightlife, while updating and extending the analyses.

The production of corporate nightlife

One of the general characteristics of neoliberal urbanization and urban entrepreneurialism is the dominance of corporate capital and the tendency towards concentration and conglomeration of ownership in cities (Harvey, 1989a). Before turning to the specific case of the UK and our three cities, it is important to comment on some global production trends. For example, Eldridge and Nofre (2018: 8) suggest a pattern of increased commercialization and marketization of this sector in cities as diverse as Lisbon, Sarajevo, Montpellier, Johannesburg, Athens and Sydney. In the US, Hae (2011) talks about a new class of nightlife entrepreneurs driving both gentrification and standardization. In Europe, four major companies are involved in the pub, bar and nightclub industry including Sperger Gaststättenbetrieb OHG, Bootshaus Cologne GmbH, Wells & Co. and Universo Pacha SA. Market (Ibis World, 2022a).

In Latin America, Gois (2018: 207) argues that the 'nightscape of Rio de Janeiro is a composition of renewed and regenerated venues in the form of bars, restaurants and nightclubs' alongside old-fashioned bars ('botequins'), the latter of which are somewhat resistant to neoliberal urban development. Regarding Asian cities, despite their earlier quote about nightlife differences, Yeo et al (2016: 383) admits things are 'shifting towards more globalised forms of entertainment spaces similar in nature to existing trends in Europe and North America'. Chew (2009), among others, highlights the growth of a Westernized nightlife in urban China.

Historically the UK pub industry was dominated by the breweries who owned 69 per cent of all pubs in 1990 (Foley, 2021: 7). Even though this monopoly was broken up by the Beer Order Act of 1989 which restricted brewery ownership to a maximum of 2,000 pubs each, the immediate result was a shift in corporate control from the brewers to the rise of multinational pub companies (or pub cos) (Chatterton and Hollands, 2003: 33–34). By the time our research was published in 2003, pub cos dominated the market, holding a record high portfolio of 32,500 pubs (55 per cent of the total) while breweries and independents held 14 per cent and 31 per cent respectively (Foley, 2021: 8). Our ownership survey of all city centre pubs in our three UK locations (Bristol, Leeds and Newcastle), showed an overwhelming dominance of corporate providers (both pub cos and brewers) with around two-thirds of all premises falling into this category. These internationally financed pub companies were crowding out both regional and independent owners and brewers through aggressive marketing, theming and branding schemes.

While the past 20 years have seen a reduction in concentration of ownership by the ten largest operators, there remain high levels of concentration and conglomeration in the UK pub industry. The branding, theming and market segmentation of licensed premises continues. For instance, Stonegate (see Table 5.1) currently controls nearly 10 per cent of all pubs in the country. In terms of revenues, the pub industry is still big business with Mitchells & Butlers plc generating almost £1.5 billion, pub chain JD Wetherspoon £1.26 billion and Stonegate £707 million (Lock, 2021). Prior to the recent expansion of Stonegate, 2019 figures show that the top four companies owned 25.5 per cent of the total market share (Seymour, 2019). This corporate trend has been aided by neoliberal-oriented city councils eager to accept and work with big chains. These corporates tend to cater to the tourist trade and more upmarket consumers, rather than meet the needs of the local population or pursue more 'social inclusionary' measures in terms of city centre use (for example, see Proctor, 2014).

Concentration in the clubbing industry also occurred during these neoliberal times with the rise of commercial superclubs capitalizing on the spoils of illegal rave culture. In *Urban Nightscapes* we mentioned the franchising of the nightclub brand Pacha which had 80 venues worldwide. In the US the top ten clubs (seven of which were located in Los Vegas) earned over US$550 million in revenue in 2016 fuelled by top-flight DJs (McIntyre, 2015).

In the UK, we highlighted companies like Po Na Group and Luminar Leisure, the latter of which ran 15 per cent of all nightclubs in the country

Table 5.1: Largest selected pub companies in the UK in 2020, by number of units

Name of company	Number of pubs
Stonegate	4,709
Mitchells & Butlers plc	1,660
JD Wetherspoon	861
Whitbread	768
New River Retail	720
Admiral Taverns	594
Trust Inns	350
Young & Co's Brewery	276
Loungers	165
Amber Taverns	154
Total	10,257 (22 per cent of 46,800)

Sources: Lock (2021; 2022)

(Chatterton and Hollands, 2003: 38). More recently, Kolioulis (2018) has talked about the 'financialization' of clubbing in London by large corporate players. While a volatile market, concentration in the clubbing industry still exists, albeit in the hands of different corporate owners. For example, the Deltic Group, before it was taken over by REKOM, was the UK's largest nightclub operator, owning 53 venues (Davies, 2020). The market share of the top three nightclubs (REKOM UK; A3D2 Ltd; The Brighton Pier Group plc) is worth around £55 million or 8.4 per cent or of the entire sector total (Ibis World, 2022b). Some commentators have remarked that clubbing under neoliberalism ownership has become far more predictable and less challenging (Glencross, 2017), especially when compared to previous eras (Hae, 2011; Hossfeld Etyang et al, 2020).

This shift in ownership pattern has had a clear influence on the style and types of premises available in UK cities. Cafe bars, theme bars and style bars dominated the city centres of Leeds and Bristol, making up 51 per cent and 50 per cent of all premises in these two cities (Chatterton and Hollands, 2003: 43). Many of these types of premises were 'branded' by either corporate brewers or pub cos. Branding, originally defined as to burn or mark a product, marks a shift towards emphasizing the 'symbolic value' of a product thereby resulting in more 'premium' pricing (Chatterton and Hollands, 2003: 25).

The club scene has also moved upmarket in terms of both style and price (Hae, 2012; Glencross, 2017). In the US, in the highest earning club, XS, a good table will cost you US$10,000 and the venue even has a cocktail that can cost you another US$10,000 (McIntyre, 2015). Although not as extreme, we found the move towards style and cafe type bars in the UK was an attempt to create a more upmarket form of nightlife. These premises target style-conscious young professionals, some sections of the student market and elements of the aspirational working class. At same time, the corporate mainstream also focused on standardized alcohol-centred or 'vertical drinking' establishments (Chatterton and Hollands, 2003: 111). The 'serial reproduction' of corporate nightlife is represented by the fact that most UK cities still contain chains like All Bar One or Stonegate's brand The Slug and Lettuce.

This has resulted in a kind of nightlife where night spaces all begin to look alike. Whole areas of cities can also be given over to being branded as a famous (or infamous) nightlife quarter. Some urban nightscapes are designed to promote a 'party city' image (Chatterton and Hollands, 2003). Focusing on the case of the Bairro Alto in Lisbon, Nofre and Martins (2017) argue that this 'Disneyfication' of neoliberal night spaces is characterized by hedonism, high levels of alcohol and drugs consumption, and race, gender and class inequalities. Additionally, profit made in these corporate premises flows out of cities and is rarely reinvested back into the local economy. Finally, it is important to recall that those that produce corporate nightlife on the ground – bar and club workers – are often poorly paid and on zero-hours contracts (Shaw, 2018).

Regulating mainstream nightlife

If one of the general features of neoliberalism is the changing role of the state to ensure 'market rule' (Peck and Theodore, 2019: 259), one would expect that the urban governance of nightlife would be primarily geared towards profit maximization and liberalization. This has certainly been the case in the UK with the development of the 24-hour city idea and local authorities supporting corporate nightlife development. Yet these actions also must be balanced with a concern over the regulation of nightlife, including drunkenness, violence, safety and vandalism.

Some researchers critiqued *Urban Nightscapes* as being too focused on ownership and corporate power in terms of explaining nightlife regulation (Hadfield, 2006; Roberts and Eldridge, 2009). Yet we always recognized that things were not so straightforward. Chatterton (2002: 23) noted that 'a number of groups often with conflicting interests, such as the local state, police, licensing magistrates, residents groups, door security firms, nightlife operators, consumers and workers, are involved in governing the night'. While this more complex picture is still very much the case in the contemporary period of neoliberal governance, some analysts have tended to interpret this fact as meaning there exists a 'nightlife consensus' rather than a more conflictual set of interests (Acuto et al, 2021; Petrovics and Seijas, 2021).[1]

If Peck and Theodore's (2019) description of neoliberalism as 'shapeshifting' is accurate, one would expect such governance to be complex and contradictory. This is particularly the case in terms of squaring the economic liberalization of nightlife with the impulse to regulate and control. In fact, both of these contrary processes can be applied at the same time – what Aalbers (2016) calls 'regulated deregulation'. An example of this might be the liberalization of nightlife through opening up the number of licences, but at the same time restricting who can apply for them in terms of meeting various by-laws and regulations (Talbot, 2011). This process can favour mainstream commercial expansion at the behest of alternative spaces (Hollands, 2016b).

Additionally, regulation is not just about laws and restrictions, but also involves more informal practices designed to subtly shape nightlife in particular ways. This can include 'policing by style' and using gentrification to regulate access (Chatterton and Hollands, 2003; Hae, 2011). Finally, some researchers have investigated the idea of the 'neoliberal policing of the self' as part of a modern nightlife regulatory regime (Haydock, 2009).

The idea of urban conurbations branding themselves as 'party cities' has never been straightforward. While the idea of the '24-hour city' represents the pinnacle of neoliberal consumption and subjectivity (Shaw, 2010), nightlife has always had a strong transgressive (Palmer, 2000) and restrictive element to it. For example, nightlife developments in cities of the Global South have been plagued by concerns about criminality and safety, not so much in clubs and bars, but in public spaces surrounding them (Oloukoï, 2018). Wolifson's (2018) study of Sydney, Australia, demonstrates the contradictions of neoliberal planning which are simultaneously designed to brand the city as a nightlife destination while at the same time imposing lockdown restrictions to reduce violence. A report by the London Assembly's police and crime committee in 2016 also found that 'areas with the most night-time violence with injury offences, tend to be those with a strong night-time economy' (Masud, 2019). The tension between opening up nightlife for economic and urban regeneration reasons continues to clash with a concern to control night-time behaviours, particularly among the young (Measham, 2004).

Hadfield (2015) has sketched out a 'wave model' of nightlife governance which is useful in historically categorizing nightlife governance. This provided a 'temporal' dimension to nightlife regulation. It also can be linked to the phase model of neoliberal urbanization discussed in previous chapters (Mayer, 2013). The first wave is the idea of relaxing nightlife restrictions in the UK (Hobbs et al, 2000) via the 24-hour city idea (Heath and Strickland, 1997). This phase fits in with the emergence of the neoliberal creative city and the desire to maximize capital accumulation into the night and buttress the general idea of branding cities as 'vibrant'. Hadfield's (2015) second wave concerns tinkering with restrictions designed to deal with social problems caused by extended hours. This involves things like introducing new drinking by-laws or imposing a levy on nightlife providers to help deal with policing and littering. Finally, he mentions a more recent third wave of governance designed to respond to continuing problems of access and exclusion. This wave coincides with the more recent conciliatory phase of neoliberal urbanization as discussed by Mayer (2013).

It might be argued that Hadfield's (2015) model is indeed a sketch and is not fleshed out in enough empirical detail. A second issue concerns the degree to which his model might be applied to understanding nightlife outside of a Western context (for example, see Case Study 5.1 on Rio de Janeiro). A final concern is that there is a tendency to periodize the waves too strictly rather than see nightlife governance as more of a mix of all three phases simultaneously.

Case Study 5.1: Urban development and governance of nightlife in Rio de Janeiro

Gois (2018) provides a detailed and comprehensive study of nightlife governance and policies in the Latin American city of Rio de Janeiro. Although commercial leisure spaces emerged in Rio in the colonial period, he suggests that the city centre went through a period of public disinvestment and economic decline in the 'lost decade' sweeping South America in the 1980s (Gois, 2018: 209). During this time the nightscape was described as 'dangerous and precarious' and was characterized by a sense of insecurity. The urban population residing there were largely working-class and elderly residents who couldn't afford to move. Plans to renew Rio's urban landscape through the development of entertainment, culture and nightlife occurred largely during the 1990s in the context of widening democracy and decentralization. This was also a period in which neoliberalism was introduced to the Brazilian economy, with an emphasis on public space renewal and private investment (Gois, 2018: 212). In the downtown area between 1984 and 2010, 150 cultural sites and more than 500 bars and restaurants opened in areas like Lapa, now a renowned nightlife destination. Downtown workers and students were later joined by tourists in terms of forming a nightlife audience. Gois (2018: 214) argues that this was the first time nightlife had become a central part of an urban redevelopment project in the city.

Gois (2018: 210) is keen to point out that the process of gentrification in the city is not so clearly associated with the urban core, as wealthy residents had moved out to the suburbs much earlier. He argues that concerns with safety, mobility and organization of nightlife were not just motivated by gentrification, but a combination of demands from owners, nightlife goers and local residents (Gois, 2018: 220). Such local developments had the effect of improving access and facilities for some, while seeking to manage certain undesirable activities and elements of the urban population. A second difference with Western neoliberal urban development and nightlife studies, Gois (2018: 215) argues, is a Latin American concern with the street and public spaces rather than the governance of nightlife premises themselves. He argues that after a decade of urban projects and policies designed to upgrade the urban environment, including populating it with more commercial nightlife spaces, there has been a shift in emphasis towards behavioural control (Gois, 2018: 217). The recent past has concentrated on increased policing of nightlife and 'unruly behaviour' and design changes to make spaces safe for tourists and other cultural activities. Overall, this case study demonstrates some of the different ways neoliberal urbanization works in the Latin American context.

A good example of mixed regulatory regimes is the recent rise of different Night Mayor schemes (Czars, Mayors, Ambassadors and Councils). Straw (2018), for example, contrasts their very different roles as lobbyists, sectoral managers or representatives of minority populations. Similarly, the impact of the pandemic on nightlife may have already taken things to another 'wave' of governance concerning nightlife recovery and survival. In some sense, this has meant that many different and sometimes conflicting nightlife actors have had to work together to lobby for an overall recovery plan (Petrovics and Seijas, 2021). This can have the effect of seeing nightlife as a rather homogeneous entity rather than recognizing that the needs and concerns of the alternative sector are clearly distinguishable from the interests of corporate providers. Hae's (2011) notion of the 'nightlife fix', whereby a new class of night-time entrepreneurs and city officials act in concert to deal with the contradictions of the night through gentrification, is instructive here. I would argue that in the current neoliberal creative city, capital and state continue to be powerful and significant players in the governance and regulation of nightlife in most cities, despite the rise of Night Mayor schemes.

Consuming neoliberal nightlife: gentrification, segregation and exclusion

One of the key arguments of *Urban Nightscapes* (Chatterton and Hollands, 2003) was that the consumption of neoliberal nightlife was segmented and exclusionary (Hollands, 2002). Central to this argument was the idea of nightlife gentrification and the exclusion of certain groups like the urban poor (Chatterton and Hollands, 2003). I would argue that this pattern is consistent with neoliberal urbanization (Mayer, 2013) and the development of the dominant creative city paradigm (Peck, 2005).

Early examples of the impact gentrification was having on nightlife divisions and exclusions abounded in our research. For instance, one nightclub owner from Leeds said, '[w]e like people to make an effort to look smart ... helps to attract a slightly better class of clientele' (nightclub owner 2, Leeds, quoted in Chatterton and Hollands, 2003: 108). A young woman from the same city experiencing such dress codes explained how it made her feel: 'It's just the way they make you feel once you're in there, the people who sort of sneer at you' (Jackie, 23 years old, Leeds, quoted in Chatterton and Hollands, 2003: 108). There was also animosity in the other direction regarding pretentious clubbers: 'I hate to see these beautiful people with their perfect make-up and their perfect hair' (Steve, focus group 2, Newcastle, cited in Chatterton and Hollands, 2003: 119), while others sought out premises where there was 'just a better class of people' (Sarah, 21 years old, Leeds, cited in Chatterton and Hollands, 2003: 116).

Also significant were negative stereotypes about the activities of 'chavs' (also see Chapter 7) on nights out. They included 'get pissed ... have a shag and have a fight', to quote one of our respondents (cited in Chatterton and Hollands, 2003: 115). In a discussion of the type of revellers inhabiting a residual nightlife area of Leeds city centre, one respondent produced the following hateful representation:

> Nasty, horrible creatures of society, who crawl out from under their stone on Thursday 'cos its dole day. They put on the same frock every week 'cos they don't wanna buy a new one until they get too fat. Mainly seen wearing the PVC skirts and boob tubes, which are too tight, sort of sagging and not nice. The over 40s, who still think that they are 18. (Mark, 22 years old, Leeds, cited in Chatterton and Hollands, 2003: 191)

This quotation clearly expressed the view that some people are not welcome in the newly gentrifying neoliberal city. There were also other 'unwanted groups' in the city at the time of our research, such as young people just 'hanging out'. Homeless youth also faced exclusion as they interfered with both retail and nightlife consumption (Chatterton and Hollands, 2003: 67, 191).

So, what, if anything, has changed regarding neoliberal nightlife consumption patterns since our research was conducted nearly 25 years ago? There is now a wide range of studies which confirms that patterns of gentrification and exclusion have continued (Talbot, 2011; Hae, 2012; Kolioulis, 2018; Wolifson, 2018, among others), albeit with slightly different inflections. For example, while our research focused on nightlife providers targeting the professional middle and service classes, others since note the impact of the creative classes. Hae (2011: 3461) says: 'Attracting professional constituencies or the creative class is expected to facilitate the post-industrialisation of the city as a solution to the declining urban economy.' Similarly, in her research on London, Kolioulis (2018: 208) suggests clubs 'have become part of the so-called "creative sector" (Florida, 2004), bringing the night-time to the centre of the debate about gentrification'. Glencross (2017) similarly argues that neoliberal nightlife today is a marker of creative distinction rather than the inclusion that characterized rave culture.

Both Hae (2012) and Kolioulis (2018) argue that 'nightlife gentrification' acts to segregate and 'price out' segments of the urban population. Kolioulis (2018: 214) suggests that the 'financialisation of clubbing' by companies backed by large corporations, means that entry to clubs becomes expensive (between £25 and £45) and hence inaccessible. Glencross (2017) concurs that neoliberal nightlife today is dominated by 'big business'. Hae (2012) notes particularly that gentrification infringes on urban inhabitants' 'right to the city'. While one might argue that gentrification is more advanced in cities like New York and London, it has also continued to develop in smaller post-industrial centres like Newcastle upon Tyne. For example, Steven Patterson of the organization NE1, suggested: 'Traditionally, Newcastle has had a reputation for what people call vertical drinking cheap alcohol, such as trebles for a pound deal. Now we have a clear movement towards mid to upmarket venues. It is absolutely fantastic for this city' (quoted in Proctor, 2014).

The use of gentrification to 'manage' and regulate nightlife is also evidenced in Wolifson's (2018) study of Sydney, Australia. She argues that the attempt to regulate nightlife there through gentrification has bolstered class inequalities. Wolifson (2018: 41) suggests that Sydney's gentrifying strategy sought to 'improve urban subjectivities and foster more civilised consumption in the city at night'. However, she goes on to argue that the more recent 'lockout law' targeting a delineated inner-city zone is effectively a class form of discrimination. Similarly, one can draw a common thread between cities of the Global North and South regarding using gentrification of the night to improve the safety image of the city and to encourage middle-class consumption and tourism. Oloukoï (2018), for example, discusses the case of Johannesburg, South Africa, arguing that night-time gentrification is seen as a way of bridging concerns about fear and criminality and encouraging a particular type of neoliberal urban development.

The irony of nightlife gentrification is that it suffers from some of the same contradictions as Florida's (2004) creative class solution (discussed in Chapter 3). Hae (2011: 3461) defines the nightlife fix as 'a process through which the nightlife that nurtures diverse and alternative sub-cultures has been largely displaced and through which neighbourhoods are left with a simulacrum of urban vibrancy'. In seeking out diverse and alternative night experiences (Florida, 2002), the creative class gentrifies and stultifies it, leading to its embourgeoisement and standardization (Hae, 2012). Resistance to this process existed in our research where there was recognition of the limits of neoliberal nightlife: 'Corporate clubs and corporate pubs have got it so wrong. … It's the bland globalisation thing' (Rick, 26 years old,

Bristol, cited in Chatterton and Hollands, 2003: 124). The next subsection looks generally at the character of alternative nightlife before moving on to a case study of opposition to its neoliberalized form in the city of Geneva.

The struggle for alternative nightlife

The shortcomings of various aspects of neoliberal nightlife, such as corporate standardization and gentrification, has led to opposition and the search for alternatives. Historically, resistance to mainstream nightlife forms was best represented by rave culture and the squatting scene, though these alternative forms have increasingly been squeezed by legislation. Despite this, in contrast to the segregated and standardized night spaces promoted by neoliberalism, 'experimental counter-spaces', characterized by informality and self-management, struggle to create more diverse types of nightlife in many cities (Hollands, 2019; Hunter-Pazzara, 2019; Berthet-Meylan, 2022; Giaever Lopez, 2022).

In *Urban Nightscapes* (Chatterton and Hollands, 2003) we characterized alternative nightlife as defining itself against the mainstream and possessing the following features: spatially on the margins of the city; having a strong sense of place; resisting conventional norms; autonomous and self-managed; lifestyle rather than profit-based; self-regulating; tolerant and diverse; solidaristic; and mixing aspects of nightlife like music and drinking/drug use, with socializing, politics, performance and art/culture (Chatterton and Hollands, 2003: 202–214). Examples we looked at included raving and the free-party scene and squatting the city and DIY nightlife. In the city of Barcelona in 2000, we charted the existence of a whole alternative network of 'social centres' – essentially squats tolerated by local city governments – providing a variety of both daytime and night-time activities. Most of these alternative networked premises in the city (21 at the time we conducted the research) contained not only bars and places to put on music and dance events, but also had cafes, libraries, meeting rooms, ran classes and engaged in other forms of creative endeavour. Many were forced to close during the property boom, though there is evidence of a renaissance of social centres in this now 'fearless city' (Sanchez Belando, 2017).

Alternative spaces in many other European cities were also closed down in the consolidation phase of neoliberal urbanization. They included famous squats in Berlin (Art House Tacheles), Prague (Villa Malada), Geneva (Rhino) and Amsterdam (Vrankrijk). The world-renowned Christiania in Copenhagen has staved off closure, but only through losing some of its original autonomy (Coppola and Vanolo, 2014). However, as Chapter 3 outlined, we have also seen the more recent rise of new types of alternative creative spaces. Although having different organizational structures and possessing an altered relationship with the local state, they are not too dissimilar to the social centres we previously studied in Barcelona. Spaces like OT301 in Amsterdam and MACAO in Milan, which were looked at earlier, while first and foremost arts-based spaces, also have strong nightlife programmes organized around music and clubbing (Hollands, 2019).

The fight for nightlife counter-spaces in Geneva

In Geneva, Berthet-Meylan (2022) has charted the rise of what she calls 'nightlife counter-spaces', which are essentially a modern variant of alternative nightlife spaces of the past. She characterizes these spaces as accessible, tolerant and informal. They experimentally and creatively combine elements of nightlife (music and dance) with art and culture. The key differences between alternative spaces of the past and these newer nightlife counter-spaces appears to be in their co-production with the local state and their more everyday forms of resistance to challenging neoliberalism (also see Hollands, 2019). It is here in Geneva (for a short profile of the city see Case Study 5.2) that we now turn, to illustrate a fightback and resurgence of alternative counter-spaces (Berthet and Bjertnes, 2011; Hollands et al, 2017).

Case Study 5.2: Geneva: a rich but divided city?

Geneva is the second largest city in Switzerland, acting as an important global business centre for finance (banking), trade and commerce. It has both a city (municipal) and state (canton) government, making it politically unique. Geneva houses the headquarters of several international corporations and organizations, including Merck Serono S.A and Procter & Gamble (both pharmaceutical companies), the Red Cross and the United Nations. As home to many international organizations (Deuber Ziegler, 2004), the city contains a diverse demographic with over 40 per cent of the population being resident foreign nationals (with around 180 nationalities being represented). It has an urban metropolitan population growth of over 1 per cent a year and is projected to keep growing. While internationally recognized for its high quality of life, in 2015 Geneva was ranked as the second most expensive city in the world in terms of goods and services (Friedman, 2015). While the city had a rich history of countercultural activity previously, neoliberal urbanization in the form of the growth of its finance and service economy, property speculation and its high cost of living, has resulted in the social polarization of cultural provision, including nightlife.

Deemed the squatting capital of Europe in the mid-1990s (Pattaroni, 2014: 60), Geneva's counterculture has suffered in the last few decades from property shortages, soaring prices/rents, legal challenges to squatting and increased gentrification (Saltmarsh, 2011). In terms of nightlife, a survey of owners, regulators and consumers of bars, pubs and clubs in the city in 2010 reinforced the general argument of Chatterton and Hollands (2003) about the mainstreaming of provision and 'squeezing' of alternative venues (Berthet et al, 2010). However, a broad alliance of young people began to fight back, holding street protests in 2010 to highlight the high cost of nightlife and a lack of alternative spaces in the city (Hollands et al, 2017).

The existence of a youthful counterculture in the city of Geneva has a long history. In the wake of the events of May 1968 in Paris, this emerged in the form of youth clubs and cultural associations (Gros, 2004). These critical spaces critiqued not only mainstream art and culture but also local and state politics. Like many cities in Europe, the alternative scene in Geneva grew and diversified considerably in the 1970s and 1980s. Espousing the values of collective management, sociability and creativity (Rossiaud, 2004), squats questioned the established order of work, leisure, culture and creativity (Pattaroni, 2014). Until the millennium, squat culture and its expansion in Geneva was facilitated and governed by informal 'trust contracts' between the countercultural population and the authorities. Spaces like Artamis (literally meaning 'friends of art'), an emblematic occupied industrial space that was home to over 200 artist/artisans, and Rhino, a squat opened in 1989 and home to the music venue Cave 12, headlined a range of alternative nightlife premises. By the mid-1990s, Geneva was the most squatted city in Europe, with an estimated 120 buildings occupied by some 2,800 inhabitants (Pattaroni, 2014: 60).

Economic and political change wrought by neoliberal policies began to alter the fortunes of the alternative sector as global property development and a growing gentrified workforce flooded into the city. Politically, the election of Daniel Zappelli, an ultraconservative General Attorney for the State of Geneva in 2002, saw the beginning of the end for much of the squatting movement in the city (Berthet and Bjertnes, 2011). By 2008, only 15 squats remained (Berthet-Meylan, 2022: 117), with Rhino and Artimis closing in 2007 and 2008, respectively. As a concession, some cultural squats were promised that they would be relocated, signalling an incorporation phase of neoliberal urbanization (Mayer, 2013).

Some resisters began to talk of the 'cultural sterilization' of alternative spaces in the city and a 'countercultural malaise' within Geneva. Its nightlife, in particular, was described as 'boring' (Saltmarsh, 2011). Previously, in 1997, a political decision to liberalize the night-time economy through the abandonment of the 'Clause du besoin' (requirements clause), a law regulating the number of night venues in Geneva since the 1930s, quickly transformed the city's nightlife from informal alternative to commercial mainstream. From 2001 to 2007 the number of registered licences for night venues in the city increased threefold to around 3,000 (Berthet et al, 2010). This primarily involved the growth of exclusive and gentrified mainstream premises at the expense of accessible and informal alternative spaces.

It was this increasingly 'polarized' night scene in Geneva that provided the context for a series of 'night protests' in 2010. It has also created a debate about the need for greater alternative provision. One alternative space central to these events is l'Usine (see Case Study 5.3), which not only was at the heart of these nightlife protests, but was a key venue fighting for self-management against overregulation in the city in 2015 (Hollands, 2018). With the closure of one mainstream (MOA) and one independent nightclub (Halle W) in September 2010 (due to breaches of zoning and health violations), l'Usine was cast into the spotlight when it was overwhelmed by young revellers from the closed clubs (Saltmarsh, 2011).

Case Study 5.3: l'Usine: fighting for alternative culture in Geneva

According to Broome (2015) l'Usine is 'one of Europe's largest self-managed cultural spaces, which groups together 18 different collectives and associations, including a radio station, a graphic design studio and a bar'. Considered to be one of the last centrally located arts/culture/nightlife venues in the city, it also houses a theatre, a cinema, artist studios, an art gallery, workshops for crafts people and a music shop. It operates in a building originally provided by the Geneva Council to the organization Etat d'Urgence (State of Emergency) in 1989. Although l'Usine has never been a squat it has always followed an autonomous ethos, practising collective, non-hierarchical decision-making in and across the numerous collectives it accommodates. 'Functioning horizontally', it is, according to one of its staff, 'all about solidarity' (quoted in Broome, 2015). Importantly, it is also affordable compared with the rest of Geneva nightlife, with reasonably priced drinks and an entry fee of around US$16–25 (Saltmarsh, 2011). Not surprisingly, perhaps, it remains immensely popular with both alternative and mainstream youth, with nearly 14 per cent of those surveyed describing it as their favourite night venue in the city (Berthet et al, 2010). Located in the middle of a popular neighbourhood, l'Usine is currently an 'alternative island' in a gentrified and commercialized district in the heart of the city centre. Funded on a four-year rolling basis by the city, it is simultaneously seen as a focal point for alternative culture in the city. It has also been subject to local state pressure regarding its management practices, permits, licensing, noise and safety.

Following a MOA-organized protest in October 2010 that involved around 1,000 young people, l'Usine took the decision to go on strike, arguing it was not responsible for the overcrowding of its premises. It closed its doors for the next two weekends, inviting the crowd to party outside the club in protest. On 22 October, as a result of an invitation of

Figure 5.1: Nightlife 'strike', Geneva, 2010

Source: Rafael Schutz (reproduced with permission)

l'Usine, 2,000 young people, a diverse combination of revellers, cultural producers, DJs, artists, politicos, and middle- and working-class youth, occupied the Plaine de Plainpalais, the marketplace in the centre of the city. Here, they staged an improvised and carnivalesque late night party with the aim of demanding more night venues (Berthet and Bjertnes, 2011). For two consecutive weekends subsequently, l'Usine announced its 'night strike' and on 30 October an unlicensed street party was attended by 2,000 people again, this time on the Place de Neuve (Saltmarsh, 2011) (see Figure 5.1). MOA reopened on 5 November and Halle W one week later.

It was not simply the decision to overturn these venue closures that is significant here. Preceding these protests, the publication of a critical nightlife research survey commissioned by the city of Geneva reiterated that there was a shortage of alternative night venues in the city. The report showed that alternative spaces made up less than 3 per cent of the total (Berthet et al, 2010). This, in turn, was followed by the organization of Etats Généraux de la Nuit, a high-profile, week-long conference on night culture which took place from 1 to 5 March 2011. As one of the keynote speakers, I reiterated ways to support and grow alternative spaces and suggested strategies for them to make wider alliances (Hollands, 2011). Out of the conference, a representative lobbying body called the Grand Council of the Night was formed. It was comprised of a range of nightlife actors including those from the alternative sector. The Council's mission was to deliberate on issues and help inform strategies and policies in relation to night-time issues and provision. More recently the Grand Council of the Night petitioned for new licensing exceptions in the city favourable to encouraging more alternative spaces to operate. This came into law in 2016 (Berthet-Meylan, 2022).

This case demonstrates that alternative visions of nightlife are both practical and possible, though some political compromises with the local creative state might be required. One consequence of the disappearance of squats has been that contemporary alternative cultural producers are forced to involve themselves in 'new deals' with city and state authorities. This happens via running their activities in premises offered by either the city or the canton and fitting in with official rules, from security to opening hours and licensing (Hollands et al, 2017). This new situation raises a wide range of issues regarding the possibility of retaining the essence of alternative nightlife, including maintaining collective management practices (Berthet-Meylan, 2022).

Improving our 'night vision': neoliberal nightlife, COVID-19 and alternatives

In this chapter we have highlighted some of the main shortcomings of neoliberal nightlife in terms of its corporate ownership, regulatory problems and exclusionary tendencies. In response to this we have suggested that resistance can occur and that nightlife counter-spaces can challenge mainstream provision by emphasizing co-production, experimentation and accessibility (Berthet-Meylan, 2022). Alternative forms of nightlife are much less alcohol-driven and more mixed in their provision of art, culture and music. They are also self-regulatory and encourage diversity and tolerance. Historically the corporate city has tended to squeeze out these more creative and informal spaces despite examples of opposition. Eldridge and Nofre (2018: 2) have noted that trends in the neoliberal city like exclusion, gentrification and over-commercialization were already beginning to threaten various aspects of nightlife prior to the advent of COVID-19 and lockdown. While the pandemic gave us the opportunity to reassess various aspects of urban life, the question is have we really given enough thought to rebuilding a night-time economy that is more diverse, creative and accessible?

It is clear that the nightlife sector has a whole has suffered more during COVID-19 than any other part of the economy. Premises were closed the longest and many were not deemed eligible for any arts recovery money. However, it was already in significant decline prior to the pandemic (Foley, 2021). For instance, 50 per cent of clubs in London had closed between 2010 and 2016, and 20 per cent of UK clubs closed their doors in 2018 (McCorry, 2021). Similarly, the number of pubs in the UK have declined from over 60,000 in 2000 to 47,200 in 2019 (Foley, 2021: 8). The decline in clubbing and pub-going has been linked to the indoor smoking ban in 2007, rising alcohol prices, a preference for socializing at home and the younger generation drinking less alcohol (Lock, 2021).

In terms of the corporate mainstream, the Night Time Industries Association stated that one-fifth of the businesses it represented would lose £40,000 each week of the extended lockdown (Ibis World, 2022b). This shows that for the big players there is still a significant amount of money to be made in the nightlife industry. Yet, an online survey conducted by the UK All-Party Parliamentary Group over a four-week period in February 2021 found that 51 per cent of staff in nightclubs had been made redundant rather than kept on furlough (Ibis World, 2022b). While some of these closures may have been independent operators who were financially forced to shut, it is reasonable to suggest that these figures also represent a significant 'disinvestment' in the workforce by corporate nightlife operators who generally undervalue their workforce. For decades, corporate pub chains and clubs have made huge amounts of capital from their business without really investing back into cities. So, what is the argument for using public money to rescue them?

Finn McCorry (2021), a club DJ and writer, makes the argument that clubbing in particular has been hard done by and deserves to be saved. She reasons that it is one of the few industries of consequence to young people. Additionally, she argues that its economic role has not been fully grasped by the government who let the sector slip through the net during COVID-19. McCorry (2021) says that '[c]lub culture has suffered during the pandemic and lost out on government support, but it is also eroded by a lack of acknowledgment of its unique position in the arts'. Only 12 venues received any cultural recovery funds in the UK. Finally, she cites the All-Party Parliamentary Group for the Night-Time Economy, which suggested that without major intervention in the night-time industry, it faces 'extinction' with 63 per cent of clubs making redundancies.

There is some merit in McCorry's (2021) argument about nightlife's importance to youth culture and its unique role in the arts. Unfortunately, her analysis does not differentiate between corporate 'super clubs' and tolerant and accessible alternative spaces. For example, take the case of Deltic, once the largest UK club operator with 53 premises. Peter Marks, chief executive of Deltic Group, was particularly vocal in the summer of 2020, saying that they had received no government support and that staff redundancies were imminent (Davies, 2020). More than 1,000 of Deltic's young staff of 2,400 were let go, but the company was sold out of administration to the corporate Swedish nightclub operator Rekom for £10 million (Hancock, 2021). Marks remained chief executive of the new organization, which merged with the Rekom Group when COVID-19 restrictions were lifted (Witts, 2020). In this case are we really to believe that the role of government in neoliberal times is to prop up corporate ownership and finances rather than support nightlife independents and bar/club staff who have suffered most during the pandemic? Eldridge and Nofre (2018: 2) ask: 'How might we make nightlife in our twenty-first century cities more sustainable, inclusive and secure?' The answer is not by supporting mainstream commercial nightlife, but rather through encouraging alternative and independent operators.

Tipping the balance between mainstream and alternative nightlife premises requires some imagination. Access to space in an era of rampant property development and the gentrifying neoliberal city is a key problem. City authorities could use their own building assets and planning powers to provide council properties and other empty spaces for alternative nightlife provision. As we have seen from the Geneva example, this plus licensing exceptions can encourage the alternative sector to survive and develop. Defining alternative nightlife spaces as arts and cultural venues and encouraging mixed use of clubs as galleries, theatres and creative hubs (and making cultural monies available) would also help. Support for the alternative sector should not be to make a city 'cool', but because this sector is genuinely creative, experimental, diverse and accessible.

More radically, cities (and national governments) might consider either repealing anti-squat legislation, or at least create a clause that buildings unoccupied for a period of time could be used as temporary alternative nightlife spaces. Similarly, while it is unlikely that we will see any movement on repealing the Criminal Justice Bill in the UK, again one might hope for an eventual relaxing of draconian fines levelled at illegal parties. While this is unlikely to happen even post-COVID-19, could a renewed free-party scene be part of a new urban creative future? Young people's desire to create self-organized nightlife events appeared to be undiminished during the COVID-19 pandemic, despite huge fines and negative publicity (Lee, 2020). Is there a way to channel this youthful energy into urban creativity and still maintain public health and safety? Nofre (2021) has suggested that we should reverse current arguments about harm and start to understand that nightlife could be an important source of social well-being, community-building and psychological mutual support for young people living through difficult post-COVID-19 times.

Nightlife, even alternative forms, also need to begin to take seriously the environmental consequences of this energy-sapping part of the urban cultural economy. One example of this is Music Declares Emergency (nd), which is a group of artists, music industry professionals and organizations that stand together to declare a climate and ecological emergency and call for an immediate governmental response. While believing in the power of music to promote the cultural change needed to create a better future, they also acknowledge the environmental impact of music industry practices and commit to taking urgent action (Music Declares Emergency, nd; see also Figure 5.2).

Figure 5.2: Music Declares Emergency t-shirt

Source: Music Declares Emergency, https://musicdeclares.shop/music-declares-emergency/
(reproduced with permission)

We need to sharpen our wider 'night vision' (Davies and Mummery, 2006) and begin to think more about providing a diversity of night-time activities beyond simply drinking and clubbing (Amid, 2018). Much more could be done to make city centres accessible to a wider range of age groups, families and under-18s, as well as becoming more female, disabled and gay friendly, ethnically diverse and open to the less well-off and urban poor. Part of increasing this accessibility requires widening the range of night-time activities on offer, as well as providing free events and subsidies for certain groupings. City centres should become a community resource again with educational, leisure and art and cultural venues open later into the evening. The creation of more safe public spaces where families can go, children can play and people can simply hang out without consuming are needed. Activities like night markets, free and subsidized outdoor festivals, cinema screenings and musical concerts could replace expensive and inaccessible mega-events. And rather than thinking of nightlife as a social problem, we should instead concentrate on night 'well-being' and 'mental health'.

Finally, we need a night-time economy based not just on corporate consumption, but one organized around diversity, accessibility and environmental sustainability. For the struggle for alternative nightlife is not simply a demand for the 'right to party', but is also part of a broader struggle to create a more just and fulfilling urban future.

Rethinking the Tourist City: Contestation and Alternative Cultural Tourism

In Chapter 2 it was noted that Harvey (1989a: 9) highlighted tourism as a significant entrepreneurial urban strategy for ailing cities. More recently, Hutton (2016: 66) further asserts that while tourism has always had a cultural dimension, over the last couple of decades 'cultural tourism' has experienced dramatic growth. As such, it has become a key urban branding tool for the neoliberal creative city.

As the creative economy has expanded globally, so too has the growth in tourism moved far beyond traditional destinations of the late 19th and early 20th centuries, like Paris, New York or London. In Europe, cities which historically have not experienced tourism previously, like Barcelona, Berlin and Prague, were by the millennium quickly becoming cultural meccas. Creative North American cities like Los Angeles, San Francisco and Chicago now vie with New York for the best tourism experience. Globally there is an avalanche of cities promoting tourism with reference to their cultural assets and creative infrastructure. In the Global South, Rio de Janeiro rose to prominence hosting the 2016 Olympic Games and attracting 1.17 million tourists during that two-week period (Kalvapalle, 2016). Hong Kong attracts 29 million visitors a year, topping the list of Asian cities, while Singapore, a city known to eagerly embraced the creativity paradigm (Luger, 2019), is ranked fourth in terms of tourist numbers with nearly 19 million visitors (Ganbold, 2022).

Despite its obvious economic benefits, growth in this sector has resulted in a rise in discontent around tourism-related issues in cities in recent years (Novy and Colomb, 2018). This signals the need for change and alternative policy solutions. While this issue has been represented most publicly by protests against noise, overcrowding, rent rises and public disorder, underlying these more 'visible' problems is the displacement and gentrification of many traditional city neighbourhoods via tourism (Salerno, 2022). Urban artists may clearly benefit from tourism but they can also be impacted negatively by many of the issues just mentioned. The pandemic also called into question neoliberal urban development strategies based around a continual growth model of tourism, while the climate crisis also disputes the sustainability of this particular sector of the cultural economy (Higgins-Desbiolles, 2020).

This chapter examines tourism within the context of the neoliberal creative city, outlining its characteristics and shortcomings. It also focuses on examples of opposition and the need for alternatives. The first part of the chapter looks at the rise of urban tourism and briefly discusses the question of 'who is a tourist', as well as distinguishes between different types of tourism. It then turns to critically analyse the main features of neoliberal tourism by linking it to urban entrepreneurialism, the cultural economy and the creative city. Finally, it examines and assesses examples of tourism contestations in Barcelona, Shanghai and Berlin. The second part of the chapter centres in on a discussion of alternative cultural tourism and uses the Prague Fringe Festival as a case study example. The chapter concludes with a brief discussion about the politics of alternative types of tourism and the need to pursue more just and sustainable forms in the future.

The rise of neoliberal tourism

Tourism, as we know it today, exists in a much different context and scale to that of the past. Very early forms of religious and educational travel can be traced back to antiquity and the middle ages. What we know as 'leisure travel', however, is associated with the industrial revolution and the development of travel technology. In the UK, historically tourism was characterized by social division and segmentation. This was largely a division between the activities of the upper and middle classes visiting exotic and often colonial locations (Gyr, 2010) and the working classes whose industrial struggles included the right for rest and recuperation in the form of nearby holiday and seaside resorts (Barton, 2005). So-called 'mass tourism' further expanded from the 1960s onward, characterized by new forms of holidaying experiences. These included European and overseas visits which were increasingly shaped by corporatization (that is, the 'package' holiday) and globalization. The 1990s also saw the creation of the 'city break' with the rise of budget airlines and a rapid growth of urban tourism in particular. Tourism is described as the world's biggest single industry (Marvell, 2006) accounting for 20 per cent of total global employment growth since 2013 (Loss, 2019) prior to the pandemic.

The growth in tourism numbers and journeys in the last 70 years has been phenomenal. In 1950 worldwide tourism as measured by international

Table 6.1: Number of flights by year, 2004–2021

Year	Number of flights (in millions)
2004	23.8
2006	25.5
2008	26.5
2010	27.8
2014	33.0
2016	35.2
2018	38.1
2020	40.3 (pre-COVID-19)
2021	22.2

Source: Salas (2022)

arrivals stood at only 25 million (World Tourism Organization, 2015: 2). By 2012 it was estimated that this figure reached 1 billion for the first time and by 2019 tourism made up 10 per cent of global GDP and was worth almost US$9 trillion (Constantin et al, 2020). The number of international tourist arrivals was projected to be 1.4 billion in 2020 before the COVID-19 pandemic hit. It is estimated that this will still reach 1.8 billion by 2030 (Novy and Colomb, 2018: 8). The number of flights in the global airline industry nearly doubled between 2004 and 2020 (pre-pandemic) (Salas, 2022; also see Table 6.1). Despite the impact of COVID-19 and environmental concerns, it is suggested that the number of air passengers is expected to actually double again in the next 20 years (FlyGreen, 2022).

Tourism generally is defined as the 'activities of persons travelling to and staying in places outside their usual environment for not more than one consecutive year for leisure, business and other purposes' (World Tourism Organization, 1995: 1). Often it is measured by numbers of international visitors or hotel guests. As we shall see in this chapter, such a generic definition and measurement belies a more complicated analyses of, first, who is defined, or rather 'perceived', as a tourist, and, second, different forms of tourism and tourist experiences. It also masks the specific nature of modern neoliberal types of tourism (Mosedale, 2021) and the possible development of alternative and more sustainable forms. We need to begin to understand tourism not simply as a monetary and numerical travel phenomenon, but as a particular type of urban relationship closely connected to the cultural economy and the neoliberal city.

We begin with the more general and seemingly simple question of who exactly is a tourist? This issue was raised by McCabe (2005) in order to get us to think differently about a range of tourism issues. His simple question asks whether we have a far too simplistic notion of what a tourist actually is, thereby confusing a range of issues related to tourism itself. Increased mobility and migration mean that cities are full of people who are neither local nor tourists. For example, urban populations are made up a range of people not local to the city they live in. They may have moved from another city within the same country or they may be an EU citizen working and living in a city in a country not of their origin. Many cities now have substantial and long-term immigrant and 'expat' communities in their midst. Overseas students attending university are another section of the urban demographic. None of these groups are local, but we would not classify them as tourists either, even though we might occasionally mistake them for such.

Finally, local inhabitants can engage with their own city 'as a tourist', attending events and tours not originally designed for them. Novy and Colomb (2019: 361) suggest that 'tourist practices intersect with other patterns of place consumption, mobility, work and leisure, and that the notion of the tourist itself as a distinguishable entity should be called into question'. While we conventionally continue to use the term tourist, it has the effect of lumping together a wide range of people and simplifying a whole range of different urban activities and practices. It also provides an easy scapegoat for urban problems rather than looking at broader issues of who cities are for, who benefits from them and how are they governed.

This point is also connected to the idea that there are different forms of tourism to be considered. Not only can these types be distinguished but they are also subject to different social judgements. Often, when the word tourism is invoked what we are really expressing are conventional forms of tourism. For example, the 'package holiday' or organized tours, aspects of which are often viewed in a negative light. One only need think of local disdain for large groups of tourists being guided around the city or, perhaps more pejoratively, unfavourable representations of 'cruise ship tourism' (Asero and Skonieczny, 2017) and stag parties or 'alcotourism' (Thurnell-Read, 2011). Another conventional but less controversial form is 'business tourism', where cities, hotels and restaurants cater for the corporate and mobile business classes (Harvey, 1989a). Ironically, this type of tourism is rarely criticized even though it often skews the cost of travel, accommodation and subsistence in a negative direction for other travellers not on expenses. Related to this, there has been a steady gentrification of tourism in most cities eager to charge premium prices for accommodation, events, food and drink (Gravari-Barbas and Guinand, 2017).

Still others have sought to distinguish the role of the 'experience economy' in travel and the idea of 'cultural tourism'. Richards (1996: 24) describes cultural tourism as 'the movement of persons to cultural attractions away from their normal place of residence with the intention to gather new information and experiences to satisfy their cultural need'. Similarly, with the rise of the internet and Airbnb, there has been a decided move away from the package holiday to more bespoke and 'individualized' tourist experiences.

It is important to keep in mind these tourism distinctions. Yet it might be argued that all of these types are variations of a neoliberal form. Wearing et al (2019: 27) state that the 'neoliberal model of tourism pursues profit at all costs with scant regard for local people, communities, or the natural environment', while Eisenschitz (2013: 98) says that 'tourism actively expresses and encourages neoliberal values and politics'. Inherent in neoliberal tourism ideology is the uncritical adoption of a limitless growth policy based on ever increasing tourist numbers. Success here, measured in tourist dollars, contributes to place-making. It also enhances a city's ranking and reputation. Developers, the well-off (tourists as well as locals) and the corporate private sector benefit, while poorer urban communities suffer. Wearing et al's (2019) quote also hints at some moral as well as environmental issues here. Tourism both reinforces neoliberal urban ideology as well as exposes some of its various contradictions.

The rise of global neoliberal tourism can be traced back to David Harvey's recognition of the shift towards place marketing and urban entrepreneurialism in the mid-1980s. Tourism, he argued, was a fundamental component of his idea of the 'spatial division of consumption'. It was also one of the main entrepreneurial strategies that cities around the world began to use to aid their ailing capital accumulation strategies (Harvey, 1989a). Since this time, many cities around the globe have seen tourism as a relatively straightforward economic driver and an important part of their urban regeneration strategy. As Novy and Colomb (2019: 361) argue, '[c]ity governments, regardless of their ideological orientation, have thus multiplied their activities to support the tourism sector, for example through investments in tourist-oriented attractions, campaigns and events'.

For example, contemporary tourism is increasingly seen as highly compatible with other amenity-based arts and cultural strategies and viewed by neoliberal city leaders and urban policy makers as a relatively low investment approach and economic boost for the private sector (Novy and Colomb, 2018: 10). Richards and Paolo Russo (2014: 4) argue that tourism 'has formed an important part of the "creative turn" with cities keen to distinguish themselves through developing creative forms of tourism that sit alongside existing cultural regeneration plans'. Alongside the selling of tourist experiences based increasing on the cultural economy, we have also seen the rise of urban 'mega events' and what some have called the 'festivalization of cities' (McGuigan, 2016; Evans, 2019). As Chapter 5 argues, tourism also relies heavily on the nightlife reputation of cities. Tourism, then, cannot be separated from wider developments in the neoliberal creative city.

The neoliberal tourist city is also an entrepreneurial one in the sense that it increasing caters for business needs and the requirements of wealthier tourists, as well as well-off locals. If we take Harvey's (1989a) argument about urban entrepreneurialism seriously, it is not difficult to notice that much tourist provision in cities mirrors meeting the needs of the global corporate business classes with the development of luxury hotels, fine dining restaurants and pricey cultural amenities. For example, Eisenschitz (2013: 103) argues that 'Los Angeles' Bunker Hill was designed by an elitist state to exclude the poor and to create an environment attractive to the middle class and the tourist'. Tourist developments like this cannot be separated from wider processes of urban entrepreneurialism, gentrification and social polarization.

In terms of neoliberal tourism's more specific features, Wearing et al (2019: 27) go on to say that 'the economic benefits generated from this global trade have been skewed towards wealthy investors'. For example, Gallo (2019) discusses seven giants that earn billions of dollars thanks to global tourism. Wearing et al (2019: 27) also suggest that economically 'many host communities receive an impoverished return, such as the creation of a few poorly paid menial jobs'. Generally, the tourism sector has been largely unregulated and left to benefit the private sector. Higgins-Desbiolles (2018) argues that urban authorities and multinational travel corporations instituted policies in the early 2000s to offset criticism of the negative impacts of tourism. They did this through promoting agendas of sustainability, corporate social responsibility and 'pro-poor' tourism. Yet the travel and hospitality industry is generally characterized as 'precarious' and riddled with low-paying jobs (Robinson et al, 2019) as the recently exposed cruise ship P&O example has demonstrated (Gheyoh Ndzi, 2022).

Tourism can also create inequities between tourists and locals while also exacerbating divisions between rich and poor locals. This is accomplished by asserting 'the right to tourism' over the 'rights of residents' (including local artists), as prime spaces are turned over to the hospitality and travel sector. For example, Eisenschitz (2013: 103) argues that the International Olympic Committee effectively governed London for a month, imposing excessive conditions with regard to security in the running of the 2012 Olympic Games. More drastically, the 2016 games in Rio de Janeiro in Brazil resulted in massive clearances of people's homes in some of the favelas (Freeman and Burgos, 2016) (see Figure 6.1). Similarly, the El Raval area of Barcelona has been highlighted as one area where cultural regeneration (Jauhiainen, 1992), and then tourism (Quaglieri Domínguez and Scarnato, 2017), have worked in tandem to gentrify the district. However, Degen's (2018) research on this area shows that it has not become quite the cultural

Figure 6.1: '67 thousand homeless people, Olympics for who?', Vila Autódromo, Rio de Janeiro, Brazil, 2016

Source: Rodolfo Rosa da Silveira (reproduced with permission)

zone intended and that it has been partly reoccupied by diverse local publics despite regeneration.

One of the other main features we see in neoliberal tourism policy has been a move towards gentrification (Gravari-Barbas and Guinand, 2017; Gotham, 2018). While part of this is motivated by branding and charging premium prices (see also Chapter 5 on nightlife), it is also about judgements about 'class tourism' (Thurnell-Read, 2011). The introduction of low-cost flights in the 1990s, for instance, meant that cities like Prague and others experienced the 'stag party' phenomena. These largely Eastern European cities initially welcomed such trade because it was bringing money into the local economy. Soon they began to see some of the downsides of this type of tourism. As a senior spokesperson for the Czech Tourism Authority said: "[W]hether its EasyJet or Ryanair especially and you know Jet2 ... they want the groups of young men who go to drink, they're good spenders they booze on the flight and you know. And we don't want them" (female, interviewed in 2017, Prague). There has been a clear shift in attracting a more gentrified and 'cultured' tourist clientele. A former councillor of culture for the city of Prague, admitted 'we want to attract young single people who are used to paying for expensive, provision, whether it be hotels, restaurants, etc' (cited in Hollands, 2009: 143).

Despite this tilt towards the corporatized, pro-business and gentrified city, neoliberal tourism ideology is more 'shape shifting' (Peck and Theodore, 2019) and complex than this (Higgins-Desbiolles, 2018). For example, like the creative city itself, it seductively argues that tourism is inherently beneficial for cities. The role of the local state is to buttress the fictitious narrative that 'tourism is good for everybody' (Assemblea de Barris per un Turisme Sostenible, 2019).

Neoliberal tourism subjectivity is also closely tied up with the experience economy and creative strategies. An example of this is the more recent shift away from the package or organized tour holidays, towards one in which tourists themselves construct their own 'authentic' travel experience. This might involve setting up one's own itinerary in a city and also seeking out places and activities not normally found on the main tourist trail. Eisenschitz (2013: 100) argues that '[c]ultural tourism justifies itself by recourse to neo-liberalism's propositions which it in turn legitimates'. Richards and Paolo Russo (2014) suggesting that even alternative varieties of tourism may be susceptible to incorporation into the neoliberal form.

This creative tourism phenomena can have some contradictory consequences for cities. First, it can result in the invasion of cities not normally touristed and neighbourhoods that have traditionally been outside of 'tourist bubbles' (Jacobsen, 2003). Second, in seeking out alternative cultures in this city, creative tourists may inadvertently begin to bring such activities back into the 'mainstream'. Organized graffiti trails, visits to alterative creative spaces or cool bars may begin to change the character of areas and places as they become incorporated as the 'edgy' element of neoliberal tourism strategies (Pattaroni, 2020).

Many of the negative neoliberal features discussed here have led to the growing dissatisfaction of sections of the local population, including artists, with the impact tourism is having on their urban environment and quality of life. This has sometimes resulted in the mobilization of these concerns into various forms of 'anti-tourist' movements, though, as argued next, this 'label' is somewhat of a misnomer. Neoliberal tourism has seemingly created a set of intractable tensions within the city. To cite Novy and Colomb:

[A]cross the globe, there has been a proliferation of manifestations of discontent and protest around tourist related issues in the city. This points to an increasing 'politicisation from below' of the impacts of the visitor economy on people in places which is the result of the qualitative and quantitative transformations of urban tourism and of the way in which tourism has been governed (or not) in contemporary cities. (Novy and Colomb, 2019: 358)

This discontent is discussed in more detail in the next section.

Protesting tourism and its discontents

Like other neoliberal urban policies, including creative city ones, tourism seems to have been accepted as a wholly positive development for cities. Traditionally it has been all about boosting visitor numbers and supporting the private tourism sector. With the growth of tourism discontent, however, there has been more of a local state shift towards the regulation of tourist impacts on cities, neighbourhoods and communities. Rather than viewing this discontent as 'anti-tourist', Novy and Colomb (2019: 359) say: 'Taking issue with tourism and its impacts is not per se "tourism-phobic", and the often-alluded-to notion of "overtourism" distracts us from the fact that there is more to consider than the volume of visitation when making sense of (urban) tourism's current problematisation, politicisation, and contestation.'

Neoliberal tourism brings into sharp focus wider issue like gentrification, mobility and migration, class discrimination and changes to the urban environment. It also connects to broader issues of who has the right to the city and the lack of 'good' tourism governance (Novy, 2018). Finally, it raises the need to conceptualize tourism in a more holistic way and to seek alternative policies and strategies.

Not all tourist-related protests are of the same character. Some are simply 'anti-tourist' in intention, going as far as relating themselves to wider populist and even anti-migration discourses (Screti, 2022). Others, organized around a specific area of the city, may come across as NIMBY (Not In My Back Yard). Still others appear quite specific or single issue oriented. Novy and Colomb (2019: 363) helpfully distinguish between protests around *negative effects* (that is, overcrowding, noise, disorder), *equity impacts* (for example, house and rent prices and gentrification, and so on), and *political contestations* around tourism (questioning how tourism is governed, or not, and how it is a symptom of wider urban processes). In the following we look at three examples of urban discontent with tourism and assess them against these different criteria.

The first example of 'protesting tourism' comes from the city of Barcelona. The 1992 Olympics Games had a dramatic effect on the cultural regeneration of the city and boosting tourism (Dodd, 2004). Since then, Barcelona has experienced a 400 per cent rise in tourist numbers and is now the fifth most visited city in Europe. Unsurprisingly, the city consistently ranks as one of the top ten creative cities in the world and is recognized as a cultural mecca in terms of its architecture, food, and nightlife.

Despite these 'successes' Barcelona is also recognized as a city that has experienced significant discontent around the tourist issue. As early as 2002, residents in the Ribera district of the city were campaigning for the restriction of nightlife, as the once quiet Passeig de Born became increasingly packed with bars and restaurants oriented towards the tourist market (Chatterton and Hollands, 2003: 64–65). Other resident associations in Barcelona's old city have also been campaigning outside city hall for years about the growth of rental apartments and the anti-social (drunken) behaviour of tourists. It was photographic evidence of three intoxicated and naked Italian tourists wandering around the city's streets in 2014 that sparked further outrage (Novy and Colomb, 2018: 1–2).

Figure 6.2: Anti-tourism sign, Barcelona

Source: Miltos Gikas/Flickr (CC BY 2.0)

Overcrowding in one of the city's main tourist attractions, Park Güell, also led to a campaign in 2013 to limit tourist numbers through a payment and booking system, even though there was local opposition to this solution (Aries-Sans and Russo, 2018). Anti-tourist signs soon became a permanent feature of the city landscape (see Figure 6.2). In 2017 the youth wing of a Catalan political party slashed the tyres of a tour bus near FC Barcelona's stadium, spraying the windscreen with the slogan 'Tourism kills neighbourhoods' and later were filmed vandalizing tourist bicycles (Burgen, 2017).

While a number of these responses may appear to be a 'knee jerk' reaction about tourism effects or motivated by a particular kind of politics, they all focus attention on its governance, or lack of it. They also reveal the failure of unregulated neoliberal tourism strategies which are based on unlimited growth and a lack of concern over their impact on transforming neighbourhoods in negative ways. One body in Barcelona, which took up a more critical and holistic position around tourism, was the Assembly of Neighborhoods for Sustainable Tourism (ABTS). To quote from a website featuring an exhibition on the assembly:

ABTS was set up in 2015 as a coordinating body for several neighbourhood and single-issue groups and organisations who share a radically critical approach to the urban model and specifically the tourism model currently in force in Barcelona. This is a struggle not against tourists, but rather against the industries that get rich off them and against the public administrations that allow and/or encourage this urban model of tourism. (Assemblea de Barris per un Turisme Sostenible, 2019)

Rather than protesting against tourists, ABTS represent Novy and Colomb's (2019) *equity critique* of tourism. Their proposal of 'tourism degrowth' would later feed into city council plans favouring a decrease in tourism and reducing overcrowding in the city (Blanco-Romero et al, 2018; Russo, and Scarnato, 2018). This development blurs into Novy and Colomb's (2019) political contestation of tourism category.

Previously, a housing activist, Ada Colau, wrote an article in *The Guardian* critical of Barcelona's neoliberal tourism strategy and, within a year and a half, found herself as head of the citizen's activism movement, Barcelona en Comú, and the elected mayor of the city (Novy and Colomb, 2018: 8). In their 2015 manifesto, the group said:

Rethinking the model of tourism is one of the first tasks at hand … while the profits from tourism are concentrated in a few hands, the costs are suffered by the great majority of the men and women of the city. It is necessary to comprehensively change this model with the participation of everyone involved. Employment in this sector can't be precarious and unsustainable. The trends towards the closure of public spaces and the expulsion of the most economically vulnerable from their neighbourhoods must be stopped. (Guanyem Barcelona, 2015: 2)

After extensive public consultation, this elected social movement produced a Strategic Tourism Plan for 2020. This was an attempt to develop a cross-sectoral approach to governing tourism 'to guarantee the general interests of the city' (Tourism Department Manager's Office for Enterprise and Tourism, 2017: 5). This represents quite a significant political change in the city about how to tackle some of the problems and issues that tourism brings to the forefront in the context of a wider urban strategy (see also Chapter 8). It not only signals *political contestation* in Barcelona, but actual *political transformation*. On the Barcelona en Comú website, they mention closing 4,900 illegal tourist flats and fining the platforms that advertised them. They also have a Tourist Accommodation Plan to prevent any more housing from being transformed into tourist accommodation in neighbourhoods with overcrowding (Tourism Department Manager's Office for Enterprise and Tourism, 2017: 92-96). Further, their 2020 strategic plan seeks to manage tourism in the city through degrowth (Blanco-Romero et al, 2018) and 'by making it compatible with the other needs of the multiple, complex and heterogeneous city that is Barcelona' (Tourism Department Manager's Office for Enterprise and Tourism, 2017: 6).

A second example of cultural tourism resistance comes from a Global South city (see Case Study 6.1).

Case Study 6.1: The visitor economy, creative entrepreneurs and conflict in a Shanghai neighbourhood

Arkaraprasertkul's (2018: 282) study of neighbourhood conflict is 'born out of the impacts of globalization and the rise of the tourism industry and the creative economy on urban space in Shanghai' and is a second example of tourism discontent. He mentions that over the past decade the government of Shanghai has pursued a 'global city agenda' and that it ranks only second to Beijing in terms of tourist numbers. It is also notable in terms of using the creative industries to develop its urban brand (O'Connor and Gu, 2020). While concerned with modernizing its image and skyscape, Shanghai's brand also involves preserving its historic monuments and local cultural heritage.

Arkaraprasertkul's (2018) research looks at a traditional neighbourhood of alley-way houses in Shanghai, known as *lilong*. It focuses on the tensions between the 'global city' discourse, the city government's preservationist ideals and the changing needs and composition of the local community. On the one hand, the city's desire to attract tourists and creative entrepreneurs has result in crowded streets, with this latter group infiltrating traditional *lilong* neighbourhoods due to cheap rents. This in turn has stimulated the development of businesses and amenities in an ageing residential neighbourhood and created conflicts over noise, overcrowding and unregulated economic activity. Arkaraprasertkul (2018) reports on a 2013 government crackdown on unofficial businesses in a particular area of the city. This is somewhat at odds with the desire to attract tourist numbers and encourage the growth of the creative industries. So, while aspects of this conflict are related to the creative city paradigm and neoliberal tourism, in this case they are also connected to the local state's need to manage entrepreneurial activity and preserve the heritage of the neighbourhood.

A third example of protesting tourism comes from the city of Berlin. Novy and Colomb (2018: 1) trace the origins of discontent back to the socio-spatial restructuring of the city with the fall of the Berlin Wall. Similarly, Hollands (2019: 737) discusses the impact the influx of artists into various neighbourhoods through the 1990s had on the character of the city. The labelling of Berlin as a 'cool city' via a public–private coalition brought with it not only artists and tourists but also gentrifiers and property developers

(Colomb, 2011). Novy (2018: 52) charts the phenomenal rise of tourist numbers which have increased four-fold since the 1990s to 28 million overnight stays in 2014, making it the third most popular tourist destination after Paris and London.

While the seeds of discontent were sewn earlier, Novy and Colomb (2018: 1) trace the first visual signs of anti-tourism in Berlin as appearing in the summer of 2011. Residential and mixed-use alternative neighbourhoods like Kreuzberg, Friedrichshain and Prenzlauer Berg had by then been transformed by the influx of artists and the impact of tourism, particularly through the rise of Airbnb. Similarly, alternative forms of culture in those neighbourhoods, like graffiti, cool bars and alternative art spaces, started to become co-opted into the city marketing strategies, with the Alternative Berlin Walking Tour being an example of this. Novy (2018: 60–61) suggests that some of the more aggressive anti-tourist sentiments, including the suggestion that visitors should practice 'balconing' (that is, jumping off balconies), were headline-grabbing but untypical. Other critics felt that the fault lay not with tourists per se, but with the failure of local government to respond policy-wise to wider economic and cultural change in the city.

One of the problems was that the most affected areas themselves had limited power to address tourism and planning issues. These powers lie mainly within the purview of the Senate which continued to support a growth tourism policy despite rising discontent. Others argued that the Senate lacked an understanding of both the tourism issue and how it was integrated with neoliberal economic and cultural growth strategies in the city. Recent interventions seem to support more of a 'tinkering strategy' here, rather than a real political contestation like Barcelona. Changes included slightly broader policy interventions including rent control legislation, an increase in social housing provision and some limits on Airbnb (O'Sullivan, 2019). On 15 April 2021, however, Berlin's rent cap (*Mietendeckel*) was declared unconstitutional because the courts ruled that only the federal government was entitled to regulate rents, showing how strong the property lobby is in the city.

A recent Senate document entitled *Sustainable and City-Compatible Berlin Tourism Plan 2018+* argues for 'creating the requisite framework conditions for a sustainable, city-compatible and socially fair tourism' (Senate Department for Economics Energy and Public Enterprises, 2018: 2). While there is some movement here in terms of recognizing that tourism is not a separate entity from other forms of urban regeneration, it still maintains a 'long-term moderate growth in tourism' (Senate Department for Economics Energy and Public Enterprises, 2018: 2). As Novy (2018: 68) argues, while there has been a *re-politicization* of the tourism issue as part of a wider feature of neoliberal urban development, further mobilization and contestation in Berlin is needed if radical change is to come about.

Alternative cultural tourism: the Prague Fringe Festival

In addition to protest and resistance against the tourism city, there are also alternative types of tourism experience and organization. We have already distinguished cultural tourism from more conventional types (Richards, 1996), yet this form is also closely associated with neoliberal values and policies. Richards and Paolo Russo (2014) similarly outline what they call creative and alternative forms of tourism, distinguished by a more engaged tourist experience often existing on the fringes of city. Previously I argued that it is important to distinguish between mainstream and alternative forms of cultural tourism and festivals (Hollands, 2010).

Hollands (2010) characterizes alternative cultural tourism as having a number of defining features beyond that mentioned by Richards and Paolo Russo (2014). First, they are 'not for profit' events and organizations motivated by a creative and artistic ethos. Second, such events prioritize the 'use value' of space over 'exchange value', often transforming and questioning the social-spatial order and urban aesthetics. Third, these alternative cultural tourism organizations usually have a collective or horizontal structure, often rejecting a producer/consumer distinction. This creates the notion of a wider and diverse creative community characterized by social bonding. Events such as this also pride themselves as being diverse, risky and accessible.

The example utilized here is the Prague Fringe Festival. First, it is important to say something general about what fringe actually is. Despite its popularity worldwide, many people might not have attended a fringe festival or know what its ethos is. In her interviews with festival directors about defining fringe, one scholar revealed themes like edgy, experimental, original, alternative and 'not mainstream' as key features (Batchelder, 2006). Historically the term has been used to refer to an event 'on the edge' of an already established art or cultural festival, with Edinburgh Fringe being the first to run alongside the 1947 Edinburgh International Festival. It can be argued that fringe has its roots in alternative culture, participatory performance and consumption and an open access philosophy. Yet not all fringes can be described as alternative cultural tourism. The Edinburgh Fringe has literally become the biggest arts festival in the world and many suggest it has become directly incorporated into the corporate and mainstream branding culture of the neoliberal city (Clark, 2012; Bob, 2019).

The Prague Fringe Festival operates on a model closer to the original Edinburgh Fringe, having its roots in alternative culture, being non-hierarchical and 'performer-led'. The argument is that it is both a practical example and a possible model for an alternative cultural tourism strategy.

Following a brief description of the Prague Fringe, I examine how it engages diverse communities of artists, locals, volunteers and audiences from around the world and seeks to create egalitarian relationships between them. Additionally, I argue it helps to build different kinds of cultural networks, bonds and social capital (Hollands, 2010).

The Prague Fringe was founded in the year 2000 by two Scots and a Geordie (a person from Newcastle upon Tyne) who were all associated previously with the Edinburgh Fringe. It has grown steadily from a small event involving 13 companies and 63 performances over five days, to over 40 companies drawn from all around the world, engaging 250 performances over eight days (2019 figures, as COVID-19 impacted on subsequent fringes). It is 'not for profit', has a skeleton staff, and is largely run by both performers and a team of volunteers. Shows cost around £9 and run from late afternoon to nearly midnight in both existing theatres and unconventional spaces, encouraging audiences to see multiple shows in a day to create a 'festival experience'. The Fringe Club, open all day and late into the evening, is open to performers, volunteers and audiences to encourage interaction and bonding.

Audience statistics reveal that the Prague Fringe is a form of alternative cultural tourism in terms of diversity and mixing. In 2011, people living in the city made up 55 per cent of its audience (25 per cent Czechs and 30 per cent non-Czechs) and 45 per cent tourists (Hollands, 2012), showing that the festival caters for locals, expats and overseas visitors alike. In 2016, the audience was made up of 30 different nationalities, with 15 different nationalities represented in the programme (Hollands, 2016a: 11). Prague Fringe is also 'female-friendly' with women making up 60 per cent of the audience and it caters for a relatively wide range of age groups and occupations (Hollands, 2016a: 10). Significantly, in terms of fulfilling the Czech Tourism Authority's brief of attracting 'repeat tourists', over 40 per cent of the fringe audience were returnees.

More important, perhaps, is the fact that much of this audience are not what one might consider to be 'typical tourists'. As one long-term Prague Fringe volunteer, writer and audience member pointed out in interview, "I've been coming here for years and years, to volunteer, to learn, to watch and to contribute creatively to the city. I'm not a f★★★ing tourist!" (interviewee, 57, female, Edinburgh). Rather than contributing to 'tourist problems', this alternative tourism experience was much more about social learning, creativity, diversity and creating a temporary community.

One of the key ways in which bonding within the Prague Fringe is expressed is through the notion of a 'fringe family'. This is similar to what Hetherington (2000) has elsewhere referred to as 'communitas', which can be described as a temporary yet intense form of community spirit, solidarity and togetherness. This point relates to the lack of distinction made between performers and audience members, as expressed by the idea of the 'festival participant': 'We prefer to refer to everyone involved in the Prague Fringe as festival participants, rather than separate them out into different categories like artists and audiences' (Carole Wears, then Prague Fringe Associate Director, cited in Hollands, 2010: 387). From one year to the next there is often a swapping of roles from audience member to volunteer and even performer or writer/director.

This phenomenon of rotating roles has an egalitarian ethos to it. Additionally, it questions conventional distinctions between cultural producers and consumers. This extends to audience members themselves, who sometimes become involved in the making of a show in terms of providing direct feedback to writers, directors and performers. Furthermore, while the festival directors are responsible for much of the early planning, curation and organization of the event prior to it happening, the actual day-to-day running of the festival is really in the hands of performers themselves, supported by a small but dedicated set of 'front of house' volunteers and technicians. While there is question mark over unpaid cultural labour, ironically, the volunteer experience was the opposite of alienation and exploitation. Rather, they spoke more about a lack of hierarchy and sense of ownership of the festival, as the following quote demonstrates: 'Where I work normally the boundaries between artists, staff and audience are rigid. The Prague Fringe festival blurs these boundaries, the upshot of which is a more participatory experience for all' (English, female volunteer, cited in Hollands, 2010: 386).

Finally, the non-hierarchical nature of the Prague Fringe also appeared to create certain kinds of social bonds, interactions and social networks. There were lots of examples of how this bonding process occurred across traditional artistic hierarchies. This included interactions between performers, venue managers, front of house volunteers and local Czech technicians. Respondents talked here about special feelings of community, intense personal interaction and mutual respect. Social media also allowed groups that met in Prague to remain in contact from one year to the next. Work and social networks formed through the Fringe could also provide new opportunities for employment and travel elsewhere. What is evident here is an informal economy of cultural networks created through social bonding not seen in more mainstream arts organizations.

To conclude this section, although only a single case, the Prague Fringe example has important implications for thinking about alterative cultural tourism policy in cities more generally. First, it emphasizes the different role alternative cultural tourism could play in cities with respect to creating social value, enhancing social capital and bonding, forging friendships and internationalizing the educational value of art and culture. The impact side of my research on the Prague Fringe (Hollands, 2017a) has sought to demonstrate to culture and tourism departments in the city both the weakness of neoliberal tourism strategies as well as the strength of alternative ones. Politicians and tourism officials in the city are beginning to see the value of alternative cultural tourism as an antidote to some of the issues caused by 'mega-events' and conventional tourism, such as overcrowding and the concentration of tourists in certain geographical areas in the city. As a city centre councillor responsible for culture and tourism issues told me, events like the Prague Fringe represent "the way forward for the future development of tourism" (male, interviewed 2017, Prague). Prague Fringe also demonstrates that alternative types of cultural tourism are possible, practical and sustainable over time.

Like all forms of alternative culture, fringe can be co-opted into neoliberal tourism policies in the form of cities selling themselves as 'edgy' and 'different'. On a bigger scale, we have talked about how the 'coolness' of Berlin and the edginess of its alternative culture has, in some sense, been partially usurped by mainstream tourism strategies. Festivals, including fringe, are particularly susceptible to such incorporation (Quinn, 2010). The corporatization of the Edinburgh Fringe was previously mentioned (Bob, 2019) and there are a number of other studies about the growth of fringes around the world that support this shift from alternative to mainstream, with Adelaide and Perth Fringe in Australia being two prime examples (Wynne, 2018; Thomasson, 2019). Even smaller and more independent fringes, like Prague, are not perfect and are also susceptible to these processes. In fact, more recently, there have been changes in its organization structure in terms of it becoming more 'formalised' organizationally and accepting private sponsorship monies, which may have begun to shift its alternative characteristics and ethos.

Towards just and sustainable forms of tourism

What a single example of alternative cultural tourism like the Prague Fringe cannot do on its own is challenge the neoliberal tourist city. This requires broader and more collective action as discussed in Chapter 4. One example of this was the 'Days of Unrest Initiative for Cultural Prague', which happened in the city in 2008 (Hollands, 2009). This was a broader collective mobilization by independent and alternative venues to force the city council to reorganize the public funding of the arts to include separate funding streams for independent arts organizations. It was a fight for recognition and value of the alternative sector. It also became a struggle which highlighted the shortcomings of neoliberal tourist policies. The Initiative sought to defend a vision of culture as a public good and save Prague from 'rampant consumerism', 'mindless commercial development' and outright 'Disneyfication' (Burke, 2008: 39). While the 'Days of Unrest' mobilization was successful in terms of creating independent culture funding streams it was not enough to shift Prague's overall neoliberal tourism strategy. Furthermore, groups outside of the cultural movement may have seen the protest as being motivated by self-interest designed to benefit only the arts sector.

The key issue is that any effective alternative cultural tourism mobilization must be linked up with wider urban concerns so protest does not appear self-serving (Novy and Colomb, 2019). In order to create real and lasting change here, it is clear that collective action cannot be limited to either a singular urban cultural movement (see Chapter 4) or be focused around just an anti-tourist stance. Rather, cultural tourism movements must embed and ally themselves with wider urban social movements concerned with gentrification, housing and equality issues. Ideally, they also need to gain access to political power, as the earlier Barcelona example demonstrates. That city's degrowth strategy towards tourism is balanced by its plans to develop alternative neighbourhood economies and obtain proper remuneration for hospitality workers. It also involves practical policies designed to tackle some of the immediate issues such as noise, overcrowding and tourist gentrification. Things like cracking down on Airbnb and restricting it in particular neighbourhoods, subsidizing educational and creative tourism and taxing business tourism, are all strategies than can be utilized here.

Policies required to re-balance the city towards alternative culture, meeting local need and creating different kinds of urban tourism, is only half the battle. As some commentators have argued, we also need to develop more justice-related and sustainable forms of tourism. Guia (2021: 504) defines sustainable tourism as 'developing, promoting and practicing tourism in a way that carries more social and environmentally friendly prospects for the ensemble of stakeholders involved, especially host communities and the environment'. How we attain this is a bigger question. Do we start to encourage people to travel less, particularly air travel? Critics point out that air travel only contributes about 8 per cent of greenhouse gases and can we really stop people from getting on planes? Raising the cost of air travel only benefits those who can afford it and punishes the less well-off. However, with the number of flights set to double in the next 20 years we will need to take actions like encouraging other forms of travel (trains) and people holidaying more locally. We will also need policies and laws which guarantee protection for indigenous communities and the natural world being affected by tourism.

The idea of justice tourism takes the social and political dimensions of alternative and sustainable tourism even further. Scheyvens (quoted in Guia, 2021: 504) defines justice tourism as a 'type of tourism which develops solidarity, mutual recognition and equity between guests and hosts, while also providing local communities with economic, social and cultural benefits, and supporting their self-determination' (for an example, see Case Study 6.2). Wearing et al give some more substance to these ideas in this rather lengthy quote:

For example, a well-managed, well-regulated, and authentic peer-to-peer tourism venture can lead to the sharing of tourists' time, knowledge, skills, enthusiasm, and energy to enhance the communities and environments where they travel. The culture of the host community is respected and the tourist is open to experiencing aspects of the other culture with a view to learning and expanding the self. This shift in the relationship of power between tourist and host culture through collaborative exchange in a nonmarket sphere enables both to interact and to learn from each other, with an eventual hybridisation and enrichment of both cultures. The tourist destination becomes a space for interaction and learning, and tourism does not damage or destroy the culture or environment of the host community and its environment. (Wearing et al, 2019: 39)

Case Study 6.2: Alternative justice tourism and Bethlehem's 'segregation wall'

An example of justice tourism from the Global South comes from the work of Isaac (2009; 2010). He looks at alternative forms of tourism in the Palestinian tourism industry, including the case of Bethlehem's 'segregation wall'. In his discussions Isaac mentions the importance of tourism for Palestine's economy and identity and the domination of their tourism industry by Israel. Isaac (2010) highlights the work of the Alternative Tourism Group (ATG), established in 1995, in particular. ATG is a Palestinian non-governmental organization concerned with tourism, which offers a critical look at the culture, history and politics of the country and its difficult relationship with Israel. The group 'operates according to the tenets of justice tourism, that is, tourism that holds as its central goals the creation of economic opportunities for the local community, positive cultural exchange between guest and host through one-on-one interaction, the protection of the environment, and political/historical education' (Isaac, 2010: 30). ATG works with a wide range of groups and delegations and runs several tours throughout Israel and Palestine highlighting faith and political issues and in particular the segregation wall in Bethlehem. According to the ATG itself, they 'accompany visitors on a journey with a purpose and with intent to both learn and unlearn through gaining accurate insights into Palestine and the struggle for justice as viewed through the eyes of Palestinians and based on their aspirations' (Kassis et al, 2016: 47–48). While Isaac (2010) views this as a social justice example of alternative tourism, other research is slightly more cautious. Higgins-Desbiolles (2018) cites a number of research studies that remain critical of power differentials in terms of 'privileged tourists' visiting such sites and the need to remain attentive to the structural foundations of contemporary injustices within tourism generally.

In conclusion, challenging neoliberal tourism requires not only building on alternatives but also thinking about how these forms can become more just and sustainable. Higgins-Desbiolles (2020: 610) calls for a post-pandemic reset towards a 'community-centred tourism framework that redefines and reorients tourism based on the rights and interests of local communities and local people'. Sheller (2018) suggests a more holistic theory of mobility justice to obtain movement equality as well as environmental sustainability.

Finally, returning to an earlier point by Novy and Colomb (2019), this chapter has argued that we need to move away from restricted notions of anti- and over-tourism and begin to analyse the issues raised in light of broader urban process and contestation of the neoliberal creative city. While tourism concerns may be the spark for protest and opposition they are underlined by wider issues of urban equity, city governance and who cities are for. Neoliberal arguments that everyone benefits from the jobs created by tourism and that the gentrification of neighbourhoods via touristification is automatically a good thing for cities, is beginning to wear thin. While tourism is seemingly difficult to regulate on its own, debates here have to be embedded within wider struggles tackling urban processes like gentrification, creativity, inequality, justice and sustainability. Only then can we begin to move away from the idea of isolated 'tourism problems' and begin to transform the neoliberal city itself.

Creative Polarization, Division and Exclusion

Previous chapters have referred to how neoliberal urbanization and the creativity paradigm are implicated in the production of social and spatial inequalities. This chapter returns to a focus on the creative city and explores its role in contributing to urban polarization, division and exclusion. Florida's (2004) initial vision was that the creative class was going to transform the urban economy in a positive direction creating economic growth and increasing social tolerance. We now find ourselves in a 'new urban crisis' (Florida, 2018) characterized by 'hyper-gentrification', housing bubbles and a widening gap between the rich and poor. The argument made here is that the neoliberal creative city has, in fact, actively contributed to this crisis (Dorling, 2017).

This chapter is organized into four sections. First, it provides a wider context by looking at how neoliberal urbanization creates increased polarization between rich and poor (Shi and Dorling, 2020) while ideologically blaming the less well-off for their worsening situation. Second, it discusses how the creative class paradigm 'maps onto' urban divisions, hiding, extending and creating new social inequalities (Gerhard et al, 2017). It focuses on the negative impact the creative class has had on the service and working classes, as well as the urban poor. It also explores how the creative class concept itself hides significant divisions and inequalities within its own ranks. Third, I explore the process of 'creative exclusions' through the idea of seeing disadvantaged youth as either a 'creative underclass' or as 'non-creative chavs'. The final section of the chapter concludes by briefly considering some alternative ways of tackling social polarization, creative divisions and exclusions.

Capitalism, neoliberalism and polarization

To preface the discussion of why the most successful neoliberal creative cities appear to be the most unequal (Florida, 2003b; 2018), it is important to examine the issue historically. Capitalism from its inception is a system based on inequality and polarization. Marx (1977) argued that it was based on a two-class model divided between the proletariat (workers) and the bourgeoise who owned the means of production. While he also recognized that capitalism produced a 'sub-class' of workers, Marx rather deterministically theorized that increasingly within capitalism people would be thrust into either of the two main classes. We know now that the class structure within this economic system is much more varied and diverse than this today. Yet as Wright (2015) points out, there is still a very rich corporate managerial class and extremely precarious and marginalized class in existence. Where Marx was more perceptive was in his general point that capitalism tended towards a growing gap between the most rich and poor. What we understand today as socioeconomic polarization. As Marx (1977: 714) once said: 'Accumulation of wealth at one pole is at the same time accumulation of misery, agony of toil, slavery, ignorance, brutality, mental degradation, at the opposite pole.'

Marx's (1977) work meticulous details this disparity historically. Yet his theory of the state as the political instrument of capitalist interests did not really envisage the creation of the welfare state and social policies designed to reduce inequalities (Lavalette and Mooney, 2000). Through working-class struggle, economic reform and state welfarism, socioeconomic polarization under Western capitalism was reduced for a period. For example, the UK became less polarized during the post-war years up until the late 1970s with 'the share of income going to the top 10% of the population fell over the 40 years to 1979, from 34.6% in 1938 to 21% in 1979, while the share going to the bottom 10% rose slightly' (The Equality Trust, nd). Similarly in the US, income inequality peaked in the 1920s, remained low through the Great Depression (Piketty and Saez, 2003) and was relatively low from 1947 through to the 1970s (Owyang and Shell, 2016).

This income narrowing came to an end in both of these major Western countries with the rise of neoliberal economics and politics. The exhaustion of industrial Fordist modes of accumulation in the 1970s and the creation of new modes of flexible capital accumulation (Harvey, 1989b: 89) demanded different modes of national and local governance. Politically, the rise of neoliberalism is best represented by Thatcherism in the UK and Reganism in the US (Harvey, 2007: 88). To facilitate market rule (Peck and Theodore, 2019) national and local states have to act to favour capital over labour. The opening up of trade barriers favouring globalization, urban entrepreneurialism, deregulation of the financial sector, lower taxes on top earners and corporations, and privatization all aided new forms of capital accumulation. Attacking workers' rights and conditions as well as challenging the welfare state were also part of this process.

Neoliberalism in the Global South has followed a slightly different path than in the North. This was partly due to different levels of industrialization and agricultural production. There was also existing polarization between a small land-owning elite and large, poor peasant class and a relatively underdeveloped welfare state in many Global South countries. Connell and Dados (2014) argue that its introduction there actually pre-dated its rise in the West. Their understanding of neoliberalism in Latin America is that it acted as a development strategy conducive to political stability via military dictatorship and extractive capitalism (in sectors like agriculture, mining, forestry, raw materials, and so on). However, when the Western model of neoliberalism was essentially re-imposed on the Global South via structural adjustment programmes designed to curb debt, it had the similar effect of worsening already existing economic polarization in many countries (Vellinga, 2002).

As Shi and Dorling (2020: 1) argue: 'Through neoliberal policies ... wealth becomes increasingly concentrated in the hands of a few who become ever wealthier'. For example, income inequality in the US was found to have increased by about 20 per cent from 1980 to 2016, while the wealth gap between America's richest and poorer families more than doubled from 1989 to 2016 (Menasce Horowitz et al, 2020). In the UK, since 1979 the early reduction of inequality has reversed sharply before flatting out (The Equality Trust, nd), with the 2021 Census showing that the top 10 per cent of population in the UK hold nearly 50 per cent of all wealth, while the bottom 10 per cent hold only 0.02 per cent (Office for National Statistics, 2022). Surveys of Latin American and Caribbean countries have found that countries that went through radical neoliberal reform packages showed greater increases in inequality (Vellinga, 2002). In Latin America, Rodríguez (2021: 2) argues that the 'consolidation of already significant inequalities, precarious jobs and informality, political closure and social exclusion, are today among the best-known legacy of neoliberal policies'. In East Asia the financial crisis of the late 1990s resulted in devastating increases in unemployment and poverty in countries like Thailand, Indonesia and Korea (Harvey, 2007: 96).

Neoliberal global capitalism produces not only socioeconomic polarization but also spatial polarization. The term, 'socio-spatial polarization' refers broadly to the growing gap between rich and poor in both socioeconomic position and geographic location. Shi and Dorling (2020: 1) argue: 'Socio-spatial inequality grows with the ascendency of neoliberalism.' Its various dimensions can be viewed at a global level and within countries, cities and even neighbourhoods. For example, the richest 10 per cent of the world's population own 76 per cent of the wealth while the poorest half own just 2 per cent (Myers, 2021). Astoundingly, in 2018, 'the 26 richest people in the world held as much wealth as half of the global population (the 3.8 billion poorest people)' (United Nations, nd). The geographical distribution of wealth is also skewed towards the Global North which controls approximately four-fifths of the world's income. In 2020, wealth rose by around 10 per cent in North America and Europe (which holds around 60 per cent of the world's total wealth), while it fell by 10 per cent in Latin America (Deshmukh, 2021). The connection between neoliberalism and the Global North and South in terms of growing wealth disparity should not be lost here. In 2015 alone, an academic report calculated that the Global North appropriated US$10.8 trillion of net worth from the South in the form of labour, land, energy and raw materials, with this loss representing 30 times their aid receipts (Hickel et al, 2022).

Over the last two decades, income inequality has increased *within* most countries with the average income gap between the top 10 per cent and bottom 50 per cent of individuals within countries doubling in this period (Myers, 2021). Bernie Fraser, economist and former Treasury secretary and Reserve Bank governor in Australia, largely blames neoliberalism and its influence on policy making for the 'disconnect between Australia's impressive economic growth story and its failure on so many markers to show progress towards a better, fairer society' (Fraser cited in Karp and Hutchens, 2018). While Sydney is the most unequal region with the top 1 per cent of earners accruing nearly 12 per cent of the total income (Wade, 2019), another academic study showed that the suburbs of Cottesloe and Subiaco, outside of Perth (see Figure 7.1), are where income inequality has increased the most in the country (Fleming-Muñoz and Measham, 2015). The average house price in Subiaco, for instance, in 2022 was AUD$1.625 million (MacDonald, 2022).

In the Global South, Laurell (2015) argues that three decades of neoliberalism in Mexico has literally destroyed society, characterized by a polarized income distribution, falling wages, increased precariousness, rising inequality and extreme violence. Health conditions have also deteriorated and disorders associated with violence, chronic stress and a changing nutritional culture have also occurred. Many countries championing neoliberal policies have experienced widening socio-spatial polarization in recent years, including the creation of stark regional inequalities (for the US see Florida, 2018; for the UK see Centre for Cities, 2018; for the Global South see Navarro, 2007).

The idea that cities have experienced increased social polarization comes largely from the work of Sassen (1991) and Friedmann (1986) in the 1980s and 1990s. Hamnett's (1994; 2021) work empirically and theoretically questions this assertion and the idea that social polarization is occurring outside of the major world cities. He argues that most global cities (in the North and South) have experienced 'professionalization' instead and that polarization is a contingent outcome in certain cities at certain times (Hamnett, 2021). However, Hamnett's argument is considerably weakened by the fact that he utilizes studies and data that look at changes in the

Figure 7.1: Rising inequality and house prices in the suburbs of Perth, Western Australia

Source: photo by the author, 2016

occupational class structure rather than income/wealth inequalities or the rise in poverty in cities. It is the growing gulf between the rich and poor that is critical here in terms of impact of neoliberalism, not the fact that there may be an expanding middle class in many cities (though Florida's [2018] work in the US and UK challenges this latter fact). Hamnett's (2021) recent work also fails to mention the rise of the urban cultural economy or discuss the relevance of creative jobs in relation to the polarization thesis. This latter point is something I take up in the next section of the chapter.

Looking at income and wealth inequalities, and studies documenting extreme poverty and riches in cities, are better indicators than occupational change to evidence socioeconomic polarization. Globally, cities with the highest income inequality are generally located in sub-Saharan Africa or the Americas, for example, Johannesburg, Cape Town and Rio de Janeiro, though US cities like Houston, Los Angeles and New York make it into the top 20 (Euromonitor International, 2017; see Table 7.1).

Behrens and Robert-Nicoud (2014) suggest that successful large cities are more likely to be places that disproportionately reward the 'most talented' people (the superstars) and disproportionately fail the 'least talented'. In 2016 the top 1 per cent of income earners took 40 per cent of all income while the bottom half had to make do with 6 per cent in the highly ranked creative city of New York City (Nijman and Wei, 2020: 3). Yet, New York was beaten into tenth place in terms of highest income inequality by such diverse US cities like Boston, New Orleans, Atlanta, Cincinnati, Providence, RI, New Haven, Washington, Miami and San Francisco in a Brookings

Table 7.1: Top 20 major cities ranked by highest income inequality in 2016

Rank	City	Palma ratio*
1	Johannesburg	13.4
2	Lagos	12.3
3	Nairobi	11.7
4	Santo Domingo	10.7
5	Cape Town	9.1
6	Kuala Lumpur	8.5
7	Rio de Janeiro	7.2
8	Guatemala City	6.4
9	Sao Paulo	4.8
10	Miami	4.8
11	Frankfurt	4.7
12	Baku	4.5
13	Salvador	4.4
14	Bogota	4.4
15	San Jose	4.4
16	Houston	4.4
17	Los Angeles	4.3
18	Jerusalem	4.3
19	New York	4.3
20	Quito	4.2

Note: * The Palma ratio, like the Gini coefficient, is another statistical method used to measure the unequal distribution of income among the population.

Source: Euromonitor International (2017)

2016 survey (Holmes and Berube, 2016). Commenting on a co-authored study of wage inequality in the US (Heinrich Mora et al, 2021), one of the authors (Geoffrey West cited in Anderer, 2021) stated:

> What was a huge surprise in this research was that, as the city grows, there's no advantage to people in the bottom 10–20th percentiles. As you go down the income deciles, the value-added for city-dwellers got less and less in a systematic way ... so much so that, in the bottom decile you get nothing at all. There's even evidence that you're losing quality of life.

In the World Atlas (2022b) inequality survey, parts of London came ahead of Johannesburg, South Africa as the most unequal city in terms of income. As

Nijman and Wei (2020: 4) argue: 'Income inequality has been increasingly exacerbated by inequality in wealth, especially the appreciation of property values.' A number of studies have documented the impact the super-rich are having on London, including Atkinson (2021) and Burrows and Knowles (2019). London has the highest poverty rate in the UK at 28 per cent due primarily to the cost of housing and living (Trust for London and WPI Economics, 2022). Again, it is hardly the exception here. Income inequality in the UK has a whole has increased by 2.2 percentage points in the ten-year period leading up to financial year ending 2020 (Office for National Statistics, 2021). This has no doubt gotten worse since the pandemic and the cost of living crisis. The Centre for Cities (2018: 68) report *City Outlook 2018* showed that Cambridge and Oxford beat London as the most unequal UK cities, followed by Reading and Brighton, among others.

Significant socio-spatial inequalities also exist at the level of urban neighbourhoods. There is a long history of studies in urban sociology around class and racial segregation going back to the Chicago School of Sociology (Park, 2013). In the US, studies of ghettoization, particularly around race and poverty, are plentiful (Johnston et al, 2003; Wilson, 2012; Candipan et al, 2021), while in the UK studies of council housing and estates and their link with class and poverty are also numerous (Campbell, 1993; Hanley, 2012). Similarly, in the Global South there are a plethora of studies of barrios, favelas and slums and their association with poverty, fear and crime (Davis, 2007; Pearlman, 2011). More recently, in the Global North, housing gentrification and the 'move back to urban centres', stimulated by the creative city paradigm, have produced new patterns of socio-spatial polarization. For example, Florida's (2018) recent work in the US has discovered a more 'patchwork metropolis' characterized by the rich sometimes living cheek by jowl with the urban poor as the former group invade inner-city areas. Koch et al (2021) also provide an interesting and nuanced study of elite and poverty based social polarization, tensions and a 'shrinking middle class' in four UK neighbourhood locations.

The evidence reveals that socio-spatial polarization is a permanent feature of neoliberalism. Further, it dominates not only the geography of the city but affects how the urban class structure has changed and evolved. Wright's (2015) work on the contemporary American class structure demonstrates that a historically large and stable middle class and a growing precarious segment of the working class is now 'bookended' by a super-rich corporate class and an extremely impoverished poor class. Hutton's (1995) UK based schema posited a 30/30/40 model of society created by neoliberalism with 30 per cent categorized as disadvantaged and marginalized, 30 per cent insecure and 40 per cent privileged. In his later work he contrasted the 'super-rich' from what he called the 'disenfranchised underclass' (Hutton, 2010). Standing (2011) further develops the idea that neoliberal capitalism creates a growing 'precariat' – an emerging class comprising the rapidly growing number of people facing lives of insecurity. Beck's (2000) analyses of work insecurity suggests a convergence of Global South and North polarization – what he called the 'Brazilianization of the West'.

These analyses of a polarized urban class structure are critical to the debate about neoliberal creative cities in two ways. First, in arguing that neoliberalism has directly resulted in a growing wealth and income gap between the rich and poor. And, second, in highlighting structural and political reasons behind the rise in precarity, exclusion and poverty in the city. They also help counteract more nefarious and neoliberal ideologies designed to justify the super-rich (though see Sayer, 2015) and combat perspectives designed to denigrate the victims of poverty, 'poor work' and precarity (Shildrick, 2018; Wacquant, 2022).

Rather than accept that socio-spatial polarization is an inherent feature of capitalism, neoliberalism favours an emphasis on individual merit and behavioural failing in terms of explaining the growth of inequality. Analysing data from both the US and the UK, Azevedo et al (2019: 83) argue that 'it is unrealistic to assume that attitudinal support for tax cuts for the wealthy and austerity programs for the poor is unrelated to the social dimension of ideology'. The belief in meritocracy (even though Sayer [2015: 6] argues that one-third of all wealth is inherited in the UK), the argument that poverty is not necessarily bad for American cities (Glaeser, 2012) and the general idea that welfare 'cheating' is endemic (Morrison, 2019) are all interconnected elements of this ideology. More specifically, the idea that the poor themselves, in terms of their behaviours and attitudes, are largely to blame for socio-spatial polarization and poverty is a central feature of neoliberal thinking in the West (Shildrick and MacDonald, 2013; Wacquant, 2022).

The idea of the 'undeserving poor' is not one confined solely to the current neoliberal period but has a long history, particularly in the US and UK (Mann, 1992; Wilson, 2012).[1] However, it is not surprising that its modern Western variant was forged in the early thrones of neoliberal economics exemplified by the rise of Margaret Thatcher's new right government elected in the UK in 1979 and during the 1980s Reganomics phase in the US. Thatcher's 'authoritarian populism' (Hall and Jacques, 1983) was characterized by an attack on both trade unionism and the welfare state, including a pre-election moral panic around welfare cheats known as 'scroungerphobia' (Deacon, 1978). In the US, sociologists like Charles Murray (1984) began talking about a growing welfare dependency culture complete with a racial inflection (see Herrnstein and Murray's [1994] later study of race and IQ). The link between these two countries' political ideologies was forged by Murray himself when he was hired by Rupert Murdoch's *Sunday Times* to investigate the so-called 'emerging British underclass problem' (Murray, 1990).

While ideas of a disenfranchised post-industrial section of the working class existed in both the UK (Westergaard, 1992) and US (Wilson, 2012), it was Murray's more blameworthy and 'cultural behaviourist' idea of the urban underclass that came to the fore in the neoliberal 1990s. Murray's (1990) thesis was essentially that the UK was experiencing a frightening and growing underclass. This was evidenced by their engagement in crime, high rates of worklessness and child illegitimacy rates. This was the 'new undeserving poor' – work-shy, promiscuous and reliant on a too generous benefit system. Wacquant (2022), more recently, looks at the negative legacy of the idea of the underclass in the US context.

Even though Murray's (1990; 1994) studies were fundamentally flawed theoretically, methodologically and empirically (Bagguley and Mann, 1992; MacDonald, 1997), the underclass thesis has spawned decades of myths and stereotypes. These 'myths' include ideas that the causes of poverty can be linked directly to the cultural behaviours of the urban poor (MacDonald et al, 2020), successive generations of 'worklessness' (MacDonald et al, 2014) and 'troubled families' (Crossley, 2018). Race continues to be a key part of the American underclass debate (Wacquant, 2022) and the idea of 'scrounging' welfare benefits continues to the present day (Morrison, 2019). Later in the chapter, I critically return to some variants of the urban underclass thesis in terms of explaining their creative incorporation and exclusion, but first I discuss the idea of 'creative divisions' within the neoliberal city.

Creative divisions

The creative city paradigm and associated policies are roughly two decades old if we take Florida's *The Rise of the Creative Class* as a significant marker. Chapter 3 demonstrated its close overlap with neoliberal ideology and the previous section set out the wider context of socio-spatial polarization. What additional effects has the creative paradigm had on the urban class structure and the unequal spatial reconfiguration of cities? Gerhard et al (2017: 4) hint at the fact that 'the current trend toward creative city policies does not reduce, but rather hides existing inequalities and even births new ones'. Oakley and Ward (2018: 15) argue that the 'last 20 years of neo-liberal cultural policies … have seen the cultural sector become more and more implicated in processes of exclusion and inequality'.

It is useful to begin with Florida's (2004) original work, *The Rise of the Creative Class*, published initially in 2002, to provide context. This research was US-based and centred on a three-class model – the rising creative class, a service class and a declining manual working class. Optimistically, Florida saw the creative class as a largely progressive force which would transform not only work and leisure, but society as a whole. In essence they would drive economic growth, promote greater tolerance and would generally benefit everyone in the city. Described by Florida (2004: 315) as 'natural leaders of the 21st century', the creative elite needed to 'reduce class divides' (Florida, 2004: 321) and 'look beyond itself and offer members of society a vision in which all can participate and benefit from' (Florida quoted in Dreher, 2002: 8). Interestingly, his original work says little about social polarization or the poorest groups in society, outside of the idea that there is a need to help make them more creative (Florida, 2004: 322). In Florida (2004) there is only a single reference each made to the 'economic underclass' (2004: 321) and 'poverty' (2004: 322).

This is not to say that Florida was completely unaware of inequalities produced by the creative revolution. Initially though he almost exclusively concentrates on divisions between his three main classes rather than explore polarization between the rich and poor. A year on from the publication of *The Rise of the Creative Class*, Florida (2003b) in his article entitled 'The new American dream' draws attention to inequality in general where the term is mentioned 18 times. Here he baldly states that 'my research suggests that rising inequality stems mainly from the very nature of the emerging creative economy' and '[c]ity-regions that rank highest in terms of creative economic strength also rank highest in income inequality' (Florida, 2003b). This is happening, according to Florida, not only because the creative class is sprinting ahead economically, but also because of a decline in working-class jobs and a growth in part-time and low-paid service employment. Again there is little space given over to the urban poor in the article with the terms 'poor', 'poorer' and 'low-income' invoked only once each.

If Florida's own data was telling him that creativity was exacerbating urban inequalities, then the overwhelming question is why did he spend the next couple of decades promoting the creative city paradigm? The answer, it seems, is his belief in the idea that creativity is necessary for urban economic growth and his faith in a 'creative meritocracy'. In response to his theory being called elitist, his mantra has always been that 'every human being is creative' (Florida, 2014: xi), they just do not have a creative job. In *The Rise of the Creative Class Revisited*, Florida (2014: xi) maintains that the 'essential task before us is to unleash the creative energies, talent, and potential of everyone else', despite its obvious link to growing inequality. While slightly more attention is given to 'hardship and inequality' and the need for a 'new social compact' in this work, the price for unleashing this creative energy is still apparently worth it. Despite Florida's (2014: ix) insistence that his creativity model was not 'neoliberal market driven', critics previously noted his libertarian creative meritocracy (Peck, 2005: 757), 'trickle down' theory of social justice (Leslie and Catungal, 2012) and economic growth imperative (Kirchberg and Kagan, 2013).

In his most recent book, *The New Urban Crisis*, Florida (2018: xxii) concedes that 'I had been overly optimistic to believe that cities and the creative class could, by themselves, bring forth a better and more inclusive kind of urbanism'. In a 2017 interview he admits that the crisis has been partly because the 'artistic, cultural creative has been so successful' (Florida cited in Sussman, 2017). In his recent book Florida is much more concerned with social polarization not only between the creative and service and working class, but also between the urban rich and poor. While sections of the creative class continue to thrive, blue-collar and service workers are much worse off. Artists and musicians are being pushed out of trendy areas of the city by the super-rich, middle-class households are shrinking and the percentage of poor households has increased significantly (Florida, 2018: 7). Blame for the crisis is largely placed on 'hyper-gentrification', property development and the super-rich. Florida's (2018) book provides ample evidence of a 'winner takes all' urbanism, a growing city of elites and the clustering of classes in different 'patchwork' configurations.

Florida's (2018) main data and examples in *The New Urban Crisis* comes largely from cities in the US, supplemented by some UK examples. But he also mentions that part of the urban crisis concerns low growth and rising poverty in the Global South (Florida, 2018: 8–9). In chapter 9, Florida (2018) quite rightly emphasizes the negative impact of globalization there and the need for 'bottom-up' approaches and infrastructure to tackle issues like poverty and economic development. However, he curiously says very little about the creativity paradigm or the impact of the creative class in cities of the Global South (for example see Case Study 7.1).

Case Study 7.1: Creative class inequalities in the Global South: the case of Latin America

Florida's idea of the creative class leading economic growth has been discussed in relation to the Global South. Robert Ramos (2009), a global cultural marketer, says that Latin America's 'rich cultural and creative resources could play a more visible and relevant role with the advent of its creative class, which if properly supported, could partake on what is increasingly an economy of ideas and innovation'. The end result, in his view, could be a Latin version of England's 'Cool Britannia' strategic creative platform back in the 1990s (Landry, 2000). Ramos, however, does not really discuss how the unleashing of such talent and creativity might also lead to increased socio-spatial polarization in cities of the Global South. Similarly, Enrique Avogadro, Secretary of Culture and Creativity in Argentina, admits poverty and inequality are still a huge problem, but suggests that the 'challenge is to transform Latin America's creative economy into a development engine for our population as a whole' (Avogadro, 2016), fuelled by its young, middle-class creative population.

An interesting case study of a city in the Global South experiencing the creative city paradigm is Cachoeira, Brazil (Baumgartner and Rothfuß, 2017: 217–237). Cachoeira is a relatively small Latin American city which has been rejuvenated by the urban creative economy – namely, culture, tourism and education. While some of this development has had positive consequences in terms of the economic revival of the city, its overall effects have been uneven, the authors argue. The building of a university and amenities like book and coffee shops and festivals have been favourable, yet there has also been housing displacement and traditional street markets replaced by branded supermarkets. This has created a kind of 'town and gown' divide with the creative parts of the city cut off from ordinary neighbourhoods. Socio-spatial polarization then also appears to be a feature of creative development in even medium-sized cities of the Global South.

Florida (2018) is clear that his recent book is not a 'mea culpa' (Wainwright, 2017) but rather a continuation of his work in *The Rise of the Creative Class*. This continuity is, in fact, part of the problem. For instance, he does not fully acknowledge the degree to which his creative class idea and accompanying policies have contributed to the very crisis he is outlining (Dorling, 2017). Florida fails to see the irony that his obsession with the ranking of cities in terms of measuring creativity actively fed into a 'winner takes all urbanism'. Also, that his construction of the creative class as an urban elite effectively contributed to what he calls a 'city of elites' (Florida, 2018).

Florida also categorically refuses to acknowledge the role his creative paradigm played in fanning the flames of hyper-gentrification (Wainwright, 2017). Outside of his 'superstar cities' category, he does not actually seem to see gentrification as that much of a problem. In the epilogue to the paperback edition, Florida (2018: 231) says 'this creative class thing worked' in most ordinary cities, evidenced by 'vibrant neighbourhoods filled with newly repurposed loft developments, boutique hotels, art galleries, theatres, cafes and restaurants'.

But this situation is precisely part of the crisis itself. For example, while the city of Glasgow was deemed the 2019 UK city of culture and creativity by the European Commission (Times Travel, 2022), one-third of the city's population rely on state benefits, homelessness persists (Toro, 2007) and its life expectancy is frightening low (Gray and Leyland, 2008). These facts question the 'trickle down' impact of such creative accolades. There is also a wealth of previous research going back years showing that property developers and the rich often track artists and creative workers' movements through the city, eventually supplanting them (Zukin, 1995; Ley, 1996; Lloyd, 2006). More recently, the artist Megan Wilson's fascinating project called 'The gentrification of our livelihoods' traced the impact on a local community of an arts organization collaborating with a creative place-making developer in the city of San Francisco. She says:

What began as a reflection on the shortcomings of creative placemaking as a tool for economic development and its implications on gentrification and community displacement has become a cautionary tale for arts and community organizations to question and better understand the potential outcomes of working with partners whose interests are rooted in financial profit. (Wilson, 2014)

Similarly, in London, the Hackney Wick and Fish Island Community Development Trust has also attempted to work with developers to slow both gentrification and the loss of artist spaces, with only partial success (Furseth, 2020).

Additionally, although Florida acknowledges two waves of Western gentrification – a 1960s housing one (Glass, 1964) and a second wave in the late 1960s and early 1970s around artists – his current discussion in *The New Urban Crisis* is really only about housing and displacement. He conveniently argues this is less of a problem than is conventionally thought (Florida, 2018: 64–67). What he largely leaves out of the discussion here is the impact creatives have had on gentrification and the variety of different forms of displacement other than just housing. For example, Pratt (2018) talks about other displacement transitions such as manufacturing to residential, manufacturing to cultural work and cultural work to residential use (also see Grodach et al, 2016).

The fact that artistic gentrification is often superseded by property development and the super-rich does not exonerate elements of the creative class from 'art washing' particular areas of the city (Pritchard, 2018). Florida exclusively ignores 'creative gentrification' stimulated by his own paradigm. This is where cities are required to cater for the creative class in order to attract them. Things like creating cool bars, trendy restaurants and upmarket coffee shops (see Figure 7.2 and Seah, 2020), as well as the takeover of industrial buildings for galleries and housing that doubles as studios. Creative city gentrification is, in fact, the thin end of the wedge in terms of pricing ordinary people out of their high street and ushering in a milieu attractive to the wealthy. It also helps contribute to spatial polarization in terms of creating changes in the urban landscape so that ordinary urban residents do not feel they belong in these spaces (Baum, 2020). The issue of whether less service or working-class people are displaced from gentrified neighbourhoods than we might think is a moot one. Those that are displaced end up in worse-off areas in terms of schools, transport and crime (Sussman, 2017), while those who stay feel out of place or cannot really afford living in their local area.

Florida's (2018: 245) recent assertion that he has been influenced by Marx's theory of class is belied by the fact that his approach is largely an occupational based one, rather than a Marxian relational perspective (Wright, 1998). His

Figure 7.2: Gentrification and 'death by cappuccino' (literally), Mitte, Berlin

Source: photo by author, 2016

creative class was always a statistical amalgamation of various occupational groupings some of whom did not deserve to be lumped together. Elements of that class, primarily the well-off super core and creative professionals, clearly have had an impact on other groups in the labour market. Florida's (2018) recent work bemoans the worsening position of the service and working classes, yet he fails to acknowledge that it is this section of the creative class that has most contributed to this situation. With regard to the service class, early on he admitted, rather patronisingly, that: 'The ranks of these people are increasing in large part because the growing numbers of busy creative workers require an army of "servants" to minister to the many things they don't have time for' (Florida, 2003b). Creative gentrification of cities and high streets also help fuel precarious, part-time and low-paid work in bars, clubs and restaurants, not to mention in the retail, tourism and leisure sectors. Florida's (2018) indignation at the fact that blue-collar and essential service workers can no longer afford to live in central areas of cities, without acknowledging that the housing boom occurred during the rise of the creative city, seems somewhat ironic.

Previously, I mentioned Florida was relatively unconcerned about the urban poor in his early creative class work (Florida, 2003b; 2004). Peck (2005: 757) referred to him giving this issue only an 'occasional glimpse' and went on to argue: 'The less creative underclasses have only bit parts in this script. Their role is secondary and contingent, in economic terms, to the driving and determinant acts of creativity. Their needs and aspirations are implicitly portrayed as wrongheaded and anachronistic, their only salvation being to get more creative' (Peck, 2005: 759). In Florida's (2014) later work he reiterates the idea of extending creativity to poorer groups. And his recent book places much more emphasis on social polarization and the plight of the least well-off as a crucial element of the urban crisis (Florida, 2018). His solutions here are more laudable including investment in infrastructure (people and places), lifting wages and safety nets, providing accessible housing and improving education.

Again Florida (2018) fails to fully acknowledge the role the creativity paradigm has played in producing spatial and socioeconomic polarization in the city. Economically, his own statistics shows a growing disposable income gap between his creative class and others (Florida, 2018: 39–40). Furthermore, Catungal et al's (2009) study of Liberty Village in Florida's own adopted city of Toronto shows how displacement of space in the creative city aided business and property development but failed to 'address attendant urban problems such as gentrification, inequality, working poverty and racialised exclusion' (Catungal et al, 2009: 1111). In many 'successful' creative cities, such as the fashion capital of Italy, Milan, poverty sits among expensive shopping areas (see Figure 7.3).

Finally, it is important to look at significant social divisions that exist within Florida's creative class itself. Numerous critics have argued that his schema puts together some very disparate groups in this class (Peck, 2005; Banks and O'Connor, 2009). This has several implications for understanding inequalities within the creative class itself. For instance, Whiting et al (2022) argue that Florida's 'statistical fantasy' includes a 'professional, managerial and scientific' occupational grouping as a significant chunk of the creative population. With decent salaries, pensions, full-time and stable employment, it is this grouping that is primarily responsible for driving up house prices and contributing to the present urban crisis. Yet, most of the group does not work within the creative industries. Florida's homogeneous creative class category also disguises a wide variety of different kinds of work within the creative industries (Scott, 2008), not to mention that it contains significant social divisions in relation to class, race and gender (Parker, 2008; Leslie and Catungal, 2012; Morgan and Ren, 2012; McLean, 2014a; McRobbie, 2016). It also does not always capture the different experiences of those working in creative occupations in many cities of the Global South (Jesus et al, 2020).

Finally, 'actual creatives', meaning artists, musicians and poets, were always a 'poor relation' of the 'supercore' category, living separate lives and having different political views then well-off professionals (Whiting et al, 2022). This former group also have very different experiences of creative work (Banks, 2017a). Bain and McLean (2013), in their discussion of the idea of the 'artistic precariat', argue that Florida's formulation distorts the material reality of many artists working in the cultural sector. This occurs through lumping them together with the supercore and creative professionals who earn relatively high incomes and have job security.

Bain and McLean (2013) say despite artists having higher levels of education than the general workforce, they are more likely to experience both poverty

Figure 7.3: Homelessness in the fashion capital Milan

Source: photo by author, 2017

and precariousness. This manifests itself by this group facing higher rates of unemployment or underemployment, holding down numerous jobs in conjunction with their artistic work and experiencing lower earnings generally (Bain and McLean, 2013: 109). Serafini and Banks (2020) even warn against viewing the artistic precariat as a homogeneous entity, on the basis that precariousness itself is unevenly distributed and that it can imply a universal condition of 'temporal poverty'. One should also consider the stage of someone's artistic career (Oakley, 2009), not to mention how their experience might be affected by a combination of factors such as class, gender and race (Leslie and Catungal, 2012).

Creative exclusions

A related concept to the idea of an artistic precariat is the notion of a 'creative underclass'. Its similarity to the artistic precariat idea lies with the relative poverty and underemployment experienced by both groups. Gornostaeva and Campbell (2012: 170) in their research based in London, UK, say it 'is made up of underemployed or underpaid talent produced by the permanent oversupply of artistic labor' and 'united by low-economic and high-cultural capital'. Outside of these parameters it is more diverse in nature with 'differences between its members related to their social origin (middle or working class), education, level of involvement in economic activities, age, and the cultural product they work on' (Gornostaeva and Campbell, 2012: 172) and the fact that they form different social networks and scenes. The more politically inclined elements here appear to be more akin to what I call 'alternative creative workers' in Chapter 3, with an emphasis on engaging with the gift economy, liminal spaces and non-commodified cultural production. This component also engages in challenging aspects of the neoliberal creative city (Hollands, 2019). Others in this category are more in the classical bohemian artistic tradition (Morgan and Ren, 2012), or are non-political struggling artists. In the US context, race also plays an important role here. Denmead's (2019) research (see Case Study 7.2), reflects not only how race and class interact, but outlines exactly how the creative city paradigm works to disadvantage less well-off groups that it claims to support.

Case Study 7.2: Youth, race and the 'creative underclass': Providence, Rhode Island, US

The creative underclass in the US has been conceptualized slightly different from that developed by Gornostaeva and Campbell (2012) and is best represented in the work of Tyler Denmead in his fascinating book *The Creative Underclass: Youth, Race and the Gentrifying City* (2019). His study, set in Providence, Rhode Island, came out of his direct involvement in an organization he founded, New Urban Arts. Its mission was to provide opportunities for disadvantaged people of colour[2] to engage with the arts. While committed to the project aims, Denmead's (2019) argument is essentially that organizations like his are hijacked by creative city developments and benefit the White, privileged creative class rather than the creative ethnic underclass. In doing so he provides compelling ethnographic and factual evidence that the conditions of the creative underclass are made worse by the advent of the creativity paradigm. They are often left with 'uncreative' and low wage service jobs, lack of affordable housing and eroded welfare support.

As background, Denmead (2019: 14–15) argues that Providence's history is steeped in the exploitation of both the indigenous and slave population, a point not lost on his argument that the contemporary creative city largely benefits the White, privileged population. In 1950 he states the city was 95 per cent White, while today 40 per cent of the population is described as Latinx (Latin American origin or descent) and Afro

Americans make up a further 16 per cent (Denmead, 2019: 16). Despite its history of poverty and social polarization, Providence was one of the first US cities to rebrand itself as an art and culture 'Renaissance City', followed 'Creative Providence' in 2002 (Denmead, 2019: 16–18). Denmead's (2019) organization, New Urban Arts, a tuition-free studio, moved to the city slightly earlier in 1998, but quickly became swept up in the drive to make Providence a creative place.

Denmead (2019: 1–2) defines the creative underclass as 'my term for minoritized and marginalized young people who have grown up in cities before they were branded creative but are summoned to enact cultural performances that become legible within the context of creative led urban renewal as creative'. Within the context of the Creative Capital programme, New Urban Art's laudable mission 'to empower young people to develop creative practice that they can sustain through their lives' (Denmead, 2019: 19) was subverted into a narrative about producing the next 'creative generation' and transforming the lives of what was called 'troubled youth' (Denmead, 2019: 25).

While remaining committed to the benefits of programmes like his in terms of developing social capital, skills and encouraging political awareness, Denmead's (2019) ethnography clearly demonstrates that the creative underclass, in the main, do not obtain good creative jobs. The best they can achieve, he argues, is poorly paid, temporary, creative work at the level of local subculture (i.e. not recognized as 'real' art or artists) or they return to low-paid, part-time service work supporting the White, privileged creative elites. This neoliberal version of creativity, the idea that anyone can succeed, has a sting in tail, as Denmead (2019: 115) says, 'when the poor fail to succeed in the creative city, their failure must have been caused by the fact that they have remained "troubled" not "transformed"'.

Moreover, the rapidly gentrifying creative city displaces neighbourhoods and creates social housing shortages. Denmead (2019: 131) also documents a significant erosion of welfare support for families living in poverty, with the state of Rhode Island decreasing its share of contributions for cash assistance to poor families from US$51.5 million in 1997 to zero dollars in 2015. Economic polarization also occurs with the top 1 per cent having an average annual income of US$884,609, surpassing historical highs, compared to an annual average income of US$18,796.28 for those working in the hotel and food services industry. The unemployment rate is also two and a half times higher for Latinx when compared to the White population (Denmead, 2019: 109).

Denmead's (2019) US study questions Florida's (2014) notion that creativity can easily be extended to more disadvantaged sectors of the urban population. In the UK the fate of working-class youth accessing the creative sector is similar. While some enter theatre and drama through youth access programmes and others study creative subjects at less prestigious universities, they too face significant barriers to working in the creative industries (Friedman et al, 2017). New research from the Creative Industries Policy and Evidence Centre shows widespread class imbalances in the UK's creative industries, with only 16 per cent of people in creative jobs coming from working-class backgrounds (Carey et al, 2020). Another study showed that over 96 per cent of jobs in London's creative economy – which generates £47 billion per year to the capital's overall economy – are held by people from advantaged socioeconomic groups (Halls, 2018).

The few that do break into the cultural industries are more likely to experience low level, poorly paid, temporary work in the creative sector, supplemented by low-paid service work to bolster their earnings (Friedman et al, 2017). One alternative creative worker that I interviewed expressed her sheer frustration with this situation:

> 'I am so beaten down by the precarity of working in the arts! As a working-class person, I don't have the security net of a wealthy family. This is the reality that people like me face when choosing a career in the sector. No wonder it remains the preserve of the white, wealthy middle classes. They are the only ones who can afford to take the risk.' (Interviewee 56, female, Newcastle, gallery curator and alternative creative freelancer)

Success for the working class in the arts is essentially the stuff of *Billy Elliot*[3] fiction (O'Brien, 2020). The situation is so dire, some UK commentators have argued, that culture is actually bad for the working class in particular (Brook et al, 2020). But what about other sections of this population that are largely excluded from this new kind of creative city altogether? In Case Study 7.3, we look at the UK case of the 'chav' and 'othering' in the neoliberal creative city.

Case Study 7.3: Exclusion in the post-industrial creative city: 'othering' chav culture in the UK

Previously, I discussed how the US-based urban underclass thesis infiltrated the UK in the 1990s through the work of Charles Murray (1990). Although MacDonald and Marsh (2005: 12) argue that this perspective began to fade quickly partly because it was voraciously challenged (Robinson and Gregson, 1992; Morris, 1994), a youthful version began to emerge in the early years of the millennium in the form of the 'chav phenomenon' (Haywood and Yar, 2006; Jones, 2011). Ironically, this new class-based 'folk devil' emerged around a similar point in time to the arrival of the popular incarnation of an element of the creative class – the 'hipster' (Hancox, 2008; Le Grand, 2019). While the hipster may have been blamed for contributing to gentrification in the UK (Hancox, 2015), they were also seen as the saviour of the economy post-Brexit (Cecil, 2016). The 'chav', on the other hand, was categorically denigrated as the 'residue' of the older industrial culture no longer required in the neoliberal creative city. Nayak (2006: 815) refers to this phenomenon as 'transposing older working-class values upon new leisure routines, forging alternative pathways that waltz around the visible power structures of the corporate [and I would add, creative] city'.

In common parlance, chavs (or more regionally) 'charvas' or 'charvers', are defined partly in opposition to the creativity paradigm as 'a young person of a type characterized by brash and loutish behaviour ... usually with connotations of a low social status' (Bennett, 2013: 146). Nayak (2006) in his research based on the post-industrial city of Newcastle upon Tyne, highlighted very negative representations of this group, some of which revolved around notions of civility and culture. For instance, descriptions of charvers as 'primitive' (2006: 824), 'knuckle-grazing', 'thick', 'morons' (2006: 822) who 'affect gruff accents, strange customs and mannerisms' (2006: 823). At the same time, we saw a proliferation of very negative and derogatory websites which picked up on the 'non-creative' side of chav culture, as this extract from Chavscum.co.uk (now taken down from the web) displayed:

> Choose life. Choose your giro. Choose having 6 kids by the age of 20. Choose TV's, stereos, Dvd players (all carefully robbed from Curry's). Choose poor health, smoking 40 a day from the age of 10, drinking shite cider and black. Choose a council flat. Choose Sport's World. Choose fake sovereigns that turn your finger green. Choose wagging school to go to get pissed down the 'dockey'. Choose losing your virginity age 12 on the field at the back of the canal.

The strapline from Chavtown.com, another derogatory website (also now taken down) was 'A user's guide to Britain's peasant underclass that are taking over our towns and cities!' Ironically, academic research on marginalized working-class youth groups in cities like Middlesbrough, Newcastle and Edinburgh show that the majority are confined to their local neighbourhood or area (MacDonald and Marsh, 2005: chapter 4; McCulloch et al, 2006) either due to 'choice' (that is, the city has little to offer them) or because of the cost of commercial leisure (Loader, 1996). Haywood and Yar (2006: 24) argue that '[c]onsumption practices now serve as the locus around which exclusion is configured' and 'the excluded are classified, identified and subjected to (increasingly intense) regimes of management'. Restrictions to the use of city centre space include things like the existence of 'charver free zones' signs and dress codes in pubs and clubs (Nayak, 2006), as well as the use of anti-social behaviour orders and biased policing based on appearance.

The chav label and stereotype has been analysed as a form of 'intense class-based abhorrence' (Haywood and Yar, 2006: 16) characterized by the stigmatization of them being 'uncultured', 'out of place' and 'flawed consumers' (Lawler, 2005; Tyler, 2006; Little, 2020). Stigma is an imposed phenomenon designed to blame, deflect and exclude. As the writer Owen Jones puts it: 'As inequality has widened it's a way of people saying that the people at the bottom deserve to be there' (Jones cited in BBC News, 2011). So not only is it a term of hatred or 'symbolic violence' (Burawoy, 2019), but it is also a way of justifying inequality in the neoliberal creative city.

This is not to argue that the creative class itself, or even the popular figure of the hipster, is somehow directly responsible for the representation of the 'chav'. Yet as Gerhard et al (2017: 8) suggest, the creative city narrative about inequality tends to revolve around two contrasting constructions – the ideal creative entrepreneur person and the non-ideal low-income subject. Le Grand (2019) also argues that representations of the chav and the hipster add up to a biased classificatory system with each feeding off one another. Finally, Threadgold (2017) in his work in Australia, shows how representations of hipsters and bogans (essentially Aussie chavs) work to create a symbolic and moral economy that produces class boundaries and continuing inequalities. So, while the hipster is also sometimes an object of derision and blamed for gentrification (Hancox, 2015), it contrasts markedly with the uncultured, non-productive and troublesome image of the 'chav'. The next section briefly discusses how we might begin to rethink and tackle socio-spatial polarization, creative divisions and exclusions in cities.

Tackling polarization, creative divisions and exclusions

This chapter has argued that socio-spatial polarization is endemic to the neoliberal city and that the dominant creativity paradigm and policies have exacerbated urban social divisions and exclusions. Furthermore, neoliberalism as an ideology can act to blame the less well-off for their plight, while significant divisions in the urban cultural economy are obscured in the dominant creative city paradigm. How might we begin to reverse such polarization and begin to tackle creative divisions and exclusions?

First, it is clear that we need to urgently address the issue of economic and geographical polarization. The notion that socio-spatial polarization is endemic to capitalism is not the same as saying that nothing can be done. Or that we cannot begin to reverse the worst effects created by neoliberalism. The narrowing of incomes is precisely what happened in two major Western economies (the US and the UK) in the period from the end of the Second World War to around the late 1970s (The Equality Trust, nd; Piketty and Saez, 2003; Owyang and Shell, 2016). Additionally, smaller income inequalities exist in numerous countries with robust economies resulting in happier and healthier populations (Wilkinson and Pickett, 2009). At the most general level, raising taxes for the rich, super-rich and global corporations, as well as regulating the financial sector so huge profits, salaries and bonuses cannot be made, might be a start. Raising minimum wages and welfare safety nets in terms of providing a universal basic income is surely back on the agenda again. Affordable housing and good quality free healthcare and education are also vital for reducing inequality. Finally, a renegotiation of the uneven economic relationship between the Global North and South is also long overdue (Hickel et al, 2022).

Neoliberal globalization and competition have made many countries wary of pursuing more fair and equitable outcomes for its citizens. It has also affected how cities operate. Neoliberal urbanization has pitted city against city in a 'winner takes all' scenario of place-making designed to attract global capital (Harvey, 1989a). This has created a handful of 'superstar cities' (Florida, 2018) and produced huge global and regional inequalities. It has also resulted in a lot of 'ordinary cities' striving to compete here, but with many, understandably, failing. However, as Chapter 2 argued, some cities have begun to realize that this global competition is a rigged game and some have begun to fight back against the pernicious effect of neoliberalism. Importantly, one of the key principals for cities embracing the 'new municipalism' is tackling socio-spatial inequalities and economic injustices in cities (Thompson, 2020). This could involve the creation of a universal basic income for all (Bregman, 2018) providing a basis for a more equal society. A reversal of many of the policies designed to promote neoliberalism would be a starting point to help tackle growing socio-spatial polarization. Rodriguez (2021) argues this has happened in several Latin American countries, including innovative anti-poverty policies (Grugel and Riggirozzi, 2018).

Second, it is critical to move away from the dominant creative city paradigm if we are to reduce socio-spatial polarization. Continuing to advance the idea that more urban creativity will reduce inequality and create greater social cohesion in cities is no longer a viable option. The creative class, rather than reducing urban inequalities, has actively added to them. Instead of concentrating on attracting creative elites (Florida, 2004), cities need to re-prioritize their key service workers and seek to rebuild their foundational economy by providing affordable housing, decent healthcare and education and good public and cultural amenities (Klinenberg, 2018).

Furthermore, within the urban cultural economy, the artistic precariat and creative underclass require 'creative justice'. Banks (2017a) argues that creative justice involves offering better quality and more fulfilling cultural work which is available to all and free from harms like discrimination. This implies the need for a basic artist income to ensure parity and equal participation. Creative workers, in turn, need to actively resist being place-making 'canaries' for property developers and the rich and become 'place defenders' of community and the less well-off (Pritchard, 2018). They also need to use their alternative networks to create cultural movements to fight for equality and join up with wider urban social movements to combat precarity (Lorey, 2015; Hollands, 2019) and gentrification (Bunce, 2018).

Finally, we need to tackle social and creative exclusion. Social exclusion, by definition, implies that there is a structural dimension to exclusion (Byrne, 1999). It can be caused by a range of social institutions including the labour market, education, health and income poverty. Social exclusion also implies that society and government have a responsibility to tackle the issue through social inclusion and cohesion policies. Of course, focusing on the excluded can also deflect our attention away from its wider causes and social inclusion often begs the question, 'included into what?' (Levitas, 1998).

Instead of blaming marginalized young people and labelling them as disconnected or troublesome, we need a society that meets their needs. In addition to providing meaningful and decent employment and tackling urban poverty through raised safety nets, we need to envisage a city that offers them citizenship and a participatory role in it (Bečević and Dahlstedt, 2022). Creating supportive social and economic policies in foundational areas like employment, education, leisure, children and families, and health policy, are urgently needed. At the same time, we need redistributive policies to equalize our workplaces and our cities. As Denmead (2019: 169) argues, no amount of youth provision will solve the problems of a suppressed minimum wage, unnecessary property development, gentrified neighbourhoods and rising house prices. Additionally, rather than being offered a creative city they cannot access or afford, marginalized young people need creative justice and real opportunities to create and engage with art and culture. We need not only inclusive reforms, but a new kind of city which goes beyond neoliberal urbanization and the dominant creative city paradigm.

To conclude, the neoliberal creative city paradigm has helped drive the housing boom and pushed the economy towards low-paid service employment and precarious work for many cultural workers. It has also produced divides between creative 'haves' and 'have nots'. It has failed the vast majority of artists and freelance creatives in cities, especially those from disadvantaged backgrounds. We need to stop relying on existing creative city ideas and policies to drive the economy and level up inequalities. This does not imply art and culture should not be an important part of a new vision to take us beyond the neoliberal city. To effect such a transformation, art and culture need to be disengaged from the marketized 'creative industries' and become a part of what has been called the 'foundational economy' (Foundational Economy Collective, 2018; O'Connor, 2022). We also need to actively pursue a more just and fairer city (Fainstein, 2010) and seek 'creative justice' in the urban cultural economy (Banks, 2017a). Finally, social and environmental sustainability must be part of any future urban plan, including the cultural field (Banks, 2020). This is the focus of the final chapter of the book.

Beyond the Neoliberal Creative City

This book began by suggesting that the development of the cultural economy has been heralded as the saviour of the modern capitalist city. Arguing against urban creativity therefore seems counter-intuitive. Yet beneath this contemporary 'urban makeover' lie a series of intractable social problems such as socio-spatial polarization, hyper-gentrification, job precarity and environmental concerns. Throughout the book I have sought to show some of the major shortcomings of the *neoliberal creative city*. This final chapter brings together criticism of this divisive type of city with the pressing need to envision a different kind of urban scenario.

The first part of the chapter briefly reviews the main limits of the neoliberal creative city. It then summarizes some of the common characteristics of alternative practices in the different fields of the urban cultural economy discussed in Chapters 3, 5 and 6 (art and culture, nightlife and cultural tourism). This is followed by three further sections concerned with going beyond the neoliberal creative city. They include resetting art and culture within a foundational economy (O'Connor, 2022), pursuing creative justice (Banks, 2017a) and striving for cultural sustainability (Oakley and Banks, 2020). A final section concludes by focusing more broadly on the issues of decommodification, the commons, urban justice and sustainability. In doing so there is not only an emphasis on *what* needs to change but *how* we might begin to think of moving towards a more truly creative, just and sustainable future.

Critique and alternatives to the neoliberal creative city

I defined the neoliberal creative city as the *state-facilitated marketization of creativity and the development of a competitive place-based urban cultural economy*. It is characterized by creative image-building, an obsession with global rankings and attracting creative workers into its orbit. There is also a focus on large-scale culture-led regeneration projects, branded arts, entertainment districts and high-value tourist attractions.

One of the arguments that has been made throughout this book is that on the surface, this type of city appears quite seductive. It is also an extremely popular urban moniker. It includes not only 'superstar cities' like London, Paris and New York, but a range of other places around the world including cities from the Global South and even smaller cities from the UK, Europe, Asia and North America. What they all appear to have in common is an almost exclusively positive focus on creativity and developing their urban cultural economies. Underneath the 'creative veneer', however, this book has revealed some significant shortcomings of this type of city, which are worth briefly summarizing.

First, the neoliberal obsession with city marketing and branding has resulted in an unhealthy global competition. Cities compete against one another creatively rather than working together to solve local and global problems. Such competition creates a handful of winners and lots of losers, akin to Florida's (2018) idea of a 'winner takes all urbanism'. Even the more 'successful' cities here can lose their 'creative advantages' or get caught up so much in cultural image-making that they forget what actually made them vibrant in the first place.

A second, related criticism, is that the neoliberal creative city prioritizes the needs of capital and profit over people and communities (Brenner et al, 2011). One of the compelling aspects of this type of city is the so-called boosting of local economies through tourism, culture and entertainment. However, what is clear is that this 'creative boom' has happened at precisely the same time as service and blue-collar workers have been falling behind sections of the creative class economically (Florida, 2018). Additionally, other sections of the creative class itself, like artists, musicians and actors, have increasingly experienced precarity and urban displacement (Bain, 2003; Bain and McLean, 2013; Wilson, 2014; Furseth, 2020; also see Figure 8.1). Chapter 2 argued that the origins of the cultural economy were steeped in urban entrepreneurialism which was designed to promote property development and attract global capital, while reducing the welfare function of urban governance (Harvey, 1989a). Chapter 7 further demonstrated that socio-spatial polarization and gentrification are endemic to the neoliberal city and that social divisions are further exacerbated in so-called 'successful' creative cities (Gerhard et al, 2017).

Finally, one of the main critiques of the neoliberal creative city is its sustainability. The fragility of an economy based largely on consumption and culture was temporarily called into question during the pandemic (O'Connor, 2020). What it exposed was that what people really require is a city that has a solid foundational economy (Foundational Economy Collective, 2018). One that creates community solidarity, mutual support

Figure 8.1: 'We lose space/you lose culture', San Francisco Art Commission Gallery, 2000

Source: Megan Wilson and Gordon Winiemko (reproduced with permission)

and good mental and physical health. While urban capitalist economies are slowly recovering from the COVID-19 pandemic, it is clear that our cities cannot continue along the same path in terms of energy use. The urban cultural economy – including nightlife, tourism, and art and culture – will have to seriously consider ways to reduce consumption and move towards becoming carbon-neutral.

One of the structuring elements of this book was to explore opposition to neoliberal urbanization as well as provide examples of alternatives in the urban cultural economy. In Chapter 2, for instance, I discussed how the 'new municipalism' (Thompson, 2020) forms a credible alternative to the limits of urban entrepreneurialism (Harvey, 1989a). Similarly, in Chapter 3 I contrasted some of the neoliberal shortcomings of the dominant creative city paradigm (Florida, 2004) with some of my own ideas about alternative creative spaces and what they could offer cities (Hollands, 2019). Chapter 4 looked at conflict in the creative city and the potential role that oppositional cultural movements could play in transforming urban politics, in conjunction with other social movements. Regarding challenging neoliberal nightlife, Chapter 5 emphasized the idea of alternative counter-spaces that emphasis co-production, experimentation, informality and access, while Chapter 6 explored the possibility of more just and sustainable forms of alternative cultural tourism.

There are existing alternatives across a range of fields of the urban cultural economy. What aspects distinguish them from neoliberal creative industries and what elements do they have in common? First, these alternative urban cultures reverse the profit versus people equation putting social need ahead of the dictates of the marketplace. Second, rather than motivated by the market they are in fact driven by creativity and self-fulfilment. Third, in place of competition they emphasis cooperation, mutual support and gift-giving. Fourth, they produce new urban forms and spaces and create socially useful work rather than alienated labour. Fifth, many of these alternative urban forms are democratic, non-hierarchical and participatory in nature. They are also more inclusive, accessible and affordable. Sixth, they are usually rooted in place, having a connection to local communities. And finally, because they are local, and primarily small-scale, they are more economically, socially and environmentally sustainable.

Essentially, this 'actually existing alternative cultural economy' represents a basis for a different urban creative future. Its sheer existence, however encouraging, does not provide either a viable alternative infrastructure or a ready-made strategy to overcome the neoliberal creative city. As I have argued, many of these alternative urban cultures themselves have their own contradictions. For instance, because most of them are local and small-scale, they all face the issue of how they might 'scale up' and form a broader and more global alternative. Second, most of them are reliant on support from the state whether it be financially or in terms of providing other resources or policies favourable to their existence. Finally, as has been suggested, many such alternative cultural forms are highly susceptible to being incorporated into neoliberal creative city strategies and policy making.

So how might we begin to conceptualize the huge task of identifying an alternative to the neoliberal creative city? Where do we even start? Rather than try and cover everything I want to concentrate on three broad themes – relocating art and culture within a foundational economy, pursuing creative justice and tackling cultural sustainability.

Resetting art and culture in the foundational economy

As a leading thinker of the cultural economy, Justin O'Connor, along with various co-writers (Banks and O'Connor, 2009; 2020; O'Connor and Shaw, 2014; O'Connor, 2020; 2022), has made a persuasive argument about decommodifying art and culture by extracting it from the creative industry marketplace. In a 2009 article written by Banks and O'Connor (2009), we see the beginning of an argument as to whether the creative industries paradigm can deliver on its promise to benefit the economy and rescue the arts, particularly considering the 2008 financial market crash. O'Connor and Shaw (2014) in their article 'What next for the creative city?', also called for new ways of envisaging an 'urban imaginary' beyond the market economy. However, it is O'Connor's most recent work on art, culture and the pandemic that is most suggestive in terms of thinking beyond neoliberal creative city limitations (O'Connor, 2020; 2022). O'Connor (2022) convincingly argues that we need to reconceptualize art and culture beyond the realm of markets by locating them within the foundational economy. What does he mean by this exactly?

First, O'Connor (2022) suggests that art and culture has been in crisis for decades now, marginalized politically and subsumed by the market. Unhelpfully, it has been usurped under the terminology of the 'creative industries', which limits our understanding of it as just another sector of the economy to be promoted, ranked and sold. Florida's creative city paradigm and the marketization and ranking of cities is an example of this, as is the UNESCO promotion of cities of the Global South as new creative centres. The positioning of 'culture as a foundation for a post-industrial economy, is as much part of the neoliberal revolution as new public management or reducing the welfare budget' says O'Connor (2022: 61).

Second, borrowing the words of Brian Eno, the musician, O'Connor defines art and culture as 'everything that you don't have to do' yet 'it is central to everything we do' (Eno cited in O'Connor, 2022: 59–60). The need to 'self-actualize' through art and culture is fundamentally human. It is also understood as a democratic right here. Culture is not restricted to art and artists but is a wider 'set of collective rituals that we're all engaged with' (Eno cited in O'Connor, 2022: 68). McGuigan (2016: 187) similarly argues that all humans engage in creative labour but not all do cultural work for a living. The implication of this is that we need to think differently about what art and culture are and come up with new cultural policies to reflect this (Hadley and Belfiore, 2018). For example, we can see art and culture in a more anthropological light, including popular culture and subculture as elements of the 'creative arts'. The work of Raymond Williams (1958) reminds us that culture is not just the 'best' and recorded forms of human expression but includes everyday working-class life as well, including inventive working-class youth subcultures (Hall and Jefferson, 1976; Hebdige, 1977). It also extends to Willis et al (1990) notion that there is a vibrant symbolic life and creativity in everyday activity and expression.

Third, O'Connor (2022) suggests that we need to rescue art and culture from the neoliberal marketplace and relocate it within what is known as the foundational economy (Foundational Economy Collective, 2018; also discussed in Chapter 2). McGuigan's (2016: 185) notion that culture is a symbolic resource shared by all, and not just a commodity, is supportive of O'Connor's assertion. O'Connor argues that the idea that art and culture is separate from, and comes after, necessity, is a recent idea related to the rise of capitalism. Indigenous people, he says, talk about culture as if it is something foundational to their lives. O'Connor makes a strong and convincing case that art and culture need to be repositioned as part of the foundational economy, which he defines as 'the economic essentials, the everyday basics required for people to live a decent life … a policy approach focusing on foundational needs such as health, care, education, housing, utilities and food supply. They place priority on social needs and ecological sustainability rather than profits, markets and growth' (O'Connor, 2022: 33). This is a model where the economy serves society rather than the other way around. One that engenders citizenship, well-being, equity and sustainability. Foundational economy politics have important points of contact with the 'new municipalism' perspective discussed in Chapter 2. This approach includes investment in basic services and infrastructure and policies designed to ensure social justice, fairness and security.

The foundational economy is one of the four economic zones identified by the Foundational Economy Collective (2018), argues O'Connor. In addition to the 'tradable competitive economy' (essentially the market economy) there is a home/community zone, an 'overlooked economy' (described as things we need to replenish like clothing, furniture, haircuts, recreation, and so on) and the 'foundational economy'. There are two major components of this latter economy. First, the 'material infrastructure' of energy, water, housing, public and private transport, cables and pipes, supermarkets and food, retail banking and ATMs. The second element is 'providential services' such as education, health, social and community services, prisons/police, public administration, funerals, and public/social housing. O'Connor argues that the foundational economy is more directed towards the local economy, providing services and value. Furthermore, he suggests that we overestimate the importance of the 'tradable competitive economy' which only makes up about 40 per cent of the total economy (O'Connor, 2022).

Despite clinging onto the coattails of the creative economy, arts and culture in the market have not been successful O'Connor (2022) argues, creating low wages, precarity and poor productivity. He suggests that this part of the sector should divest itself from the creative industries and instead seek alignment with the foundational economy, thus opening up new definitions and possibilities. As he puts it:

> Is this not the moment to 'pivot', to embrace the idea of art and culture as part of the social foundations, providing the kind of public value we seek in health, education and social services, but on its own specific terms? It would mean dis-investing from a self-image of a cutting edge, high-tech, globally competitive, fast growing industry and re-locating to the foundational economy, contributing to social value and equity rather than GDP growth. (O'Connor, 2022: 43)

O'Connor (2022: 51) suggests that, ironically, the literature on heterodox economies 'rarely mentions art and culture' and this is potentially damaging. Either it is left to flounder in the marketplace and currently faces cuts in state subsidies, or it is seen as either elitist or part of the overlooked economy (as something we choose [or not] to spend our disposable income on). Instead, O'Connor makes the argument that it is much more than this. He reminds us that libraries, galleries, museums, concert halls, parks and recreation spaces were part of that era of provision of infrastructure and services within the welfare state and democratic citizenship (see also Klinenberg, 2018). Going beyond a simplistic needs and wants argument, he argues for a 'capabilities' approach to art and culture. O'Connor also suggests that participation here can be envisaged as a universal human right and an essential part of citizenship. Art and culture as collectively provided goods 'allow individuals to make informed choices about "a life worth living"' (O'Connor, 2022: 67).

Finally, O'Connor (2022: 64) argues that 'some communally provided or guaranteed art and culture ought to be provided as an essential part of the social infrastructure'. This is not to discount the market altogether. Practically art and culture currently are a 'mixed economy' of public, private and not-for-profit provision. However, we need to redefine 'core' aspects of it as 'a basic urban need' and artists and cultural workers as providing an 'essential service' (see Figure 8.2). One alternative creative worker interviewed expressed the view: "We have to say we are doing a public job" (interviewee 54, male, Paris, director of a creative cooperative workspace).

O'Connor persuasively suggests that some basic cultural provision is guaranteed by the state, with the implication that artists should receive a guaranteed basic income. State expenditure on art and culture, however, should not be seen as a subsidy for market failure or reduced to arts education. O'Connor also argues that cultural democratization and participation are crucial here (also see Hadley and Belfiore, 2018). O'Connor's thinking is highly suggestive and we return to some of these ideas after turning to the notions of 'creative justice' and 'cultural sustainability'.

Creative justice

Florida (2004) claimed that the creativity paradigm was the next stage in an economic evolution from the industrial past and that creative workers would lead blue-collar and service workers to a new prosperous age and economy. As Chapter 7 revealed, however, Florida's model has only served to exacerbate existing neoliberal socio-spatial polarization and exclusion, adding new divisions like 'artistic precariat' and 'creative underclass'. The COVID-19 pandemic meanwhile has simply brought to light long-term

Figure 8.2: 'Artwork is work'

Source: photographer unknown (reproduced with permission of the subject of the photograph, Elisa Murcia Artengo)

problems of cultural sector wage stagnation, precarity and creative inequalities (O'Connor, 2022: 45).

Banks (2017a: 41) sees creative justice as 'the preservation or development of "good" or better kinds of cultural work, including work that enables people to flourish and live well in an objective sense'. In developing this concept, he puts forward three propositions necessary to theorize this notion fully. The first is *objective respect* for the qualities of cultural objects and cultural work (including what is produced, as well as how it is produced). Key here is distributive justice in relation to cultural work. The idea that '[i]n short, people should be given equal opportunity to try and enter the cultural workplace (should they wish to) and should then be treated fairly and justly within it, as they navigate through it' (Banks, 2017b: 4). The second proposition is *parity of participation* (essentially a cultural form of affirmative action) in terms of economic distribution, cultural recognition and political representation. The third concept is the *reduction of harms*, including examples like exploitation in the cultural field (or self-exploitation), overwork, stress, bullying, intimidation, domination, aggression or violence, as well as forms of class-, gender- and race-based discrimination and misrecognition (Banks, 2017b: 6).

The relevance of Bank's notion of creative justice for this book relates to the way in which it allows us to think differently about the dominant versus an alternative creative economy. In terms of his notion of objective respect as a criterion for creative justice, it is clear that the market-led creative city paradigm largely values creative ranking, economic growth and cultural-led inward investment. An alternative creative economy would instead value art and culture that contributes to communities and the common good, not urban branding (Belfiore, 2020).

Similarly, as Chapter 7 clearly demonstrated, the neoliberal creative city reinforces social polarization, division and exclusion. With regard to parity of participation, cultural work in the dominant creative city paradigm is riven with class, gender and racial inequalities (Leslie and Catungal, 2012; McLean, 2014a; Friedman et al, 2017) in addition to increasing precarity (Bain and McLean, 2013). Alternative creative spaces and groups, in contrast, are much less hierarchical and socially inclusive (Vail and Hollands, 2013; Hollands, 2019). Finally, the creative industries are highly unjust (Brook et al, 2020) and characterized by exploitation (including self-exploitation), stigma (including classism, racism and gender inequality), precarity and other social harms. If art and culture were part of an alternative foundational economy, creative justice, economic security and well-being would be central concerns.

Banks (2018) argues that Florida's (2018) more recent progressive policy prescriptions regarding tackling urban inequalities, while welcome, are really designed to reinstate the dominance of the creative class. They also mark a return to an economic growth model rather than leading to a new system of creative equality. Banks and O'Connor (2020: 14) further argue that cultural justice is also connected to issues around cultural participation and citizenship. In other words, creative justice is not just limited to parity of participation in cultural work. Affirmative action in the cultural economy for under-represented groups, while welcome, will not in itself result in creative justice and equality. We need to shift our focus, Banks (2022) argues, from a distributive to a contributive model of justice based on what people contribute to society. This will involve considering issues of social justice generally in the city (Fainstein, 2010), including the right to not just participate but reshape a cultural and urban commons (Harvey, 2009; Marcuse, 2009:b). We return to this issue in what follows, but first consider the notion of cultural sustainability.

Sustainability in the cultural economy

Links between environmental sustainability and the creative economy are seldom made, and when they are, the connection is often fallacious. As Oakley and Banks (2020: 1) suggest: 'Culture and the arts – where they are considered at all in environmental debates – are generally viewed as either benign low carbon activities that bring pleasure and meaning, or as irrelevant in the face of existential crisis.' In reality, 'the cultural and creative industries are highly resource-intensive and often flagrantly and dangerously polluting' (Banks, 2020: 14). The argument that cultural production is inherently 'green' (Oakley and Ward, 2018: 5) is undermined by the corporate nature of digital software, film/TV and communication companies which often attempt to project a 'clean technology' image. For example, Apple has pledged to become carbon-neutral across its entire business, manufacturing supply chain and product life cycle by 2030 (Harris, 2020). The truth is that even with the use of recycling and greener production technologies, the demand for such products as iPhones and tablets means that sustainability gains are far eclipsed by the need for increased production and redundant technology turnover rates (Banks, 2020: 14). Similarly, claims that cultural products are sustainably produced are often undermined by energy-draining transport, circulation and logistical systems that undergird them (Banks, 2018: 369–370).

Digital technologies, for example, have overtaken aerospace in the production of greenhouse gases (Oakley and Banks, 2020: 2) and the average big budget film production produces 2,840 tonnes of CO_2 (equivalent to running nearly 600 cars for a year), with 50 per cent coming from fuel, 30 per cent from energy utilities and 16 per cent from air travel (Ro, 2022). Besides being major polluters and resource consumers, creative corporate companies also have engaged in dubious employment and extractive practices. As Banks and Serafini (2020: 19) argue, 'many hundreds of thousands of low-paid and poorly treated workers are working in degraded or unsafe environments, involved in the global extraction and supply chain of raw materials, and in processes of manufacture producing the creative economy goods that Global North countries most avidly consume'.

These issues are even more important as the creative economy is continually heralded as way out of economic recession (Banks, 2018). Despite the economic downturn initiated in 2008, not to mention the impact of the pandemic and the current cost of living crisis, the mantra continues to be one of growth once again. Banks question the return to a growth perspective and 'the orthodoxy that identifies growth as the primary social objective of creative economy policy' (Banks, 2020: 15). If we are to help alleviate the inevitable environmental crisis, the cultural industries themselves will have to develop different ways of sourcing, organizing, producing and distributing their cultural content (Oakley and Banks, 2020: 2). Hawkes (2001) argues culture should, in fact, be the fourth pillar of sustainability (alongside economic, social and environmental varieties). In what ways might alternative forms of culture help push us in the right direction, towards what some have called 'sustainable prosperity' (Jackson, 2016) or 'degrowth' models (Kallis, 2018)?

Banks (2018; 2020) explores the general concept of degrowth and attempts to apply it to the creative economy. The concept clearly implies opposition to unlimited neoliberal economic growth due to finite resources, while at the same time highlighting ideas like 'sharing', 'simplicity', 'conviviality', 'care' and the 'commons' (see also Kallis et al, 2015: 3). Furthermore, degrowth places strong emphasis on social justice issues, collective well-being and mutualism. Oakley and Ward (2018: 5) use the term sustainable prosperity, defined as the idea that 'people everywhere have the capability to flourish as human beings – within the ecological and resource constraints of a finite planet'.

With respect to applying the concept of degrowth to the cultural economy, Banks (2020) develops the idea of 'creative degrowth' or 'creative post-growth'. He says: 'In seeking positive solutions, theorists of cultural industries work and organisations have proposed alternative economic models that privilege community subsistence and mutual aid over unfettered economic growth, and new research on cultural co-ops and non-profits, and different kinds of "sharing" economy is rapidly emerging' (Banks, 2020: 11–12). The argument is that we need to begin to prioritize cultural economies that foreground commitments to overall human well-being rather than GDP, capital accumulation and city rankings (Banks, 2018). Some commentators use the South American inspired term 'buen vivir' here to refer to the importance of a more collective, holistic and ecological sense of well-being as a social priority (Salazar, 2015).

This book has looked at a range of small-scale examples like alternative creative spaces, nightlife counter-spaces and alternative forms of cultural tourism that possess many of qualities of 'creative sustainability' discussed. Other examples of 'creative post-growth' come from Banks' joint work with Serafini in Latin America (Banks and Serafini, 2020). Here they 'highlight the existence and emergence of some incipient "ecological", "alternative" or "post-growth" forms of cultural industries production that appear to offer different ways of thinking and doing the creative economy' (Banks and Serafini, 2020: 17). What is interesting about their examples is that often they have come out of failed neoliberal growth model societies where people have had to resort to new alternative ways of 'surviving, producing, sharing and living' (Banks and Serafini, 2020: 22).

Their first case study is a publishing project that emerged in Buenos Aires, Argentina in 2003 called Eloísa Cartonera. The founders of this non-profit cooperative publish hand-made books with cardboard covers that they buy from '*cartoneros*' (people who collected cardboard on the street). In addition to providing employment to these people they also began to train them to paint book covers and produce affordable cultural products. As Banks and Serafini (2020: 23–24) argue, not only do they provide decent employment and training, but they also use recycled material and help provide 'literature for all'. Additionally, the model has been scaled up and there are now various *cartonera* publishers all over Latin America. Their second example is a community radio station concerned with social, political and environmental issues called El Brote which emerged in 2015. Actively involved with the 'anti-extractivist movement at the local and regional levels' (Banks and Serafini, 2020: 25) and embedded in the community, El Brote is also involved in a sharing and gift economy with other cooperatives.

While Banks and Serafini (2020) admit that such examples are often small-scale, fragile and localized, as well as emerging from an economic crisis, they do provide examples of alternative cultural production that are more environmentally sustainable. Similarly, it might be suggested that there is much to learn from other Global South cities who are trying to move beyond neoliberal extractivist and economistic models of the creative industries, in terms of their emphasis on informality, inclusion, and social and environmental justice (see Serafini, 2020; Dinardi, 2020).

What is to be done ...

This book has argued that there is a strong rationale for moving beyond the neoliberal creative city. Furthermore, this chapter has suggested that within the urban cultural economy there is a need to decommodify art and culture, pursue creative justice and tackle the issue of cultural sustainability. In and of themselves, these changes will not take us beyond the neoliberal urbanization. This is because transformations in the cultural field cannot happen in isolation. Even if we could change the dominant creative city paradigm into something more alternative it would not effectively challenge neoliberalism. Moving art and culture into the foundational part of the economy will not be effective if we have not been able to ensure that foundation itself. Just as a guaranteed artist income would need to be accompanied by a universal basic income for all workers. And a cultural commons is not secure without a wider urban commons to fit into. Similarly, achieving creative justice within the cultural field, though laudable, would not eradicate the basis of social inequities in the city. Finally, achieving sustainability in the urban cultural economy will not be sufficient to tackle climate change on its own.

In order to move beyond the neoliberal creative city, we need to begin to decommodify and protect the foundational economy itself through creating an urban commons. We also need to seek social justice and the right to remake the city and achieve urban sustainability generally. The question is not so much what to do here as how to begin the process.

Vail argues that any political economy designed to 'transcend the market' would have to:

> [R]eorient incentives for production and exchange away from profit maximization and self-interest towards reciprocity, fairness and sustainability; establish limits on the rights of market actors to dispose of their property as they see fit; weaken the forces of destructive competition and acquisitiveness while still preserving the capacity for innovation; lessen market dependency and forms of market compulsion that reduce well-being and human flourishing; and provide the necessary public goods that ensure basic needs and share risks across the population. (Vail, 2022: 295–296)

In his book Vail (2022) uses the work of Polyani and focuses particularly on the idea of 'decommodification'. In the classic treatment, decommodification is 'the extent to which individuals are able to maintain a livelihood without recourse to the market' (Esping Anderson cited in Vail, 2022: 298). Vail (2022: 298), however, argues for a wider definition, suggesting that 'decommodification is any political, social or cultural process that reduces the scope and influence of the market in everyday life'. He cites many existing examples like fair trade, ethical consumption, open-source software, cultural commons, public goods, social enterprises, micro-credit, mutual aid, working time reduction and basic income, among others.

Interesting, Vail (2022: 298) notes that some of these examples actually deploy market mechanisms. Numerous other writers point out that challenging market society does not mean the end of markets. Vail (2022) argues that decommodification means a reduction in the scope or influence of markets, not their complete disappearance. Even the Marxist Eric Olin Wright (1998) has said no one believes that markets will completely disappear. O'Connor (2022) similarly argues in terms of art and culture, that markets are still 'in the mix', but should not determine the mix. Other writers talk of a reversal where markets serve society rather than the other way around like Mulgan's (2015) idea of 'servant capitalism' or Hutton's (2005) 'stakeholder capitalism'. One idea is that markets will probably be structured more locally in terms of sustainability at least, if not in terms of control, though it is important not to fall into an economic form of the 'local trap' (that is, do local economies, like local politics, always provide us with more democratic control?). Also, are ideas like servant or stakeholder capitalism a pipedream or simply neoliberalism in yet another shapeshifting disguise (Peck and Theodore, 2019)? Can something that has led us into this mess really provide a solution or way out?

Another aspect of decommodification is the idea of the 'commons'. Commoning for Lijster et al (2022: 19) is 'a process of sharing and opening up some object or activity, retracting it from capitalist exchange, and which runs counter to opposing forces one could call "enclosure", "commodification", or "privatisation"'. The notion of commons is closely related to the idea of the foundational economy. If we define the latter concept as the essential and everyday basics required for people to live a decent life, then we would probably want the main elements of the foundational economy to be held in common rather than market-led.

The urban commons or common city is when the process described by Lijster et al (2022) and the foundational economy is largely shared and enacted at the urban or city level. Harvey (2009: 49) defines the urban commons as 'a public sphere of active democratic participation', while Chatterton (2019: 94) describes it in terms of common physical attributes, socially produced goods and shared spaces. The idea of an urban commons is important because Chatterton (2019: 95) argues that community is a productive level for building commons.

Examples that might help make up a future urban commons include things like citizen initiatives, cooperatives, non-profit companies, mutual housing associations, social centres, crowdfunding platforms, ethical banks and anti-speculation foundations (Patti and Polyák, 2017). Through the study of community land trusts and ecovillages in cities, Bunce's (2018) research demonstrates how residents can engage in alternative practices of everyday urban living and community-based empowerment necessary for shaping a different urban future. This might also include a cultural commons, whereby art and culture are separated from the marketplace and located within a shared and foundational economy (O'Connor, 2022). One of the reasons behind the 'absence' of culture here is the way in which some alternative creative spaces have been viewed as 'self-interested' rather than as part of the community or an aspect of a wider urban social movement (Hollands, 2019).

The idea of decommodification and the commons also raises issues of fairness and equality. Social justice must be at the top of the list if we are to begin to challenge neoliberal urbanization. While there are examples of urban struggles here in terms of identity politics (the Black Lives Matter movement, for example), it is not just a simple case of giving under-represented social groups an equal chance to become unequal. There are also debates as to how to best achieve social justice in the city. Perhaps the most well-known example is the work of Susan Fainstein. For the last 20 years, she has worked towards developing this idea of a just city. Fainstein proposes a theory of justice in which equity, democracy and diversity should be the cornerstones of urban development. Her two main concerns are, first, under what conditions can conscious action produce a better city for all citizens?

And, second, how do we evaluate what outcomes would truly be better and more just?

There is no doubt that Fainstein's (2010) work provides a critique of neoliberal urbanization and reacts to the social and spatial inequality engendered by capitalism. It does so within a pragmatic framework including planners, politicians and activists/social movements. According to Fainstein (2009), urban planning provides a real and practical challenge to neoliberalism, unlike utopian urban visions and Marxist class-based approaches. She also critiques the latter perspective for overlooking other kinds of injustices and inequalities in the city. And it is clear that within existing laws and agreements, there are ways that the public, communities and social movements can engage with urban planning to try and ensure their interests. For example, in the UK, Community Land Trusts, not-for-profit organizations that are made up of community members, have been used to challenge city-centre developments designed purely for profit (Engelman et al, 2016). While focused largely around housing, they can also include running local pubs and shops, creating play areas and nature walks and building workspaces, including creative ones. Similarly, in the US, Community Benefits Agreements are legal contracts signed by a developer and community groups which spell out the benefits of any development.

Fainstein's work provides useful principals and pragmatic solutions to creating a more just city. It has also been a 'taking off' point for more radical ideas about the right to the city (Harvey, 2009) and the idea of 'commons planning' (Marcuse, 2009a). Harvey (2009: 46), in his article 'The right to the just city', argues that Fainstein operates with a concept of justice that is designed to mitigate the worst outcomes of an unjust system. For him, the right to the just city is the right to remake it differently through struggle not through some kind of false consensus (Harvey, 2009: 49). Marcuse (2009a: 91) argues that while the 'call for the Just City is compelling' and that distributional justice is important, it is not sufficient. Rather, he asserts we need to address the structural conditions of inequality and come up with real alternatives. 'Commons planning' as opposed to 'justice planning' deals with issues of power, not just inequality, and hence 'we need to deal with the ownership, control and use of the commons' (Marcuse, 2009a: 101). In his postscript chapter, Marcuse (2009b: 246–247) brings us back to the idea of creative justice and the cultural economy when he mentions that the right to the city includes 'the right to a full, free, creative life for all'. The role that artists and creative workers might play here in leading such a movement is, however, an ambivalent one (see Mould, 2015; Hollands, 2019; Muller, 2019).

Finally, it is important to locate sustainability in the cultural economy within wider debates about economic, social and environmental sustainability. Creative sustainability, along with other sectors of the economy, must embrace alternative ways of production, distribution and consumption, and this means thinking about 'post-growth models' (Kallis, 2018). Chatterton (2019) similarly reminds us that cities, as the biggest environmental polluters, will have to make significant moves towards becoming car-free, biodiverse zones. We will also increasingly require a commons city in order to ensure social stability. We need to think about sustainability as a whole social process involving a range of things like mental health, well-being and social cohesiveness, as well as bettering the environment. Stren and Polese (2000: 16–17) define social sustainability as 'fostering an environment conducive to the compatible cohabitation of culturally and socially diverse groups while at the same time encouraging social integration, with improvements in the quality of life for all segments of the population'. The concept should not however be reduced to social inclusion within neoliberalism, but rather associated with greater equality and the right to participate in the city generally (Davidson, 2010: 874).

... and how?

If we know essentially what needs to be done and what alternatives to the neoliberal creative city already exist, a more fundamental question is how do we begin to make such changes? 'Actually existing forms of neoliberalism' have been in place for over four decades and the creativity paradigm for over two. Although there have been examples of crisis and opposition to these political philosophies and their respective and parallel policies, they have also exhibited significant staying power, variation and 'shape-shifting' properties (Peck and Theodore, 2019). In a sense, this has allowed neoliberal urbanization to remain dominant despite its various limitations (Joy and Vogel, 2021). There are numerous obstacles here including economic scaremongering, ideology and the advent of right-wing populism in the political sphere. What kind of thinking, and more importantly action, will be required to 'tip the balance' away from neoliberal capitalism?

One view is that economic change and crisis within capitalism comes about in long waves. Husson and Louçã (2012) discuss the implications of this perspective on the period of late capitalism and neoliberalism, arguing that we are in both a regulatory and a system crisis. Another macro-approach to crisis concerns various left versions of an automated future economy (Benanav, 2022). This idea does have implications for creative work, leisure and what Chatterton (2019) calls 'joyful doing'. The first approach, however, does not really help us to figure out what to do now to effect more rapid change. The second perspective represents a progressive, yet somewhat optimistic, form of urban economic transformation through technological determinism. Perhaps the most convincing idea about crisis is the environmental one, which suggests an incompatibility between capitalism

Figure 8.3: Just Stop Oil stencil

Source: photo by author, 2022

as an economic system and the survival of the planet (Dawson, 2019). Despite its various contradictions, neoliberal capitalism has been particularly skilful in combating crises, shifting the blame and reinventing itself. Even Harvey himself, the architect of urban crisis theory, has argued capitalism will not go away on its own (Harvey and Wachsmuth, 2011).

Can crisis ever be an effective lever of change? Certainly climate change has done much to concentrate the neoliberal mindset, albeit many groups suggest that we are moving far too slow and environmental damage is now potentially irreversible (see Just Stop Oil, 2022 and Figure 8.3). At the time, it was thought that the 2008 financial crisis might lead to structural economic change (Elliott, 2018), and more recently there has been some speculation that the pandemic might find a chink in the neoliberal armour (Kilic,

2021). While all of these crises may have given the world pause for thought, many argue that opportunities for change were lost and that we are quickly returning to a 'new normal' of social polarization and precarity (Michael-Ryan, 2020). Oxfam reported that regarding the impact of the COVID-19 pandemic on income inequality, 2020 marked the steepest increase in the global billionaires' share of wealth on record with their wealth increasing by US$3.9 trillion from 18 March 2020 to the end of the year. By contrast, global workers' combined earnings fell by US$3.7 trillion, according to the International Labour Organization, as millions lost their jobs around the world (Institute for Policy Studies, nd). In the cultural realm, O'Connor (2020) argued that there were missed opportunities for change amidst the scramble for arts workers and organizations to survive financially.

At the other end of the political spectrum are ideas about more immediate and everyday forms of action that are needed to challenge neoliberal capitalism. Cooper (2014: 2), for instance, talks about everyday utopias as 'networks and spaces that perform regular daily life ... in a radically different fashion ... creating the change they wish to encounter, building and forging new ways of experiencing social and political life'. In a similar fashion Wright (2010) talks about 'real utopias' and eroding capitalism from within. Another useful attempt to think about this is Chatterton and Pusey's (2020) idea of 'post-capitalist praxis'. By praxis they are referring to the combination of theory and practice where ideals and practical change are inextricably linked.

In their article on post-capitalist praxis Chatterton and Pusey (2020: 28) seek to explore 'the diverse ways that post capitalist's subjects, economies and communities can be fostered beyond capitalism'. In doing so, they look at action and initiatives in three areas. The first is the move away from an emphasis on private property to creating an 'urban commons'. This might involve co-ownership, co-production and co-management of not only urban social goods but also social spaces in the city. The second is a move towards 'socially useful production' emphasizing the social and shared economy. The third set of actions is to move away from alienating capitalist labour towards what they call 'joyful doing', activity that is both socially useful and undertaken freely. Although Chatterton and Pusey (2020) do not specifically mention the role the urban cultural economy might play here, alternative creative spaces, experimental nightlife counter-spaces and just and sustainable cultural tourism, discussed in previous chapters, very much fit into this general idea of a post-capitalist praxis.

The idea of a post-capitalist praxis also raises a second important issue concerning at which social, political and spatial level we challenge the neoliberal creative city? One of the problems we raised in earlier chapters was that small-scale alternative creative spaces, while challenging the neoliberal city in some way, were limited in their overall effect. Chapter 4 argued that such spaces needed to form more collective urban cultural movements and link up with even wider social and political coalitions to effect change. Chatterton (2019: 4) similarly talks about a 'rapidly emerging constellations of connected experiments' that begin to link bottom-up initiatives with top-down change, creating a meso level of political transformation. Vail (2022: 320) argues that 'reforms will need to impact on the entire capitalist institutional order at multiple political levels (local, national, global) and across multiple social spheres (political economy, nature, social reproduction, democracy)'. This will require democratization of the state and its relationship to civil society. O'Connor (2022: 55) concurs and suggests that the cultural transformation he advocates will require change at many levels. This ranges from citizen control and participation to the actions of social and cultural movements, groups and communities, as well as at the local and national state level.

This entail big transformations and is a tall order. While retaining Vail's (2022) sentiment that neoliberal transformation will require change at multiple levels, what role can cities in particular play here? Chatterton (2019: 95) argues that post-capitalist praxis is not only about creating socially useful work outside of capitalism, but also finding new ways of producing urban space. Communities are a productive level for building an urban commons. Additionally, he argues that cities appear to be at the centre of the most acute problems in addition to being centres of 'disruptive innovations' (Chatterton, 2019: 9).

It is clear from Chatterton's book title, *Unlocking Sustainable Cities: A Manifesto for Real Change*, and his strapline, 'Think Big, Act Small, Start Now', that he believes that significant change can occur within cities (also see Joy and Vogel, 2021). O'Connor (2022) envisages art and culture as part of a new local and sustainable economy, even though this sector is often missing from the foundational economy and new municipalism debates. As he argues, 'much of the cultural ecosystem is rooted in local, everyday economies' (O'Conner, 2022: 106). Both O'Connor (2022) and Chatterton (2019) agree that such commons planning will require new urban alliances, forms of cooperation and, indeed, political compromises. It will also require real shifts in decision-making power and resources to municipalities.

There are already numerous ways progressive local states and alternative political platforms, in conjunction with civil society, can use statutory planning powers, legal precedents and public assets to challenge the neoliberal city. For instance, rather than invest in large-scale public–private projects which tend to benefit the private sector, they could pursue public–common projects designed to build up the social economy and community infrastructure (Klinenberg, 2018). Instead of selling off public buildings for private development projects and gentrified housing, they could be used as social, community and cultural centres. Rather than financially support large arts organizations and buildings, local government could instead fund community theatre and temporary spaces, freelancers, socially engaged artists, the creative precariat and creative underclass and others to produce culture. Practical examples of 'radical municipalism' have already been mentioned in terms of previous discussions of the 'foundational economy' and 'fearless cities'.

One case of radical municipalism that I would like to briefly return to here, for inspiration, is the social movement platform Barcelona en Comú (Barcelona in Common). In addition to being successfully elected to run the city for two consecutive terms, they have sought to both challenge neoliberal urbanization (Colau, 2019) and provide an alternative form of urban governance emphasizing civic participation. For instance, their pre-election manifesto entitled 'Why do we want to win back Barcelona?' included key principles and commitments like: guaranteeing a good life for all including the right to quality healthcare, decent housing, public education and well-being; providing a socially and environmentally fair economy (including a new tourism model); and democratizing public institutions including promoting local initiatives and networks of self-managed public goods and services (Guanyem Barcelona, 2015). The manifesto was clear that the current tourism economy had to change, highlighted by the comment 'We don't want a city that sells its urban heritage to the highest bidder' (Guanyem Barcelona, 2015: 2). Barcelona en Comú is also one of the few fearless cities giving due attention to the role culture can play in a foundational economy. For example, in 2021 they presented their Cultural Rights Plan including nine government measures and 100 concrete actions including the right to create as well as access culture. They also favour the development of projects and spaces emphasizing cultural participation, circulation and co-production (Barcelona Institute of Culture, 2022).

Of course, one case, however exemplary, is just that, a single example. Not to mention that the election and re-election of a radical social movement is fairly unique. Harvey (2012) also warns against the idea of socialism in one city as a solution. However, just as many cities have entered into the neoliberal creative city competition, perhaps there is the beginning of a new confederation of 'fearless cities' now emerging, inspired by the Barcelona example (Barcelona en Comú, 2019; Russell, 2019). For instance, Joy and Vogel (2021), highlight Seattle, Washington and Jackson, Mississippi as two other examples of cities attempting to forge a more progressive and cooperative urban path. As a well-known proponent of municipalism as a progressive force argues: 'If we are to transition from the death spiral society that decades of neoliberalism have foisted upon us to a new rational society that delivers on the promise of humankind, we must create a global network of fearless cities, towns and villages' (Bookchin, 2019: 16). Harvey (2012) himself mentions that such a network, if it could be fostered, might form the basis of a wider challenge to global neoliberalism.

Whatever the case, there remain numerous obstacles to this transformation. For example, many cities and communities are hamstrung by both national neoliberal policies and a lack of adequate local resources to finance radical change, including addressing urban and regional inequalities (for the case of the UK, for instance, see Lee et al, 2016; Atkins and Hoddinott, 2022). Neoliberal ideology also creates fear and doubt by arguing that cities require inequality and poverty in order to function. Glaeser (2012), a well-known US urban theorist, contentiously makes the point that inequality in cities is not necessarily bad as they require poor workers to do particular jobs. He says American cities 'don't make people poor; they attract poor people' (Glaeser cited in Piramal Raje, 2015) and this is an urban strength not weakness. Behrens and Robert-Nicoud (2014) further suggest that cities do not 'require aggressive local redistributive policies, for such policies attract the poor and repulse the rich, leading to the bankruptcy of local governments'. Finally, innovative cities in the Global South are often hampered from developing large-scale alternative economies due to their colonial past and Global North extractivist and debt policies. They are sometimes also plagued by authoritarian governments, populism and militarism, not to mention a lack of financial resources generally. Major changes will be required to remove these various economic, political and ideological barriers.

Although I am in no way a social forecasting urban sociologist I want to finish on the question of *when* we might begin to move beyond the current neoliberal creative city towards one that is democratically creative, just and sustainable. Part of the reason for doing so is connected to what the research is saying and part of it is related my own life course in conjunction with the trajectory of neoliberal capitalism. One way to think of this prediction is as a combination of Gramscian 'optimism of the will' and Solnit's (2016) progressive idea of hope as 'an embrace of the unknown'!

I was born a full decade after the post-war social democratic contract with capitalism which had a welfare state, a national health care system and affordable and relatively accessible education. During this period there were at least discussions about making art and culture available to all. Jobs were full-time and long-term, housing was affordable and the cost of living was reasonable. Yet I have also lived through 40 years of neoliberal transformation where union power has been weakened, inequality grew and the cost of higher education has increased exponentially. The price of housing is at an all-time high and there is a lack of affordable social accommodation. The cost of living in many countries, particularly the UK, has risen significantly with food and fuel poverty rife. The labour market, even for creative workers in the Global North, is precarious. Well-being and happiness levels are at an all-time low. And art and culture struggle to gain a foothold in the marketplace, fail to attract adequate public funding, or achieve real democratization.

Neoliberal urbanization has not only transformed nearly two-thirds of my own life but has encompassed my son and my grandson's entire lives. I think it is finally time to move away from an economic system that makes more billionaires while a greater percentage of the urban population experience problems feeding themselves and keeping warm (Bregman, 2018). It is time to move away from urban entrepreneurialism as a local economic strategy and start to build a foundational economy that meets people's everyday needs. Finally, it is time for cities to stop individually competing in creative city rankings and instead join a collective confederation of 'fearless cities' designed to solve the most pressing urban problems of the day. An alternative urban cultural economy has a role to play here in creating and documenting this reimagining of the world – how it currently is and how it could be.

If neoliberalism and the dominant creative city are both 'dead, if not still dominant' (Smith, 2008; Luger, 2017), a combination of both reason and hope tells me that together we can reverse many of the negative aspects of this kind of city in my lifetime. I would also like to believe that in my grandson's lifespan we will have moved sufficiently towards quite a different society and urban environment. One in which many of the alternatives that I document will have flourished and evolved into something much more permanent. One in which the city is not only accessible and participatory, but exciting and vibrant too (in an alternative way!). And one in which urban society is characterized by real levels of creativity, justice and sustainability, rather than competition, inequality and environmental degradation.

As I said in the introductory chapter of the book, there is no blueprint to follow and the path forward will not be an easy one. To cite Peck and Theodore:

> All of this implies that the long-awaited arrival of 'postneoliberalism,' whatever its variegated shape, will surely not be a single event, or globally synchronized threshold moment, but rather an extended and geographically uneven interregnum, marked by atrophying consensus, regulatory ruptures, crisis-assisted transformations, social conflicts, squalid compromises, reactionary opportunism, and the unruly emergence of actually existing alternatives from across the political spectrum. (Peck and Theodore, 2019: 259)

Echoing these sentiments, the way forward will not be smooth and neoliberal capitalism will not cede power easily. There will be many conflicts, ruptures and compromises along the way. But we owe it to the next generation to provide them with something better, more ethical and certainly more joyful. I hope this book has helped, in whatever small way, to illuminate the debate and point us beyond the neoliberal creative city towards a more truly creative, just and sustainable urban future.

Notes

Chapter 1

[1]   This is not to suggest that these three fields cover the urban cultural economy in its entirely. See Hutton (2016) for a fuller discussion of different elements.

[2]   This subtitle is a reference to Richard Florida's *Who's Your City? How the Creative Economy Is Making Where You Live the Most Important Decision of Your Life* (Florida, 2008), a book which perhaps best represents his obsession with creativity rankings.

[3]   Jesus et al (2020) suggest that when applying the creativity paradigm in Global South cities we should be aware of several significant differences, including: fewer resources for educational programmes to produce a sizable creative class; marked differences in terms of salaries and working conditions for creative professionals; varying socio-political and cultural realities with accentuated urban problems such as violence, drug trafficking, the presence of militias and paramilitary groups; and divergent capacities for the provision of soft and even basic hard infrastructure. The key issue here is to remain aware of such imbalances and variations, while still asserting that the creative city idea is indeed global in scope.

[4]   While this latter aspect might have been somewhat altered by the impact of the COVID-19 pandemic on stimulating government spending to keep the capitalist economy going, many argue that neoliberalism is still very much alive and well as both an ideology and a political project. For a recent discussion of the UK see Duncan (2022) for instance.

[5]   In terms of the Global South, there are three schools of thought that are central to this point about neoliberalism – one that it is not always directly relevant, one that it is highly relevant and one that suggests we need to consider the different institutions, cultures and processes through which is applied. Smit (2021) highlights the first position which argues that neoliberalism does not always fully explain all Global South urbanization processes (Parnell and Robinson, 2012) because of higher levels of poverty and informality, relatively weaker government capacities and pre-existing inequalities. The second position, that it is highly relevant, relates to Smith's (2002) argument that neoliberalism flourished in cities of the Global South precisely because there was not a strong welfare state tradition. A third position, which this book supports, emanates from Peck et al's (2018) point that we need to understand how national and local conditions are key to understand the variegated way in which neoliberalism works in practice ('actually existing neoliberalism'). Murray (2004: 158) notes 'that neoliberal urbanism is particularly prominent in the growing cities of the global South which aspire to be "world class" cities'. This is consistent with arguments that the neoliberal creative city is a paradigm taken up by many major cities in the Global South, even though this adoption needs to be seen in the context of some of differences alluded to in note 3.

[6]   While Storper (2016) reiterates some of the general arguments that there is a gap between the idea and reality of neoliberalism, his main argument seems to be that neoliberal policies are a national not a municipal issue. He also makes the curious assertion that there is little

evidence of urban austerity or cuts in public welfare. These claims appear to ignore the fact that UK cities have borne the brunt of national austerity policies post-2008 due to cuts and changes to how local government is funded (Harris et al, 2019). Additionally, Storper's (2016) article plays down the impact 30 years of urban entrepreneurialism has had on cities (see Harvey, 1989a; also Chapter 2). Nor does he engage with the significant rise of the cultural economy and creative city strategies which are shot through with neoliberal tendencies (Peck, 2005). Finally, his article also appears to ignore more general neoliberal urbanization trends such as work precarity, social polarization and urban gentrification.

[7] The Gini coefficient is a statistical method used to measure the unequal distribution of income among the population.

Chapter 2

[1] While Harvey's (1989a) article focuses mainly on the UK and the US (with a couple of mentions of Europe), his work on the history of neoliberalism (Harvey, 2007) and his book *Rebel Cities* (Harvey, 2012) very much considers cities of the Global South as examples. As I go on to argue later in this chapter, some of the more recent writing on applying Harvey's notion of urban entrepreneurialism to cities are located in Global South regions like Asian, Africa and Latin America.

[2] The Fearless City Network, although inspired and headed by Barcelona en Comú, does contain Global South representation with four cities from Asia, four from Latin America and one from Africa listed as members, with the rest coming from Europe and the US (Barcelona en Comú, 2019).

[3] The 'local trap' is one in which the local scale is assumed to be inherently more democratic than other geographical scales, like national or global ones (Purcell and Brown, 2005). While this is often true, it is not automatically the case.

Chapter 3

[1] There is less focus on Landry's (2012; 2000) approach here as it is less neoliberal in orientation, despite it having some corporate elements and a concern with regeneration and growth (see Segovia and Hervé, 2022). His early work with Bianchini focused more heavily on participatory creativity and the use of local resources rather than neoliberal globalized formulas (see Landry and Bianchini, 1995).

Chapter 5

[1] Contemporary researchers of night-time governance (Acuto et al, 2021) appear to adopt a rather functionalist model where everyone's interests are broadly similar. As such the dominance of neoliberal capitalism and exclusion of the urban poor are not really highlighted in this work (that is, neither neoliberalism nor the urban poor are found in their book index).

Chapter 7

[1] There is a tendency to blame underdevelopment for high poverty rates in the Global South rather than the poor themselves (Brennan, 2018). Within countries like South Africa, the poverty scapegoats tend to be immigrants who undercut the indigenous poor in terms of 'taking their jobs' and working for lower rates of pay (see Dewa, 2022).

[2] Denmead (2019) uses the term 'people of colour' to include Latino and Afro American residents.

[3] *Billy Elliot* is a play and film of an aspiring young ballet dancer from a working-class background living in a mining village who achieves his dream of performing at the Royal Opera House.

References

Aalbers, M.B. (2016) 'Deregulated regulation', in S. Springer, K. Birch and J. MacLeavy (eds) *The Handbook of Neoliberalism*, London: Routledge, pp 563–573.

Abrahamson, M. (2014) *Urban Sociology: A Global Introduction*, Cambridge: Cambridge University Press.

Acuto, M., Seijas, A., McArthur, J. and Robin, E. (2021) *Managing Cities at Night: A Practitioner Guide to the Urban Governance of the Night-Time Economy*, Bristol: Bristol University Press.

Adams, B. (2019) 'In Detroit, a new type of agricultural neighborhood has emerged', *Yes Solutions Journalism*, [online] 5 November, Available from: https://www.yesmagazine.org/social-justice/2019/11/05/food-community-detroit-garden-agriculture

Alexandri, M.B. and Raharja, S.J. (2020) 'Development strategy of Bandung creative city through the performance improvement of creative industries', *International Journal of Business and Globalization*, 24(4): 560–568.

Althusser, L. (1971) *Lenin and Philosophy and Other Essays*, New York: Monthly Review Press.

Amid, A. (2018) 'Mashhad, Iran: Challenging the concept of a twenty-four-hour city', in J. Nofre and A. Eldridge (eds) *Exploring Nightlife: Space, Society and Governance*, London: Rowman & Littlefield, pp 85–98.

Amin, A. and Thrift, N. (2007) 'Cultural-economy and cities', *Progress in Human Geography*, 31(2): 143–161.

Amsterdam Alternative (nd) 'About Amsterdam Alternative', *Amsterdam Alternative*, [online], Available from: https://amsterdamalternative.nl/about

Anderer, J. (2021) 'As cities grow, the rich get richer and the poor "get nothing at all"', *Study Finds*, [online] 19 August, Available from: https://www.studyfinds.org/rich-get-richer-poor-get-nothing/

Anders, L. (2011) 'Alternative initiatives, cultural intermediaries and urban regeneration: The case of La Friche (Marseille)', *European Planning Studies*, 19(5): 795–811.

Andersson, I. and James, L. (2018) 'Altruism or entrepreneurialism? The co-evolution of green place branding and policy tourism in Växjö, Sweden', *Urban Studies*, 55(15): 3437–3453.

Anttiroiko, A.V. (2015) 'City branding as a response to global intercity competition', *Growth and Change*, 46(2): 233–252.

Apel, D. (2015) *Beautiful Terrible Ruins: Detroit and the Anxiety of Decline*, London: Rutgers University Press.

Aries-Sans, A. and Russo, P. (2018) 'The right to Gaudí: What can we learn from the commoning of Park Güell, Barcelona?', in C. Colomb and J. Novy (eds) *Protest and Resistance in the Tourist City*, London: Routledge, pp 247–263.

Arkaraprasertkul, N. (2018) 'The abrupt rise (and fall) of creative entrepreneurs: Socio-economic change, the visitor economy and social conflict in a traditional neighbourhood of Shanghai, China', in C. Colomb and J. Novy (eds) *Protest and Resistance in the Tourist City*, London: Routledge, pp 282–301.

Artist-led Research Group (2019) 'Ecologies & economies of the artist-led: Space, place, futures', a report from a symposium in Leeds, 26–27 October 2018, [online], Available from: https://artistledresearchgroup. files.wordpress.com/2019/06/arg_a4_book_2.1.pdf

Asero, V. and Skonieczny, S. (2017) 'Cruise tourism and sustainability in the Mediterranean: Destination Venice', in L. Butowski (ed) *Mobilities, Tourism and Travel Behavior: Contexts and Boundaries*, [online], Available from: https://www.intechopen.com/chapters/58056

Assemblea de Barris per un Turisme Sostenible (2019) 'Touristification/ Tourism degrowth', Barcelona Cultura, Ajuntament de Barcelona/Institut de Cultura, [online], Available from: https://ajuntament.barcelona.cat/ lavirreina/en/online-exhibitions/touristification-tourism-degrowth/374

Atkins, G. and Hoddinott, S. (2022) 'Local government funding in England', *Institute for Government*, [online] 7 January, Available from: https://www. instituteforgovernment.org.uk/explainers/local-government-funding-england

Atkinson, R. (2021) *Alpha City: How London was Captured by the Super-Rich*, London: Verso.

Avogadro, E. (2016) 'Is Latin America ready for a creative economy?', *World Economic Forum*, [online] 17 June, Available from: https://www.weforum. org/agenda/2016/06/is-latin-america-ready-for-a-creative-economy/

Azevedo, F., Jost, J., Ruthmund, T. and Sterling, J. (2019) 'Neoliberal ideology and the justification of inequality in capitalist societies: Why social and economic dimensions of ideology are intertwined', *Journal of Social Issues*, 75(1): 49–88.

Bader, I. and Scharenberg, A. (2010) 'The sound of Berlin: Subculture and the global music industry', *International Journal of Urban and Regional Research*, 34(1): 76–91.

Bagguley, P. and Mann, K. (1992) 'Idle, thieving, bastards: Scholarly representations of the "underclass"', *Work, Employment and Society*, 6(1): 113–126.

Bain, A. (2003) 'Constructing contemporary artistic identities in Toronto neighbourhoods', *The Canadian Geographer*, 47(3): 303–317.

Bain, A. and McLean, H. (2013) 'The artistic precariat', *Cambridge Journal of Regions, Economy and Society*, 6(1): 93–111.

Bain, A. and Landau, F. (2018) 'Artist intermediaries in Berlin: Cultural intermediation as an interscalar strategy of self-organizational survival', *Urban Research & Practice*, 11(3): 247–262.

Banks, M. (2017a) *Creative Justice: Cultural Industries, Work and Inequality*, London: Rowman & Littlefield.

Banks, M. (2017b) 'What is creative justice?', *CAMEo Cuts 1*, June, Leicester: Research Institute for Cultural and Media Economies, University of Leicester.

Banks, M. (2018) 'Creative economies of tomorrow? Limits to growth and the uncertain future', *Cultural Trends*, 27(5): 367–380.

Banks, M. (2020) 'Creative economy, de-growth and aesthetic limitation', in K. Oakley and M. Banks (eds) *Cultural Industries and Environmental Crisis: New Approaches for Policy*, Cham: Springer, pp 11–24.

Banks, M. (2022) 'Cultural work and contributive justice', *Journal of Cultural Economy*, DOI: 10.1080/17530350.2022.2058059

Banks, M. and O'Connor, J. (2009) 'After the creative industries', *International Journal of Cultural Policy*, 15(4): 365–373.

Banks, M. and O'Connor, J. (2020) '"A plague upon your howling": Art and culture in the viral emergency', *Cultural Trends*, 30(1): 3–18.

Banks, M. and Serafini, P. (2020) 'Towards post-growth creative economies? Building sustainable cultural production in Argentina', in I. Kiriya, P. Kompatsiaris and Y. Mylonas (eds) *The Industrialization of Creativity and Its Limits: Values, Politics and Lifestyles of Contemporary Cultural Economies*, Cham: Springer, pp 17–29.

Barcelona en Comú (2016) 'How to win back the city en comú: Guide to building a citizen municipal platform', [online] March, Available from: https://archive.org/details/win-the-city-guide/mode/2up

Bacelona en Comú (2019) *Fearless Cities: A Guide to the Global Municipalist Movement*, Oxford: New Internationalist.

Barcelona Institute of Culture (2022) Barcelona Cultural Rights Plan, Barcelona City Council, second and revised and expanded edition, [online] November, Available from: chrome-extension://efaidnbmnnnibpcajpcgl clefindmkaj/https://www.barcelona.cat/aqui-es-fa-cultura/sites/default/files/2022-11/ENG_PlaDretsCulturals_0.pdf

Barton, S. (2005) *Working-Class Organisations and Popular Tourism, 1840–1970*, Manchester: Manchester University Press.

Batchelder, X. (2006) 'The world's largest arts festival, the Edinburgh Festival Fringe: Mechanics, myth and management', PhD thesis, The Ohio State University, Columbus, [online], Available from: https://etd.ohiolink.edu/apexprod/rws_olink/r/1501/10?clear=10&p10_accession_num=osu1149104422

Baum, T. (2020) 'Changing employment dynamics within the creative city: Exploring the role of "ordinary people" within the changing city landscape', *Economic and Industrial Democracy*, 41(4): 954–974.

Baumgartner, W.H. and Rothfuß, E. (2017) 'Creative inequality in the mid-sized university city: Socio-spatial reflections on the Brazilian rural–urban interface: The case of Cachoeira', in U. Gerhard, M. Hoelscher and D. Wilson (eds) *Inequalities in Creative Cities. Issues, Approaches, Comparisons*, New York: Palgrave Macmillan, pp 217–237.

BBC News (2011) 'Why is "chav" still controversial?', *BBC*, [online] 3 June, Available from: https://www.bbc.co.uk/news/magazine-13626046

BBC News (2022) 'Middlesbrough fails again in bid for city status', *BBC*, [online] 20 May, Available from: https://www.bbc.co.uk/news/uk-england-tees-61522979

Bečević, Z. and Dahlstedt, M. (2022) 'On the margins of citizenship: Youth participation and youth exclusion in times of neoliberal urbanism', *Journal of Youth Studies*, 25(3): 362–379.

Beck, U. (2000) *The Brave New World of Work*, Cambridge: Polity Press.

Behrens, K. and Robert-Nicoud, F. (2014) 'Do cities widen the gap between rich and poor?', *World Economic Forum*, [online] 24 July, Available from: https://www.weforum.org/agenda/2014/07/cities-urbanization-rich-poor-inequality/

Belfiore, E. (2020) 'Whose cultural value? Representation, power and creative industries', *International Journal of Cultural Policy*, 26(3): 383–397.

Benanav, A. (2022) *Automation and the Future of Work*, London: Verso.

Bennett, J. (2013) 'Chav-spotting in Britain: The representation of social class as private choice', *Social Semiotics*, 23(1): 146–162.

Berthet-Meylan, M.A. (2022) 'Nightlife as counter-space in the neoliberal city: Experimentation, co-production and resistance in Geneva's night-time economy', PhD thesis, Leeds University, [online], Available from: https://etheses.whiterose.ac.uk/30684/

Berthet, M.A. and Bjertnes, V. (2011) 'Reclaim the city! Reclaim nightlife!', *Eurozine*, [online] 3 August, Available from: https://www.eurozine.com/reclaim-the-city-reclaim-nightlife/

Berthet, M.A., Nada, E. and Association pour la Reconversion des Vernets (2010) 'Voyage au bout de la nuit: Recherche sur la vie nocturne Genevois', *Department de la Culture*, Geneva, [online] 10 September, Available from: https://www.academia.edu/2313763/Voyage_au_bout_de_la_Nuit

Blanco-Romero, A., Blázquez-Salom, M. and Cànoves, G. (2018) 'Barcelona, housing rent bubble in a tourist city: Social responses and local policies', *Sustainability*, 10(6): 1–18.

Boas, T.C. and Gans-Morse, J. (2009) 'Neoliberalism: From new liberal philosophy to anti-liberal slogan', *Studies in Comparative International Development*, 44(2): 137–161.

Bob, B.P. (2019) 'There's no Edinburgh in the festival', *YouTube*, [online] 5 August, Available from: https://www.youtube.com/watch?v=Ex5a Y7AZ4Ug

Boltanski, L. and Chiapello, E. (2017) *The New Spirit of Capitalism*, London: Verso.

Bookchin, D. (2019) 'The future we deserve', in Barcelona en Comú, *Fearless Cities: A Guide to the Global Municipalist Movement*, Oxford: New Internationalist, pp 12–16.

Booth, K. and O'Connor, J. (2018) 'Planning for creative effects: The Museum of Old and New Art', *Australian Planner*, 55(2): 65–72.

Borchi, A. (2018) 'Culture as commons: Theoretical challenges and empirical evidence from occupied cultural spaces in Italy', *Cultural Trends*, 27(1): 33–45.

Boren, T. and Young, C. (2016) 'Conceptual export and theory mobilities: Exploring the reception and development of the "creative city thesis" in the post-socialist urban realm', *Eurasian Geography and Economics*, 57(4–5): 588–606.

Boren, T. and Young, C. (2017) 'Artists and creative city policy: Resistance, the mundane and engagement in Stockholm, Sweden', *City, Culture and Society*, 8: 21–26.

Bregman, R. (2018) *Utopian for Realists and How We Get There*, London and New York: Bloomsbury.

Brennan, K. (2018) 'Identifying the multiple causes of poverty in Africa', *Borgen Project*, [online] 28 January, Available from: https://borgenproject. org/causes-of-poverty-in-africa/

Brenner, N. and Theodore, N. (2002) 'Cities and the geographies of "actually existing neoliberalism"', *Antipode*, 34(3): 349–379.

Brenner, N. and Theodore, N. (eds) (2004) *Spaces of Neoliberalism: Urban Restructuring in Northern America and Western Europe*, Oxford: Blackwell.

Brenner, N., Marcuse, P. and Mayer, M. (eds) (2011) *Cities for People, Not for Profit: Critical Urban Theory and the Right to the City*, London: Routledge.

Brezborn, U. and Weismann, S. (eds) (2016) *KuLe: Art and Life. A House in Berlin Since 1990*, Berlin: Revolver Publishing.

Brook, O., O'Brien, D. and Taylor, M. (2020) *Culture is Bad for You: Inequality and the Cultural and Creative Industries*, Manchester: Manchester University Press.

Broome, O. (2015) 'L'Usine: Fight for your right to party', *Artefact*, [online] 13 January, Available from: http://www.artefactmagazine.com/2015/01/13/genevas-emerging-electronic-music-scene/

Brown-Saracino, J. (ed) (2010) *The Gentrification Debates: A Reader*, London: Routledge.

Bryan-Wilson, J. (2009) *Art Workers: Radical Practice in the Vietnam Era*, Berkeley: University of California Press.

Bunce, S. (2018) 'Alternatives to gentrification: Exploring urban community land trusts and urban ecovillage practices', in L. Lees and M. Phillips (eds), *Handbook of Gentrification Studies*, Cheltenham: Edward Elgar Publishing, pp 413–427.

Burawoy, M. (2019) *Symbolic Violence. Conversations with Bourdieu*, Durham, NC and London: Duke University Press.

Burgen, S. (2016) 'How to win back the city: The Barcelona en Comú guide to overthrowing the elite', *The Guardian*, [online] 22 June, Available from: https://www.theguardian.com/cities/2016/jun/22/barcelona-comun-guide-how-win-city-elite

Burgen, S. (2017) 'Barcelona anti-tourism activists vandalise bikes and bus', *The Guardian*, [online] 1 August, Available from: https://www.theguardian.com/world/2017/aug/01/barcelona-anti-tourism-activists-vandalise-bikes-and-bus

Burke, J. (2008) 'Prague elite fights "vulgar" invaders', *The Observer*, [online] 11 May, Available from: https://www.theguardian.com/artanddesign/2008/may/11/art.books

Burrows, R. and Knowles, C. (2019) 'The "HAVES" and the "HAVE YACHTS": Socio-spatial struggles in London between the "merely wealthy" and the "super-rich"', *Cultural Politics*, 15(1): 72–87.

Business Traveller (2021) 'Top global cities for entrepreneurial success', *Business Traveller*, [online] 14 June, Available from: https://businesstravelerusa.com/special-reports/top-global-cities-entrepreneurial-success/

Byrne, D. (1999) *Social Exclusion*, Buckingham: Open University Press.

Campbell, B. (1993) *Goliath: Britain's Dangerous Places*, London: Methuen.

Candipan, J., Phillips, N.E., Sampson, R.J. and Small, M. (2021) 'From residence to movement: The nature of racial segregation in everyday urban mobility', *Urban Studies*, 58(15): 3095–3117.

Carey, H., Florisson, R., O'Brien, D. and Lee, N. (2020) 'Getting in and getting on: Class, participation and job quality in the UK's creative industries', *Multiple: Creative Industries Policy and Evidence Centre*, University of Edinburgh and Work Advance, [online], Available from: https://pec.ac.uk/research-reports/getting-in-and-getting-on-class-participation-and-job-quality-in-the-uks-creative-industries

Castells, M. (1968) 'Y a-t-il une sociologie urbaine?', *Sociologie du Travail*, 1: 72–90.

Castells, M. (1977) *The Urban Question: A Marxist Approach*, Cambridge, MA: MIT Press.

Castells, M. (1978) *City, Class, and Power*, London: Macmillan.

Castells, M. (1983) *The City and the Grassroots: A Cross-Cultural Theory of Urban Social Movements*, London: Arnold.

Castells, M. (1996) *The Rise of the Network Society*, Cambridge, MA and Oxford: Blackwell.

Castells, M. (1997) *The Power of Identity*, Cambridge, MA and Oxford: Blackwell.

Castells, M. (1998) *End of Millennium*, Cambridge, MA and Oxford: Blackwell.

Castells, M. (2012) *Networks of Outrage and Hope: Social Movements in the Internet Age*, Cambridge: Polity.

Catungal, J.P., Leslie, D. and Hii, Y. (2009) 'Geographies of displacement in the creative city: The case of Liberty Village, Toronto', *Urban Studies*, 46: 1095–1114.

Cecil, N. (2016) 'London hipsters "key to boosting British economy after Brexit"', *Evening Standard*, [online] 9 September, Available from: https://www.standard.co.uk/news/london/london-hipsters-key-to-boosting-brit ish-economy-after-brexit-a3341091.html

Centre for Cities (2018) *City Outlook 2018*, London: Centre for Cities, [online], Available from: https://www.centreforcities.org/wp-content/uploads/2018/01/18-01-12-Final-Full-Cities-Outlook-2018.pdf

Chakrabortty, A. (2018) 'In 2011 Preston hit rock bottom. Then it took back control', *The Guardian*, [online] 31 January, Available from: https://www.theguardian.com/commentisfree/2018/jan/31/preston-hit-rock-bot tom-took-back-control

Charles, T. (2021) 'How Middlesbrough's developing creative quarter will provide an ongoing economic boost', *Tees Valley Arts*, [blog], Available from: https://www.boroculture.org.uk/2022/05/11/how-middles broughs-developing-creative-quarter-will-provide-an-ongoing-econo mic-boost/

Chatterton, P. (2002) 'Governing nightlife: Profit, fun and (dis)order in the contemporary city', *Entertainment Law*, 1(2): 23–49.

Chatterton, P. (2019) *Unlocking Sustainable Cities: A Manifesto for Real Change*, London: Pluto Press.

Chatterton, P. (2020) 'Coronavirus: We're in a real-time laboratory of a more sustainable urban future', *The Conversation*, [online] 27 April, Available from: https://theconversation.com/coronavirus-were-in-a-real-time-lab oratory-of-a-more-sustainable-urban-future-135712?utm_source=faceb ook&utm_medium=bylinefacebookbutton&fbclid=IwAR3sAGx-9e4rz_ zdmwGjD2PEqAOW2gzfFxco_nRRI_7no3REm2ucy3po2N8

Chatterton P. and Hollands, R. (2001) *Changing our Toon: Youth, Nightlife and Urban Change in Newcastle*, Newcastle: Newcastle University.

Chatterton, P. and Hollands, R. (2003) *Urban Nightscapes: Youth Cultures, Pleasure Spaces and Corporate Power*, London: Routledge.

Chatterton, P. and Hollands, R. (2004) 'The London of the north? Youth cultures, urban change and nightlife', in R. Unsworth and J. Stillwell (eds), *Twenty-first Century Leeds: Geographies of a Regional City*, Leeds: Leeds University Press, pp 265–290.

Chatterton, P. and Pusey, A. (2020) 'Beyond capitalist enclosure, commodification and alienation: Postcapitalist praxis as commons, social production and useful doing', *Progress in Human Geography*, 44(1): 27–48.

Chew, M.M. (2009) 'Research on Chinese nightlife cultures and night-time economies', *Chinese Sociology and Anthropology*, 42(2): 3–21.

Chien, S.S. and Wu, F. (2011) 'Transformation of China's urban entrepreneurialism: The case study of the city of Kunshan', *Cross Currents: East Asian History and Culture Review*, 1(1), [online] 1 December, Available from: https://escholarship.org/content/qt7qn1q8cx/qt7qn1q8cx.pdf

Citroni, S. (2017) 'The contradictions of creative activism: Situated meanings and everyday practices in a Milan case-study', *City, Culture and Society*, 8: 43–50.

City of Edmonton (2012) 'Edmonton, a city well built', *YouTube*, [online] 12 May, Available from: https://www.youtube.com/watch?v=mi_wn9J_7rQ

City of Melbourne (2021) 'City of Melbourne creative strategy 2018–2028', Melbourne: City of Melbourne, [online] September, Available from: https://www.melbourne.vic.gov.au/SiteCollectionDocuments/com-creative-strategy.PDF

Clark, N. (2012) 'Thirst for profit sucks spirt from fringe stage', *Independent*, [online] 5 August, Available from: http://www.independent.co.uk/arts-entertainment/theatre-dance/news/thirst-for-profits-sucks-spirit-from-fringe-stage-8008987.html

Coffield, E., Markham, K., Richter, P., Huggan, R., Butler, D., Wainwright, E. and Prescott, R. (2019) 'More than meanwhile spaces', *Newcastle University*, [online] March, Available from: https://thenewbridgeproject.com/wp-content/uploads/2019/03/MTMS.-Final-Digital-Publication.pdf

Colau, A. (2019) 'Epilogue: Transforming fear into hope', in Barcelona En Comú, *Fearless Cities: A Guide To the Global Municipalist Movement*, Oxford: New Internationalist, pp 145–148.

Colomb, C. (2011) *Staging the New Berlin: Place Marketing and the Politics of Urban Reinvention Post-1989*, London: Routledge.

Connell, R. and Dados, N. (2014) 'Where in the world does neoliberalism come from? The market agenda in southern perspective', *Theoretical Sociology*, 43: 117–138.

Constantin, M., Saxon, S. and Yu, J. (2020) 'Reimagining the $9 trillion tourism economy: What will it take?', *Travel, Logistics & Infrastructure, McKinsey and Company*, [online] 5 August, Available from: https://www.mckinsey.com/industries/travel-logistics-and-infrastructure/our-insights/reimagining-the-9-trillion-tourism-economy-what-will-it-take

Cooper, D. (2014) *Everyday Utopias: The Conceptual Life of Promising Spaces*, Durham, NC and London: Duke University Press.

Coppola, A. and Vanolo, A. (2014) 'Normalising autonomous spaces: Ongoing transformations in Christiania, Copenhagen', *Urban Studies*, 52(6): 1152–1168.

Cornelissen, S. (2017) 'Entrepreneurial urban governance and development in Africa: Challenges, opportunities and lessons from South Africa', in U. Engel and G.R. Olsen (eds) *The African Exception*, London: Routledge, pp 121–138.

Cossu, A. and Francesca Murru, M. (2018) 'Macao before and beyond social media: The creation of the unexpected as a mobilisation logic', in P. Serafini, J. Holtaway and A. Cossu (eds) *artWORK: Art, Labour and Activism*, London: Rowman & Littlefield, pp 65–86.

Creative Class Group (2016) 'Buenos Aires: A creative city?', [online] November, Available from: http://www.creativeclass.com/_wp/wp-content/uploads/2019/01/FINAL-Art-Basel-Buenos-Aires-Report.pdf

Crossley, S. (2018) *Troublemakers: The Construction of 'Troubled Families' as a Social Problem*, Bristol: Policy Press.

Cudny, R., Comunian, R. and Wolaniuk, A. (2020) 'Arts and creativity: A business and branding strategy for Lodz as a neoliberal city', *Cities*, 100: 1–10.

Cultural Workers Organize (2013) '"Messages of rupture": An interview with Emanuele Braga on the MACAO occupation in Milan', *Scapegoat: Landscape, Architecture, Political Economy*, 4: 179–187.

Currier, J. (2012) 'Selling place through art: The creation and establishment of Beijing's 798 Art District', in P. Daniels, K.C. Ho and T. Hutton (eds) *New Economic Spaces in Asian Cities: From Industrial Restructuring to the Cultural Turn*, London: Routledge, pp 184–201.

Dadusc, D. and Dee, E.T.C. (2015) 'The criminalisation of squatting: Discourses, moral panics and resistances in the Netherlands, England and Wales', in L. O'Mahony, D. O'Mahony and R. Hickey (eds) *Moral Rhetoric and the Criminalisation of Squatting: Vulnerable Demons?*, New York: Routledge, pp 109–132.

Dalakoglou, D. (2018) 'Another small death of Amsterdam', *Alternative Amsterdam*, [online] 25 September, Available from: https://amsterdamalternative.nl/articles/6313

Davidson, M. (2010) 'Social sustainability and the city', *Geography Compass*, 4(7): 872–880.

Davies, R. (2020) 'UK nightlife industry facing "financial armageddon"', *The Guardian*, [online] 20 August, Available from: https://www.theguard ian.com/business/2020/aug/20/uk-nightlife-industry-facing-financial- armageddon

Davies, R. and Mummery, H. (2006) *Nightvision: Town Centres for All*, London: The Civic Trust.

Davis, J. (2021) *The Caring City: Ethics of Urban Design*, Bristol: Bristol University Press.

Davis, M. (2007) *Planet of Slums*, London: Verso.

Dawson, A. (2019) *Extreme Cities: The Peril and Promise of Urban Life in the Age of Climate Change*, London: Verso.

Deacon, A. (1978) 'The scrounging controversy: Public attitudes towards the unemployed in contemporary Britain', *Social Policy and Administration*, 12(2): 120–135.

De Beukelaer, C. (2021) 'Friction in the creative city', *Open Cultural Studies*, 5(1): 40–53.

Degen, M. (2018) 'Timescapes of urban change', *Sociological Review*, 66(5): 1074–1092.

De Neve, J.-E. and Krekel, C. (2020) 'Cities and happiness: A global ranking and analysis', *World Happiness Report*, [online] 20 March, Available from: https://worldhappiness.report/ed/2020/cities-and-happiness-a-glo bal-ranking-and-analysis/

Denmead, T. (2019) *The Creative Underclass: Youth, Race, and the Gentrifying City*, Durham, NC and London: Duke University Press.

Department of Culture, Media and Sport (2001) *Creative Industries Mapping Document*, London: DCMS and the Creative Industries Task Force.

Deshmukh, A. (2021) 'This simple chart reveals the distribution of global wealth', *Visual Capitalist*, [online] 20 September, Available from: https:// www.visualcapitalist.com/distribution-of-global-wealth-chart/

Detroit Metro Times (2014) 'ICYMI: Forbes rates Detroit #9 on its "America's most creative cities" list', *Detroit Metro Times*, [online] 27 July, Available from: https://www.metrotimes.com/news/icymi-forbes-rates-detroit-9- on-its-americas-most-creative-cities-list-2203026

Deuber Ziegler, E. (2004) 'Sédiments, traditions et héritages culturels: XVIe- XXe siècle', *Equinoxe*, 24: 17–29.

Dewa, C. (2022) 'Migrants scapegoated in South Africa as inequality and unemployment surge', *Open Democracy*, [online] 29 March, Available from: https://www.opendemocracy.net/en/5050/migrants-scapegoated- in-south-africa-as-inequality-and-unemployment-surge/

Dickinson, M. (1999) *Rogue Reels: Oppositional Film in Britain 1945–90*, London: British Film Institute.

Dinardi, C. (2020) 'Re-thinking the creative economy through informality and social inclusion: Changing policy directions from Latin America', in K. Oakley and M. Banks (eds) *Cultural Industries and Environmental Crisis: New Approaches for Policy*, Cham: Springer, pp 79–93.

Diss, K. (2016) 'Perth's Fringe Festival gives PIAF a run for its money', *ABC News*, [online] 18 February, Available from: https://www.abc.net.au/news/2016-02-19/piaf-fringe-festival-celebrates-its-biggest-ever/7182114

Dodd, A. (2022) '£5m boost to make Middlesbrough "the most creative town in the UK"', *The Northern Echo*, [online] 12 March, Available from: https://www.thenorthernecho.co.uk/news/19988498.5m-boost-make-middlesbrough-the-creative-town-uk/

Dodd, D. (2004) 'Barcelona: The making of a cultural city', in M. Miles, T. Hall and I. Borden (eds) *The City Cultures Reader* (2nd edn), London: Routledge, pp 177–198.

Dorling, D. (2017) '*The New Urban Crisis* by Richard Florida review: "flawed and elitist ideas"', *The Guardian*, [online] 26 September, Available from: https://www.theguardian.com/books/2017/sep/26/richard-florida-new-urban-crisis-review-flawed-elitist-ideas

d'Ovidio, M. and Cossu, A. (2017) 'Culture is reclaiming the creative city: The case of Macao in Milan, Italy', *City, Culture and Society*, 8: 7–12.

d'Ovidio, M. and Rodríguez Morató, A. (2017) 'Introduction to SI: Against the creative city: Activism in the creative city: When cultural workers fight against creative city policy', *City, Culture and Society*, 8: 3–6.

Draaisma J. (2016) 'Cultural incubators: The squats of the 21st century?', in A. Wageningen and V. Mamadouh (eds) *Urban Europe: Fifty Tales of the City*, Amsterdam: Amsterdam University Press, pp 199–208.

Dreher, C. (2002) 'Be creative – or die', *Salon*, [online] 6 June, Available from: https://www.salon.com/2002/06/06/florida_22/

Duncan, J. (2022) 'The death of neoliberalism? UK responses to the pandemic', *The International Journal of Human Rights*, 26(3): 494–517.

Economist Intelligence Unit (2021) 'The Global Liveability Index 2021: How the Covid-19 pandemic affected liveability worldwide', [online], Available from: https://pages.eiu.com/rs/753-RIQ-438/images/global-liveability-index-2021-free-report.pdf

Edsor, B. (2017) 'This northern UK city has beat out the likes of Cuba and Chile for the title of "best place to visit in 2018"', *Business Insider*, [online] 20 December, Available from: https://www.businessinsider.in/This-northern-UK-city-has-beat-out-the-likes-of-Cuba-and-Chile-for-the-title-of-best-place-to-visit-in-2018/articleshow/62179262.cms

Eisenschitz, A. (2013) 'The politicisation and contradictions of neo-liberal tourism', *International Journal of Tourism Policy*, 5(1/2): 97–112.

Eldridge, A. and Nofre, J. (2018) '"Shaken not stirred": An introduction to *Exploring Nightlife*', in J. Nofre and A. Eldridge (eds) *Exploring Nightlife: Space, Society and Governance*, London: Rowman & Littlefield, pp 1–16.

Elliott, L. (2018) 'Ten years after the financial crash, the timid left should be full of regrets', *The Guardian*, [online] 30 August, Available from: https://www.theguardian.com/commentisfree/2018/aug/30/financial-crash-capitalism-banking-crisis

Emanuele, V. (2017) 'Rebel cities, urban resistance and capitalism: A conversation with David Harvey', *Verso Books*, [online] 9 February, Available from: https://www.versobooks.com/blogs/3088-rebel-cities-urban-resistance-and-capitalism-a-conversation-with-david-harvey

End Poverty Edmonton (2019) 'Who are the "1 in 10" experiencing poverty in Edmonton?', *Tamarack Institute*, [online] 19 September, Available from: https://www.tamarackcommunity.ca/latest/who-are-the-1-in-10-experiencing-poverty-in-edmonton#:~:text=The%20Edmonton%20region%20has%201,%2439%2C000%20a%20year%20or%20less.&text=9%2C705%20lone%20parent%20families%20are,8%2C460%20families%20are%20female%2Dled

Engelen, E., Froud, J., Johal, S., Salento, A. and Williams, K. (2017) 'The grounded city: From competitivity to the foundational economy', *Cambridge Journal of Regions, Economy and Society*, 10(3): 407–423.

Engelman, U., Rowe, M. and Southern, A. (2016) 'Community land trusts: A radical or reformist response to the housing question today?', *ACME: An International Journal for Critical Geographies*, 15(3): 589–615.

The Equality Trust (nd) 'How has inequality changed? Development of UK income inequality', *The Equality Trust*, [online], Available from: https://equalitytrust.org.uk/how-has-inequality-changed

Ersoy, A. and Larner, A. (2020) 'Rethinking urban entrepreneurialism: Bristol Green Capital – in it for good?', *European Planning Studies*, 28(4): 790–808.

Euromonitor International (2017) 'Income inequality ranking of the world's major cities', *Euromonitor International*, [online] 31 October, Available from: https://www.euromonitor.com/article/income-inequality-ranking-worlds-major-cities

Evans, G. (2002) *Cultural Planning: An Urban Renaissance? An International Perspective on Planning for the Arts, Culture and Entertainment*, London: Routledge.

Evans, G. (2009) 'Creative cities, creative spaces and urban policy', *Urban Studies*, 46(5/6): 1003–1040.

Evans, G. (2017) 'Creative cities: An international perspective', in J. Hannigan and G. Richards (eds) *The SAGE Handbook of New Urban Studies*, London: SAGE, pp 311–329.

Evans, G. (2019) *Mega-Events: Placemaking, Regeneration and City-Regional Development*, London: Routledge.

Fainstein, S. (2009) 'Planning and the just city', in P. Marcuse, J. Connolly and J. Novy (eds) *Searching for the Just City: Debates in Urban Theory and Practice*, Oxon: Routledge, pp 39–59.

Fainstein, S. (2010) *The Just City*, Ithaca: Cornell University Press.

Farrer, J. (2018) 'Nightlife and Night-Time Economy in Urban China', in W. Wu and M. Frazier (eds) *The SAGE Handbook of Contemporary China*, London: SAGE Publications Ltd, pp 1112–1130.

Fleming-Muñoz, D.A. and Measham, T. (2015) 'Rich and poor: Which areas of Australia are most unequal?, *The Conversation*, [online] 27 September, Available from: https://theconversation.com/rich-and-poor-which-areas-of-australia-are-most-unequal-42409

Florida, R. (2002) 'The rise of the creative class', *Washington Monthly*, [online] May, Available from: https://washingtonmonthly.com/2002/05/01/the-rise-of-the-creative-class/

Florida, R. (2003a) 'Cities and the creative class', *City & Community*, 2(1): 3–19.

Florida, R. (2003b) 'The new American dream', *Washington Monthly*, [online] March, Available from: https://washingtonmonthly.com/2003/03/01/the-new-american-dream/

Florida, R. (2004) *The Rise of the Creative Class: And How it's Transforming Work, Leisure, Community and Everyday Life*, New York: Basic Books.

Florida, R. (2005) *Cities and the Creative Class*, New York: Harper Business.

Florida, R. (2008) *Who's Your City? How the Creative Economy is Making Where You Live the Important Decision of Your Life*, New York: Basic Books.

Florida, R. (2014) *The Rise of the Creative Class, Revisited*, New York: Basic Books.

Florida, R. (2018) *The New Urban Crisis: Gentrification, Housing Bubbles, Growing Inequality and What We Can Do About It*, London: One World.

Florida, R. (2019) 'The changing geography of America's creative class', *Bloomberg*, [online] 27 August, Available from: https://www.bloomberg.com/news/articles/2019-08-27/the-changing-geography-of-america-s-creative-class

Florida, R. and Pedigo, S. (2017) 'The consumer redefined: The creative class', *lemiami.com/labs and the Creative Class Group*, [online], Available from: https://www.creativeclass.com/_wp/wp-content/uploads/2017/04/FINAL-LE-MIAMI-REPORT.pdf

FlyGreen (2022) 'Sustainable flying: Is sustainable air travel possible?', *FlyGreen*, [online], Available from: https://flygrn.com/page/sustainable-air-travel

Flynn, T. (2021) *The Brasilia of the North? Sixty Years of Regeneration*, Newcastle: Tyne Bridge Publishing.

Foley, N. (2021) 'Pub statistics: Briefing paper No 8591', *House of Commons Library*, [online] 22 April, Available from: https://researchbriefings.files. parliament.uk/documents/CBP-8591/CBP-8591.pdf

Foundational Economy Collective (2018) *Foundational Economy: The Infrastructure of Everyday Life*, Manchester: Manchester University Press.

Freeman, J. and Burgos, M. (2016) 'Accumulation by forced removal: The thinning of Rio de Janeiro's favelas in preparation for the games', *Journal of Latin American Studies*, 49(3): 549–577.

Friedman, M. (2015) 'Here are the most (and least) expensive cities in the world', *Esquire*, [online] 18 September, Available from: https://www. esquire.com/lifestyle/money/news/a38051/what-are-the-most-expens ive-cities/

Friedman, S., O'Brien, D. and Laurison, D. (2017) '"Like skydiving without a parachute": How class origin shapes occupational trajectories in British acting', *Sociology*, 51(5): 992–1010.

Friedmann, J. (1986) 'The world city hypothesis', *Development and Change*, 17(1): 69–83.

Fuchs, C. (2012) 'Some reflections on Manuel Castells' book "Networks of Outrage and Hope. Social Movements in the Internet Age"', *tripleC: Communication, Capitalism & Critique. Open Access Journal for a Global Sustainable Information Society*, 10(2): 775–797.

Fukuma, T. (2022) 'Return to the artspaces of the future', *Symposium: Towards an Alternative Vision of Creative and Cultural Third-places: Exploring Sustainable Models in Europe*, Université Sorbonne Nouvelle & La Station – Gare des Mines, Paris, 24–25 November.

Furseth, J. (2018) 'The battle to save east London: Is this finally the end? The death of Hackney Wick', *Huck*, [online] 11 October, Available from: https://www.huckmag.com/perspectives/reportage-2/the-battle-to-save-east-london-is-this-finally-the-end/

Furseth, J. (2020) 'Future of the Wick', *The Wick: Keeping the Creative Flame Alive*, [online] 13 November, Available from: https://jessicafurseth.com/2020/11/13/future-of-the-wick/

Gallo, A. (2019) '7 giants that earn billions of dollars thanks to the global tourism', *Ecobnb*, [online] 10 October, Available from: https://ecobnb.com/blog/2019/10/giants-global-tourism/

Ganbold, S. (2022) 'Leading city destinations in Asia in 2019, by number of international arrivals', *Statista*, [online] 15 February, Available from: https://www.statista.com/statistics/381848/leading-city-destinations-by-num ber-of-arrivals-asia/#:~:text=In%202019%2C%20Hong%20Kong%20 was,international%20tourist%20arrivals%20in%202019

Garrahan, P. and Stewart, P. (1992) *The Nissan Enigma: Flexibility at Work in a Local Economy*, London: Mansell.

Gerhard, U., Hoelscher, M. and Wilson, D. (2017) 'Introduction. Inequalities in the creative city: A new perspective on an old phenomenon', in U. Gerhard, M. Hoelscher and D. Wilson (eds) *Inequalities in Creative Cities: Issues, Approaches, Comparisons*, Cham: Springer, pp 3–14.

Gheyoh Ndzi, E. (2022) 'P&O: Sacking of 800 staff shows just how precarious UK jobs can be', *The Conversation*, [online] 18 March, Available from: https://ray.yorksj.ac.uk/id/eprint/6204/1/pando-sacking-of-800-staff-shows-just-how-precarious-uk-jobs-can-be-179589

Giaever Lopez, M. (2022) 'Temporary autonomous home: Free parties and migration on the margins of the urban night', *Crossings: Journal of Migration & Culture*, 13(1): 27–42.

Glaeser, E. (2012) *Triumph of the City: How Urban Spaces Make Us Human*, London: Pan Macmillan.

Glass, R. (1964) 'Aspects of change', in Centre for Urban Studies (ed) *London: Aspects of Change*, London: MacGibbon and Kee, pp xiii–xlii.

Glencross, T. (2017) 'The neoliberal night out: Why clubbing doesn't feel radical anymore', *Vice*, [online] 5 April, Available from: https://www.vice.com/en/article/9a7jgv/the-neoliberal-night-out-why-clubbing-doesnt-feel-radical-anymore

Gofton, L. (1983) 'Real ale and real men', *New Society*, 66: 271–273.

Gois, M.P.F. (2018) 'Policies for nightlife and the democratic city: From urban renewal to behaviour control in Rio de Janeiro, Brazil', in J. Nofre and A. Eldridge (eds) *Exploring Nightlife: Space, Society and Governance*, London: Rowman & Littlefield, pp 207–222.

Gornostaeva G. and Campbell, N. (2012) 'The creative underclass in the production of place: Example of Camden Town in London', *Journal of Urban Affairs*, 34(2): 169–188.

Gotham, K. (2018) 'Assessing and advancing research on tourism gentrification', *Via Tourism Review*, 13: 1–11.

Gottdiener, M. (2001) *The Theming of America: American Dreams, Media Fantasies, And Themed Environments* (2nd edn), Oxford: Westview Press.

Gould, L. (2021) 'Top global for cities entrepreneurial success', *Business Traveller*, [online] 15 June, Available from: https://www.businesstravelerusa.com/business-traveler-usa-story/top-global-cities-entrepreneurial-success/

Gowling, A. (2013) 'Amsterdam fourth most creative global city', *I Am Expat*, [online] 23 August, Available from: https://www.iamexpat.nl/expat-info/dutch-expat-news/amsterdam-fourth-most-creative-global-city

Gravari-Barbas, M. and Guinand, S. (2017) *Tourism and Gentrification in Contemporary Metropolises: International Perspectives*, London: Routledge.

Gray, L. and Leyland, A.H. (2009) 'A multilevel analysis of diet and socio-economic status in Scotland: Investigating the "Glasgow effect"', *Public Health Nutrition*, 12(9): 351–1358.

Grodach, C. (2017) 'Urban cultural policy and creative city making', *Cities*, 68: 82–91.

Grodach, C., Foster, N. and Murdoch, J. (2016) 'Gentrification, displacement and the arts: Untangling the relationship between arts industries and place change', *Urban Studies*, 55(4): 807–825.

Gros, D. (2004) 'Du désir de révolution à la dissidence: Constitution de la mouvance alternative genevoise et devenir de ses acteurs', *Equinoxe*, 24: 32–42.

Grugel, J. and Riggirozzi, P. (2018) 'Neoliberal disruption and neoliberalism's afterlife in Latin America: What is left of post-neoliberalism?', *Critical Social Policy*, 38(3): 547–566.

Gu, X., Lim, M.K. and O'Connor, J. (2020) *Re-imagining Creative Cities in 21st Century Asia*, Cham: Palgrave Macmillan.

Guanyem Barcelona (2015) 'Why do we want to win back Barcelona? Principles and commitments to guide the way', *Guanyem Barcelona*, [online], Available from: https://guanyembarcelona.cat/wp-content/uploads/2014/06/priciples.pdf

Guia, J. (2021) 'Conceptualizing justice tourism and the promise of posthumanism', *Journal of Sustainable Tourism*, 29(2–3): 503–520.

Gyr, U. (2010) 'The history of tourism: Structures on the path to modernity', *European History Online*, [online], Available from: http://ieg-ego.eu/en/threads/europe-on-the-road/the-history-of-tourism

Haben und Brauchen (2012) 'Manifesto', [online] January, Available from: http://www.habenundbrauchen.de/wp-content/uploads/2012/01/HB_web_english_neu.pdf

Habibi, Z. (2020) 'Whose cultural memory? Disruptive tactics by the creative collectives in George Town, Malaysia', in X. Gu, M.K. Lim and J. O'Connor (eds) *Re-imagining Creative Cities in 21st Century Asia*, Cham: Palgrave Macmillan, pp 113–128.

Hadfield, P. (2006) *Bar Wars: Contesting the Night in Contemporary British Cities*, Oxford: Oxford University Press.

Hadfield, P. (2015) 'The night-time city. Four modes of exclusion: Reflections on the *Urban Studies* special collection', *Urban Studies*, 52(3): 606–616.

Hadley, S. and Belfiore, E. (2018) 'Cultural democracy and cultural policy', *Cultural Trends*, 27(3): 218–223.

Hae, L. (2011) 'Dilemmas of the nightlife fix: Post-industrialisation and the gentrification of nightlife in New York City', *Urban Studies*, 48(16): 3449–3465.

Hae, L. (2012) *The Gentrification of Nightlife and the Right to the City: Regulating Spaces of Social Dancing in New York City*, London: Routledge.

Haines, G. (2021) 'The world's best cities for mental wellbeing, according to data crunchers', *Positive News*, [online] 9 July, Available from: https://www.positive.news/society/the-worlds-best-cities-for-mental-wellbeing/

Hall, S. and Jefferson, T. (eds) (1976) *Resistance Through Rituals: Youth Subcultures in Post-War Britain*, London: Hutchinson.

Hall, S. and Jacques, M. (1983) *The Politics of Thatcherism*, London: Lawrence & Wishart.

Hall, T. and Hubbard, P. (1996) 'The entrepreneurial city: New urban politics, new urban geographies?', *Progress in Human Geography*, 20(2): 153–174.

Halls, E. (2018) 'When will we give working class creatives the support they deserve?', *GQ*, [online] 27 October, Available from: https://www.gq-magazine.co.uk/article/working-class-creatives

Hamnett, C. (1994) 'Social polarisation in global cities: Theory and evidence', *Urban Studies*, 31(3): 401–424.

Hamnett, C. (2021) 'The changing social structure of global cities: Professionalisation, proletarianisation or polarisation', *Urban Studies*, 58(5): 1050–1066.

Hancock, A. (2021) 'Nightclub nightmare: Industry fears for its post-Covid future', *Financial Times*, [online] 9 April, Available from: https://www.ft.com/content/20faa49c-4723-4eea-b167-7160391196ab

Hancox, D. (2008) 'In defence of hipsters', *The Guardian*, [online] 8 September, Available from: https://www.theguardian.com/commentisfree/2008/sep/03/fashion

Hancox, D. (2015) 'Never mind the hipsters: It's the property developers who are ruining our cities', *The Guardian*, [online] 28 September, Available from: https://www.theguardian.com/commentisfree/2015/sep/28/hipsters-property-developers-gentrification-cereal-killer-cafe

Hanley, L. (2012) *Estates: An Intimate History*, London: Granta Books.

Hanna, T., Guinan, J. and Bilsborough, J. (2018) 'The "Preston model" and the modern politics of municipal socialism', *Open Democracy*, [online] 12 June, Available from: https://neweconomics.opendemocracy.net/preston-model-modern-politics-municipal-socialism/

Hannigan, J. (1998) *Fantasy City: Pleasure and Profit in the Postmodern City*, London: Routledge.

Harrebye, S. (2015) 'The ambivalence of creative activism as a reorganization of critique', *Culture and Organization*, 21(2): 126–146.

Harris, J. (2020) 'Are Apple products environmentally friendly?', *Ecologist*, [online] 16 September, Available from: https://theecologist.org/2020/sep/16/are-apple-products-environmentally-friendly

Harris, T., Hodge, L. and Phillips, D. (2019) 'English local government funding: Trends and challenges in 2019 and beyond', *Institute for Fiscal Studies*, [online] November, Available from: https://ifs.org.uk/sites/default/files/output_url_files/English-local-government-funding-trends-and-challenges-in-2019-and-beyond-IFS-Report-166.pdf

Harvey, D. (1973) *Social Justice and the City*, London: Arnold.

Harvey, D. (1985a) *Consciousness and the Urban Experience: Studies in the History and Theory of Capitalist Urbanization*, Baltimore: Johns Hopkins University Press.

Harvey, D. (1985b) *The Urbanization of Capital*, Baltimore: Johns Hopkins University Press.

Harvey, D. (1989a) 'From managerialism to entrepreneurialism: The transformation in urban governance in late capitalism', *Geografiska annale*, 71B(1): 3–17.

Harvey, D. (1989b) *The Condition of Postmodernity*, Oxford: Basil Blackwell.

Harvey, D. (1989c) *The Urban Experience*, Oxford: Basil Blackwell.

Harvey, D. (1996) *Justice, Nature and the Geography of Difference*, Cambridge: Blackwell.

Harvey, D. (2000) *Spaces of Hope: Towards a Critical Geography*, Edinburgh: Edinburgh University Press.

Harvey, D. (2001) 'Globalization and the "spatial fix"', *Geographische Revue: Zeitschrift für Literatur und Diskussion*, 3(2): 23–30.

Harvey, D. (2007) *A Brief History of Neo-liberalism*, Oxford: Oxford University Press.

Harvey, D. (2009) 'The right to the just city', in P. Marcuse, J. Connolly and J. Novy (eds) *Searching for the Just City: Debates in Urban Theory and Practice*, Oxon: Routledge, pp 40–51.

Harvey, D. (2012) *Rebel Cities: From the Right to the City to the Urban Revolution*, London: Verso.

Harvey, D. (2018) *The Limits to Capital*, London: Verso.

Harvey, D. and Wachsmuth, D. (2011) 'What is to be done? And who the hell is going to do it?', in N. Brenner, P. Marcuse and M. Mayer (eds) *Cities for People, Not for Profit: Critical Urban Theory and the Right to the City*, London: Routledge, pp 264–274.

Hawkes, J. (2001) *The Fourth Pillar of Sustainability: Culture's Essential Role in Public Planning*, Melbourne: Common Ground.

Haydock, W. (2009) '"Binge" drinking, neo-liberalism and individualism', *9th Conference of the European Sociological Association*, Lisbon, Portugal, [online] 2–5 September, Available from: http://eprints.bournemouth. ac.uk/21033

Haywood, K. and Yar, M. (2006) 'The "chav" phenomenon: Consumption, media and the construction of a new underclass', *Crime Media Culture*, 2(1): 9–28.

Heath, J. and Potter, A. (2006) *The Rebel Sell: How the Counter Culture Became Consumer Culture*, Chichester: Capstone Publishing.

Heath, T. and Strickland, R. (1997) 'The twenty-four hour city concept', in T. Oc and S. Tiesdfll (eds) *Safer City Centres: Reviving the Public Realm*, London: Chapman, pp 170–183.

Hebdige, D. (1977) *Subculture: The Meaning of Style*, London: Methuen.

Heinrich Mora, E., Heine, C., Jackson, J.J., West, G.B., Chuqiao Yang, V. and Kempes, C.P. (2021) 'Scaling of urban income inequality in the USA', *Journal of The Royal Society Interface*, 18: 1–18.

Herrnstein, R.J. and Murray, C. (1994) *The Bell Curve: Intelligence and Class Structure in American Life*, New York: The Free Press.

Hesmondhalgh, D. (2019) *The Cultural Industries* (4th edn), London and Thousand Oaks: SAGE.

Hesmondhalgh, D. and Baker, S. (2013) *Creative Labour: Media Work in Three Cultural Industries*, London: Routledge.

Hetherington, K. (2000) *New Age Travellers: Vanloads of Uproarious Humanity*, London: Cassell.

Hickel, J., Dorninger, C., Wieland, H. and Suwandi, I. (2022) 'Imperialist appropriation in the world economy: Drain from the global south through unequal exchange, 1990–2015', *Global Environmental Change*, 73: 1–13.

Higgins-Desbiolles, F. (2018) 'The potential for justice through tourism', *Via Tourism Review*, 13, [online], Available from: https://journals.openedit ion.org/viatourism/2469

Higgins-Desbiolles, F. (2020) 'Socialising tourism for social and ecological justice after COVID-19', *Tourism Geographies*, 22(3): 610–623.

Hobbs, D., Lister, S., Hadfield, P., Winlow, S. and Hall, S. (2000) 'Receiving shadows: Governance and liminality in the night-time economy', *British Journal of Sociology*, 51: 701–717.

Hollands, R. (1995) *Friday Night, Saturday Night: Youth Cultural Identification on the Post-Industrial City*, Newcastle: Newcastle University.

Hollands, R. (2002) 'Divisions in the dark: Youth cultures, transitions and segmented consumption spaces in the night-time economy', *Journal of Youth Studies*, 5(2): 153–171.

Hollands, R. (2008) 'Will the real smart city please stand up? Intelligent, progressive or entrepreneurial?', *City: Analysis of Urban Trends, Culture, Theory, Policy, Action*, 12(3): 303–320.

Hollands, R. (2009) 'Cultural workers of the world unite, you've nothing to lose but your theatres: "Dny Neklidu" ("Days of Unrest") and the Initiative for a Cultural Prague', *City: Analysis of Urban Trends, Culture, Theory, Policy, Action*, 13(1): 139–145.

Hollands, R. (2010) 'Engaging and alternative cultural tourism? The case of the Prague Fringe Festival (PFF)', *Journal of Cultural Economy*, 3(3): 379–394.

Hollands, R. (2011) 'Corporate or creative city? The role of alternative nightlife in creating a diverse and vibrant after dark economy', a keynote address presented at the event 'States General of the Night', sponsored by Geneva City Council, Geneva, Switzerland, 4 March.

Hollands, R. (2012) '2011 Prague Fringe Festival audience survey', Newcastle University, [online] October, Available from: //efa2idnbmn nnibpcajpcglclefindmkaj/http://2012.praguefringe.com/fileadmin/user _upload/2011_Prague_Fringe_Festival_Audience_Survey__FINAL_.pdf

Hollands, R. (2015) 'Critical interventions into the corporate smart city', *Cambridge Journal of Regions, Economy and Society*, 8(1): 61–77.

Hollands, R. (2016a) 'Prague Fringe audience survey & impact report', Newcastle University, [online], Available from: https://issuu.com/pragu efringe/docs/prague_fringe_audience_survey___imp/16

Hollands, R. (2016b) 'Revisiting urban nightscapes: An academic and personal journey through 20 years of nightlife research', in T. Thurnell-Read (ed) *Drinking Dilemmas: Space, Culture and Identity*, London. Routledge, pp 13–27.

Hollands, R. (2017a) '"Loving your work": Engagement, impact, and the Prague Fringe', *Discover Society*, 46, [online] 5 July, Available from: https:// archive.discoversociety.org/2017/07/05/lovin-your-work-engagment-imp act-and-the-prague-fringe/

Hollands, R. (2017b) 'Urban cultural movements and the struggle for alternative creative spaces', Major Research Fellowship Final Report, Leverhulme Trust, 22 November.

Hollands, R. (2018) 'Creative dark matter rising? Struggling over the future of alternative cultural spaces in the city of Geneva', *Discover Society* (DS58), [online] 3 July, Available from: https://archive.discoversociety.org/2018/ 07/03/creative-dark-matter-rising-struggling-over-the-future-of-alternat ive-cultural-spaces-in-the-city-of-geneva/

Hollands, R. (2019) 'Alternative creative spaces and neo-liberal urban transformations: Lessons and dilemmas from three European case studies', *City: Analysis of Urban Trends, Culture, Theory, Policy, Action*, 23(6): 732–750.

Hollands, R. and Vail, J. (2012) 'The art of social movement: Cultural opportunity, mobilisation, and framing in the early formation of the Amber Collective', *Poetics*, 40(1): 22–43.

Hollands, R. and Vail, J. (2015) 'Place imprinting and the arts: A case of the Amber Collective', *Local Economy*, 30(2): 173–190.

Hollands, R., Berthet, M.A., Nada, E. and Bjertnes, V. (2017) 'Urban cultural movements and the night: Struggling for the "right to the creative (party) city" in Geneva', in J. Hannigan and G. Richards (eds) *The SAGE Handbook of New Urban Studies*, London: SAGE, pp 295–310.

Holmes, N. and Berube, A. (2016) 'City and metropolitan inequality on the rise, driven by declining incomes', *Brookings*, [online] 14 January, Available from: https://www.brookings.edu/research/city-and-metropolitan-inequal ity-on-the-rise-driven-by-declining-incomes/

Hossfeld Etyang, J., Nyairo, J. and Sievers, F. (2020) *Ten Cities: Clubbing in Nairobi, Cairo, Kyiv, Johannesburg, Berlin, Naples, Luanda, Lagos, Bristol, Lisbon 1960 – March 2020*, Leipzig: Spector Books.

Hough, P. (2019) 'The most creative cities on earth', *Think!Creative*, [online] 27 September, Available from: https://www.linkedin.com/pulse/most-creative-cities-earth-paul-hough/

Hunter-Pazzara, B. (2019) '"12th Street is Dead": Techno-heritage and neoliberal contestation in the Maya Riviera', *Social Sciences*, 8(8): 1–17.

Husson, M. and Louçã, F. (2012) 'Late capitalism and neo-liberalism: A perspective on the current phase of the long wave of capitalist development', in L. Grinin, T, Devezas and A. Korotayev (eds) *Kondratieff Waves: Dimensions and Prospects at the Dawn of the 21st Century*, Volgograd: Uchitel Publishing House, pp 176–187.

Hutton, T. (2016) *Cities and the Cultural Economy*, London: Routledge.

Hutton, W. (1995) *The State We're In: Why Britain Is in Crisis and How to Overcome It*, Harmondsworth: Penguin Random House.

Hutton, W. (2005) 'Did I get it wrong?', *The Guardian*, [online] 9 January, Available from: https://www.theguardian.com/politics/2005/jan/09/politicalcolumnists.comment

Hutton, W. (2010) 'Extract: Them and us: Politics, greed and inequality – why we need a fair society', *The Guardian*, [online] 26 September, Available from: https://www.theguardian.com/books/2010/sep/26/them-and-us-will-hutton

Ibis World (2022a) 'Pubs, bars & nightclubs in the EU: Market research report', *Ibis World*, [online] 28 March, Available from: https://www.ibisworld.com/eu/industry/pubs-bars-nightclubs/3445/

Ibis World (2022b) 'Nightclubs in the UK: Market research report', *Ibis World*, [online] 25 February, Available from: https://www.ibisworld.com/united-kingdom/market-research-reports/nightclubs-industry/

Immergluck, D. (2001) 'The financial services sector and cities: Restructuring, decentralization, and declining urban employment', *Economic Development Quarterly*, 15(3): 274–288.

inkifi (nd) 'The world's most creative cities', *inkifi*, [online], Available from: https://inkifi.com/most-creative-cities/

Instant Offices (2021) 'Most entrepreneurial city in the UK 2021', *Instant Offices*, [online], Available from: https://www.instantoffices.com/blog/featured/entrepreneurial-city-uk-2021/#:~:text=Most%20Entrepreneurial%20Cities,were%20registered%20outside%20the%20capital

Institute for Policy Studies (nd) 'Global inequality', *Inequality.org*, [online], Available from: https://inequality.org/facts/global-inequality/

Isaac, R.K. (2009) 'Alternative tourism: Can the segregation wall in Bethlehem be a tourist attraction?', *Tourism and Hospitality Planning & Development*, 6(3): 247–254.

Isaac, R.K. (2010) 'Alternative tourism: New forms of tourism in Bethlehem for the Palestinian tourism industry', *Current Issues in Tourism*, 13(1): 21–36.

Jackson, T. (2016) *Prosperity without Growth: Foundations for the Economy of Tomorrow*, London: Routledge.

Jacobsen, J.K.S. (2003) 'The tourist bubble and the Europeanisation of holiday travel', *Journal of Tourism and Cultural Change*, 1(1): 71–87.

Jansen, N. (2014) 'The OT301 history in words', in F. Keizer (ed) *Autonomy by Dissent: EHBK/ OT301*, Amsterdam: Abnormal Data Processing, pp 247–275.

Jauhiainen, J. (1992) 'Culture as a tool for urban regeneration: The case of upgrading the "barrio el Raval" of Barcelona', *Built Environment*, 18(2): 90–99.

Jessop, B. (1997) 'The entrepreneurial city: Reimagining localities, redesigning economic governance or restructuring capital', in N. Jewson and S. McGregor (eds) *Transforming Cities: Contested Governance and New Spatial Divisions*, London: Routledge, pp 28–41.

Jesus, D.S.V., Kamlot, D. and Dubeux, V.J.C. (2020) 'A critique of the creative economy, creative city and creative class from the Global South', *International Journal of Business Administration*, 11(4): 1–12.

John, A. and McDonald, B. (2020) 'How elite sport helps to foster and maintain a neoliberal culture: The "branding" of Melbourne', *Australia, Urban Studies*, 57(6): 1184–1200.

Johnson, E. (2019) 'This is the only African city to make the top 5 world's most creative cities list', *Face 2 Face Africa*, [online] 23 July, Available from: https://face2faceafrica.com/article/this-is-the-only-african-city-to-make-the-top-5-worlds-most-creative-cities-list/4

Johnson, H. (2020) 'Global nightlife claims $1,500 billion loss due to COVID-19 pandemic', *Travel Daily Media*, [online] 9 September, Available from: https://www.traveldailymedia.com/global-nightlife-claims-1500-billion-loss-due-to-covid-19-pandemic/

Johnston, R., Poulsen, M. and Forrest, J. (2003) 'Ethnic residential concentration and a "new spatial order"? Exploratory analyses of four United States metropolitan areas, 1980–2000', *International Journal of Population Geography*, 9(1): 39–56.

Jones, K.E., Michael, G. and Rob, S. (2019) 'Urban virtues and the innovative city: An experiment in placing innovation in Edmonton, Canada', *Urban Studies*, 56(4): 705–721.

Jones, O. (2011) *Chavs: The Demonization of the Working Class*, London: Verso.

Jordison, S. (2003) *Crap Towns: The 50 Worst Places to Live in the UK*, London: Boxtree.

Joy, M. and Vogel, R.K. (2021) 'Beyond neoliberalism: A policy agenda for a progressive city', *Urban Affairs Review*, 27(5): 1372–1409.

Just Stop Oil (2022) 'Just stop oil', [online], Available from: https://just stopoil.org/

Kallis, G. (2018) *Degrowth*, Newcastle: Agenda.

Kallis, G., Demaria, F. and D'Alisa, G. (2015) 'Introduction: Degrowth', in G. D'Alisa, F. Demaria and G. Kallis (eds) *Degrowth: A Vocabulary for a New Era*, London and New York: Routledge, pp 1–18.

Kalvapalle, R. (2016) 'Rio de Janeiro welcomed 1.17 million tourists in two weeks', *Marca*, [online] 24 August, Available from: https://www.marca. com/en/olympic-games/2016/08/24/57bda7a0468aeb3e158b4596.html

Karp, P. and Hutchens, G. (2018) 'Neoliberalism has caused "misery and division", Bernie Fraser says', *The Guardian*, [online] 16 October, Available from: https://www.theguardian.com/business/2018/oct/17/neoliberal ism-has-caused-misery-and-division-bernie-fraser-says

Kassis, R., Solomon, R. and Higgins-Desbiolles, F. (2016) 'Solidarity tourism in Palestine: The Alternative Tourism Group of Palestine as a catalyzing instrument of resistance', in R. Isaac, C.M. Hall and F. Higgins-Desbiolles (eds) *The Politics and Power of Tourism in Palestine*, Abingdon: Routledge, pp 37–52.

Kaymas, S. (2020) 'Is development possible without cultural policies? Rethinking creative industries and sustainable development in the case of Turkey', *Creative Industries Journal*, 13(1): 72–92.

Keizer, F. (ed) (2014) *Autonomy by Dissent: EHBK/ OT301*, Amsterdam: Abnormal Data Processing.

Kilic, S. (2021) 'Does COVID-19 as a long wave turning point mean the end of neoliberalism?', *Critical Sociology*, 47(4–5): 609–623.

King, D. (2016) 'WTF?! (What the Fr★nge?!)', World Infringement Congress presentation, *YouTube*, [online] 19 November, Available from: https:// www.youtube.com/watch?v=gpKmPor2kk8

Kirchberg, V. and Kagan, S. (2013) 'The role of artists in the emergence of creative sustainable cities: Theoretical clues and empirical illustrations', *City, Culture and Society*, 4: 137–152.

Klinenberg, E. (2018) *Palaces for the People: How to Build a More Equal and United Society*, London: Bodley Head.

Koch, A. (2016) 'On art and life in a vanished wonderland', in U. Brezborn and S. Weismann (eds) *KuLe: Art and Life. A House in Berlin Since 1990*, Berlin: Revolver Publishing, pp 140–144.

Koch, I., Fransham, M., Cant, S., Ebrey, J., Glucksberg, L. and Savage, M. (2021) 'Social polarisation at the local level: A four-town comparative study on the challenges of politicising inequality in Britain', *Sociology*, 55(1): 3–29.

Kolioulis, A. (2018) 'More day in the night? The gentrification of London's night-time through clubbing', *Bollettino della Società Geografica Italiana serie 14*, 1(2): 207–218.

Kong, L. and O'Conner, J. (eds) (2009) *Creative Economies, Creative Cities*, Dordrecht: Springer.

Krätke, S. (2010) "'Creative cities" and the rise of the dealer class: A critique of Richard Florida's approach to urban theory', *International Journal of Urban and Regional Research*, 34(4): 835–853.

Landry, C. (2000) *The Creative City: A Toolkit for Urban Innovators*, London: Earthscan.

Landry, C. (2012) *The Origins & Futures of the Creative City*, Bournes Green: Comedia.

Landry, C. and Bianchini, F. (1995) *The Creative City*, London: Demos.

Laurell, A.C. (2015) 'Three decades of neoliberalism in Mexico: The destruction of society', *International Journal Health Services*, 45: 246–264.

Lavalette, M. and Mooney, G. (eds) (2000) *Class Struggle and Social Welfare*, London: Routledge.

Lawler, S. (2005) 'Disgusted subjects: The making of middle-class identities', *The Sociological Review*, 53(3): 429–446.

Lee, A. (2020) 'Britain's illegal coronavirus raves are impossible to police', *Wired*, [online] 20 June, Available from: https://www.wired.co.uk/article/uk-coronavirus-raves-party-police

Lee, N., Sissons, P. and Jones, K. (2016) 'The geography of wage inequality in British cities', *Regional Studies*, 50(10): 1714–1727.

Lees, L., Slater, T. and Wyly, E. (2013) *Gentrification*, New York: Routledge.

Lefebvre, H. (1996) *Writings on Cities*, Oxford: Wiley-Blackwell.

Le Grand, E. (2019) 'Conceptualising social types and figures: From social forms to classificatory struggles', *Cultural Sociology*, 13(4): 411–427.

Leitner, H., Peck, J. and Sheppard, E. (2007) *Contesting Neoliberalism: Urban Frontiers*, London: Guilford Press.

Leslie, D. and Catungal, P. (2012) 'Social justice and the creative city: Class, gender and racial inequalities', *Geography Compass*, 6(3): 111–122.

Levitas, R. (1998) *The Inclusive Society? Social Exclusion and New Labour*, London: Macmillan.

Levy, H. (2019) 'Mi Casa takes the stage in Bushwick', *Arts in Bushwick*, [blog], Available from: https://artsinbushwick.org/mi-casa-takes-the-stage-in-bushwick/

Ley, D. (1996) *The New Middle Class and the Remaking of the Central City*, Oxford: Oxford University Press.

Lijster, T., Volont, L. and Gielen, P. (2022) 'Cultural commoning in the city', in L. Volont, T. Lijster, and P. Gielen (eds) *The Rise of the Common City*, Brussels: Academic and Scientific Publishers, pp 15–32.

Little, C. (2020) 'The chav youth subculture and its representation in academia as anomalous phenomenon', *M/C Journal*, 23(5), [online], Available from: https://doi.org/10.5204/mcj.1675

Lloyd, R. (2006) *Neo-Bohemia: Art and Commerce in the Postindustrial City*, London: Routledge.

Loader, I. (1996) *Youth, Policing and Democracy*, London: Macmillan.

Lock, S. (2021) 'Largest selected pub companies in the UK 2020, by number of units', *Statista*, [online] 18 June, Available from: https://www.statista.com/statistics/310844/ten-leading-independent-pub-companies-in-the-united-kingdom-uk-by-number-of-pubs-owned/

Lock, S. (2022) 'Number of pubs in the United Kingdom (UK) from 2000 to 2020', *Statista*, [online] 4 March, Available from: https://www.statista.com/statistics/310723/total-number-of-pubs-in-the-united-kingdom/

López, A.M. (2021) 'Tourist numbers in Barcelona's hotels 1990–2020', *Statista*, [online] 14 September, Available from: https://www.statista.com/statistics/452060/number-of-tourists-in-barcelona-spain/

López Morales, E. (2009) 'Urban entrepreneurialism and creative destruction: A case-study of the urban renewal strategy in the peri-centre of Santiago de Chile, 1990–2005', PhD thesis, University College London, [online], Available from: https://core.ac.uk/download/pdf/1687572.pdf

Lorey, I. (2006) 'Governmentality and self-precarization: On the normalization of cultural producers', *transversal texts*, [online] January, Available from: https://transversal.at/transversal/1106/lorey/en

Lorey, I. (2015) *State of Insecurity: Government of the Precarious*, London: Verso.

Loss, L. (2019) 'Tourism has generated 20% of total world employment since 2013', *Tourism Review News*, [online] 7 October, Available from: https://www.tourism-review.com/tourism-industry-is-the-pillar-of-economy-news11210

Luger, J. (2017) 'Whither the creative city? The comeuppance of Richard Florida', *urbanculturalstudies*, [online] 28 September, Available from: https://urbanculturalstudies.wordpress.com/2017/09/28/whither-the-creative-city-the-comeuppance-of-richard-florida/

Luger, J. (2019) 'When the creative class strikes back: State-led creativity and its discontents', *Geoforum*, 106: 330–339.

MacDonald, K. (2022) 'The Perth regions that have had double-digit house price growth in 2022', *The West Australian*, [online] 29 August, Available from: https://www.perthnow.com.au/business/property/the-perth-regions-that-have-had-double-digit-house-price-growth-in-2022-c-8047714

MacDonald, R. (ed) (1997) *Youth, the 'Underclass' and Social Exclusion*, London: Routledge.

MacDonald, R. and Marsh, J. (2005) *Disconnected Youth: Growing Up in Britain's Poor Neighbourhoods*, Basingstoke: Palgrave Macmillan.

MacDonald, R. and Giazitzoglu, A. (2019) 'Youth, enterprise and precarity: Or, what is, and what is wrong with, the "gig economy"?', *Journal of Sociology*, 55(4): 724–740.

MacDonald, R., Shildrick, T. and Furlong, A. (2014) 'In search of "intergenerational cultures of worklessness": Hunting the yeti and shooting zombies', *Critical Social Policy*, 34(2): 199–220.

MacDonald, R., Shildrick, T. and Furlong, A. (2020) '"Cycles of disadvantage" revisited: Young people, families and poverty across generations', *Journal of Youth Studies*, 23(1): 12–27.

Magness, P.W. (2019) 'The fairytale of hegemonic neoliberalism', American Institute for Economic Research, [online] 5 June, Available from: https://www.aier.org/article/the-fairytale-of-hegemonic-neoliberalism/

Malanga, S. (2004) 'The curse of the creative class', *City Journal*, [online], Available from: https://www.city-journal.org/html/curse-creative-class-12491.html

Malmo Tourism (2018) 'Sweden's art scene shows its alternative side in Malmö', *The Local*, [online] 28 September, Available from: https://www.thelocal.dk/20180928/swedens-art-scene-shows-its-alternative-side-in-malmo-malmostad-tlccu/

Mann, K. (1992) *The Making of an English 'Underclass'? The Social Divisions of Welfare and Labour*, Bucks: Open University Press.

Manning, J. (2018) 'Newcastle is "most entrepreneurial city in the UK", new report says', *Chronicle Live*, [online] 15 May, Available from: https://www.chroniclelive.co.uk/business/business-news/newcastle-most-entrepreneurial-city-uk-14661349

Marcuse, P. (2009a) 'From justice planning to commons planning', in P. Marcuse, J. Connolly and J. Novy (eds) *Searching for the Just City: Debates in Urban Theory and Practice*, Oxon: Routledge, pp 91–102.

Marcuse, P. (2009b) 'Post-script: Beyond the just city to the right to the city', in P. Marcuse, J. Connolly and J. Novy (eds) *Searching for the Just City: Debates in Urban Theory and Practice*, Oxon: Routledge, pp 240–254.

Martel, P. and Sutherland, C. (2018) 'Durban's back of port project: A local spatial knowledge production process framed by urban entrepreneurialism', *Urban Forum*, 29: 397–412.

Martin-Iverson, S. (2021) 'The value of the underground: Punk, politics, and creative urbanism in Bandung, Indonesia', *Cultural Studies*, 35(1): 110–135.

Marvell, A. (2006) 'Tourism: The world's biggest single industry', *The Independent*, [online] 21 September, Available from: https://www.independent.co.uk/student/magazines/tourism-the-world-s-biggest-single-industry-5330650.html

Marx, K. (1977) *Capital: A Critique of Political Economy* (Volume 1): *Part 1, The Process of Capitalist Production*, Moscow: Progress Publishers.

Marx, K. and Engels, F. (1981) *The Communist Manifesto*, Penguin: Harmondsworth.

Massey, D. (1991) 'Flexible sexism', *Environment and Planning D: Society and Space*, 9: 31–57.

Masud, F. (2019) 'The growing importance of the night-time economy', *BBC News*, [online] 17 November, Available from: https://www.bbc.co.uk/news/business-49348792

May, T. (2017) 'A creative's guide to Gothenburg & West Sweden: Compact and walkable creativity to inspire', *Creative Boom*, [online] 1 November, Available from: https://www.creativeboom.com/features/the-creatives-guide-to-gothenburg-west-sweden/

Mayer, M. (2006) 'Manuel Castells' The City and the Grassroots', *International Journal of Urban and Regional Research*, 30(1): 202–206.

Mayer, M. (2013) 'First world urban activism', *City: Analysis of Urban Trends, Culture, Theory, Policy, Action*, 17(1): 5–19.

McCabe, S. (2005) 'Who is a tourist? A critical review', *Tourist Studies*, 5(1): 85–106.

McCarthy, N. (2016) 'The world's most creative cities', *Forbes*, [online] 3 November, Available from: https://www.forbes.com/sites/niallmccarthy/2016/11/03/the-worlds-most-creative-cities-infographic/?sh=2a76ad1f4dc1

McCorry, F. (2021) 'UK nightclubs need financial help – and respect for their cultural importance', *The Guardian*, [online] 23 March, Available from: https://www.theguardian.com/music/2021/mar/23/uk-nightclubs-need-financial-help-and-respect-for-their-cultural-importance

McCulloch, K., Stewart, A. and Lovegreen, N. (2006) '"We just hang out together": Youth cultures and social class', *Journal of Youth Studies*, 9(5): 539–556.

McDonough, T. (ed) (2010) *The Situationists and the City: A Reader*, London: Verso.

McGlinn, M. (2018) 'Translating neoliberalism: The European social fund and the governing of unemployment and social exclusion in Malmö, Sweden', PhD Thesis, Malmö University, Faculty of Culture and Society, [online], Available from: https://mau.diva-portal.org/smash/get/diva2:1404314/FULLTEXT01.pdf

McGuigan, J. (2009) 'Doing a Florida thing: The creative class and cultural policy', *International Journal of Cultural Policy*, 15(3): 291–300.

McGuigan, J. (2016) *Neoliberal Culture*, Basingstoke: Palgrave Macmillan.

McIntyre, H. (2015) 'America's 10 biggest nightclubs earned over $550 million in revenue last year', *Forbes*, [online] 26 May, Available from: https://www.forbes.com/sites/hughmcintyre/2015/05/26/americas-10-biggest-nightclubs-earned-over-550-million-in-revenue-last-year/?sh=5cf771264514

McLean, H. (2014a) 'Digging into the creative city: A feminist critique', *Antipode*, 46(3): 669–690.

McLean, H. (2014b) 'Cracks in the creative city: The contradictions of community arts practice', *International Journal of Urban and Regional Research*, 38(6): 2156–2173.

McLeod, G. (2002) 'From urban entrepreneurialism to a "revanchist city"? On the spatial injustices of Glasgow's renaissance', *Antipode*, 34: 602–624.

McRobbie, A. (2016) *Be Creative: Making a Living in the New Culture Industries*, Cambridge: Polity.

Measham, F. (2004) 'Play space: Historical and socio-cultural reflections on drugs, licensed leisure locations, commercialisation and control', *International Journal of Drug Policy*, 15(5–6): 337–345.

Menasce Horowitz, J., Igielnik, R. and Kochhar, R. (2020) 'Trends in income and wealth inequality', *Pew Research Centre*, [online] 9 January, Available from: https://www.pewresearch.org/social-trends/2020/01/09/trends-in-income-and-wealth-inequality/

Michael-Ryan, J. (2020) 'The blessings of COVID-19 for neoliberalism, nationalism, and neoconservative ideologies', in J. Michael Ryan (ed) *COVID-19: Global Pandemic, Societal Responses, Ideological Solutions*, London: Routledge, pp 1–8.

Milburn, K. and Russell, B. (2018) 'What can an institution do? Towards public-common partnerships and a new common-sense', *Renewal*, 26(4): 45–55.

Miles, M. (2013) 'A post-creative city?' *RCCS Annual Review*, 5 [online], Available from: http://journals.openedition.org/rccsar/506

Miles, M. (2015) *Limits to Culture: Urban Regeneration vs Dissident Art*, London: Pluto Press.

Miles, S. and Miles, M. (2004) *The Consuming City*, Basingstoke: Palgrave.

Ministry of Housing, Communities & Local Government (2019) 'English indices of deprivation', *GOV.UK*, [online] 26 September, Available from: https://www.gov.uk/government/statistics/english-indices-of-deprivation-2019

Mitchell, D. (2003) *The Right to the City: Social Justice and the Fight for Public Space*, New York: Guilford Press.

Montreal Infringement Festival (2016) 'Montreal Infringement Festival', [online], Available from: http://infringemontreal.org/archived-pages/2016-festival/montreal-infringement-festival-2016/

Morgan, G. and Ren, X. (2012) 'The creative underclass: Culture, subculture, and urban renewal', *Journal of Urban Affairs*, 34(2): 127–130.

Morris, K. (2017) 'Edmonton tourism numbers up 3.5% over 2016', *Global News*, [online] 20 December, Available from: https://globalnews.ca/news/3928048/edmonton-tourism-numbers-up-3-5-over-2016/#:~:text=Edmonton%20saw%203.3%20million%20overnight,hit%203.5%20million%20by%202020.&text=Perhaps%20the%20most%20surprising%20numbers,in%20visitors%20coming%20from%20overseas

Morris, L. (1994) *Dangerous Classes*, London: Routledge.

Morrison, J. (2019) *Scroungers: Moral Panics and Media Myths*, London: Zed Books.

Mosedale, J. (ed) (2021) *Neoliberalism and the Political Economy of Tourism*, London: Routledge.

Moseley, F. (1991) *The Falling Rate of Profit in the Postwar United States Economy*, London: Palgrave Macmillan.

Mould, O. (2015) *Urban Subversion and the Creative City*, London: Routledge.

Mould, O. (2018) *Against Creativity*, London: Verso.

Mulgan, G. (2015) *The Locust and the Bee: Predators and Creators in Capitalism's Future* (updated edn), Princeton: Princeton University Press.

Müller, A.-L. (2019) 'Voices in the city: On the role of arts, artists and urban space for a just city', *Cities*, 91: 49–57.

Murray, C. (1984) *Losing Ground: American Social Policy, 1950–1980*, New York: Basic Books.

Murray, C. (1990) *The Emerging British Underclass*, London: IEA.

Murray, C. (1994) *Underclass: The Crisis Deepens*, London: IEA.

Murray, M.J. (2004) 'The spatial dynamics of postmodern urbanism: Social polarisation and fragmentation in São Paulo and Johannesburg', *Journal of Contemporary African Studies*, 22(2): 139–164.

Music Declares Emergency (nd) 'Mission', [online], Available from: https://musicdeclares.shop/music-declares-emergency/

Myers, J. (2021) 'These charts show the growing income inequality between the world's richest and poorest', *World Economic Forum*, [online] 10 December, Available from: https://www.weforum.org/agenda/2021/12/global-income-inequality-gap-report-rich-poor/

Nathan, M., Kemeny, T., Pratt, A. and Spencer, G. (2016) *Creative Economy Employment in the United States, Canada and the United Kingdom: A Comparative Analysis*, London: Nesta.

Navarro, V. (2007) 'Neoliberalism as a class ideology: Or, the political causes of the growth of inequalities', *International Journal of Health Services*, 37(1): 47–62.

Nayak, A. (2006) 'Displaced masculinities: Chavs, youth and class in the post-industrial city', *Sociology*, 40(5): 813–831.

Newcastle City Council (nda) 'Build forward better: Our medium-term plan for 2021–22 and 2022–23', [online], Available from: https://www.newcastle.gov.uk/sites/default/files/Build%20Forward%20Better%20-%20our%20medium-term%20plan%20for%202021-22%20and%202022-23_1.pdf

Newcastle City Council (ndb) 'Build forward better: Our medium-term plan for 2021–22 and 2022–23: Appendix 1 – Revenue and capital plan 2021–22', [online], Available from: https://www.newcastle.gov.uk/sites/default/files/Appendix%201%20-%20Revenue%20and%20capital%20plan%202021-22_1.pdf

Newman, J. (2014) 'Landscapes of antagonism: Local governance, neoliberalism and austerity', *Urban Studies*, 51(15): 3290–3305.

Nijman, J. and Wei, Y.D. (2020) 'Urban inequalities in the 21st century economy', *Applied Geography*, 117: 1–8.

NiON (2010) 'Not in our name! Jamming the gentrification machine: A manifesto', *City: Analysis of Urban Trends, Culture, Theory, Policy, Action*, 14(3): 323–325.

Nkula-Wenz, L. (2019) 'Worlding Cape Town by design: Encounters with creative cityness', *Economy and Space*, 51(3): 581–597.

Nofre, J. (2020) 'Because the night belongs to us', *Emulations – Revue de Sciences Sociale*s, 33: 129–138.

Nofre, J. (2021) 'Nightlife as a source of social wellbeing, community-building and psychological mutual support after the Covid-19 pandemic', *Annals of Leisure Research*, [online], Available from: https://www.tandfonl ine.com/doi/full/10.1080/11745398.2021.1964991

Nofre, J. and Martins, J.C. (2017) 'The Disneyfication of the neoliberal urban night', in P. Guerra and T. Moreira (eds) *Keep it Simple Make it Fast! An Approach to Underground Music Scenes*, Porto: University of Porto Press, vol 3, pp 113–124.

Nofre, J. and Eldridge, A. (2018) *Exploring Nightlife: Space, Society and Governance*, London: Rowman & Littlefield.

Norman, A. (2021) 'The UK's sub-regional inequality challenge', *Centre for Progressive Policy*, [online] 12 January, Available from: https://www.prog ressive-policy.net/publications/the-uks-sub-regional-inequality-challe nge#:~:text=Of%20the%20290%20OECD%20regions,across%20the%20 290%20OECD%20regions

North, P. and Nurse, A. (2014) 'Beyond entrepreneurial cities: Towards a post-capitalist grassroots urban politics of climate change and resource constraint', *Metropoles*, 15: 1–20.

Novy, J. (2018) 'The selling (out) of Berlin and the de- and re-politicization of urban tourism in Europe's "capital of cool"', in C. Colomb and J. Novy, *Protest and Resistance in the Tourist City*, London: Routledge, pp 52–72.

Novy, J. and Colomb, C. (2013) 'Struggling for the right to the (creative) city in Berlin and Hamburg: New urban social movements, new "spaces of hope"?', *International Journal of Urban and Regional Research*, 37(5): 1816–1838.

Novy, J. and Colomb, C. (2018) 'Urban tourism and its discontents: An introduction', in C. Colomb and J. Novy, *Protest and Resistance in the Tourist City*, London: Routledge, pp 1–29.

Novy, J. and Colomb, C. (2019) 'Urban tourism as a source of contention and social mobilisations: A critical review', *Tourism Planning & Development*, 16(4): 358–375.

Oakley, K. (2009) 'From bohemia to britart: Art students over 50 years', *Cultural Trends*, 18(4): 281–294.

Oakley, K. and O'Connor, J. (eds) (2015) *The Routledge Companion to the Cultural Industries*, London: Routledge.

Oakley, K. and Ward, J (2018) 'The art of the good life: Culture and sustainable prosperity', *Cultural Trends*, 27(1): 4–17.

Oakley, K. and Banks, M. (2020) 'Cultural industries and environmental crisis: An introduction', in K. Oakley and M. Banks (eds) *Cultural Industries and the Environmental Crisis: New Approaches for Policy*, Cham: Springer, pp 1–10.

O'Brien, D. (2020) 'Class and the problem of inequality in theatre', *Studies in Theatre and Performance*, 40(3): 242–250.

O'Brien, P. and Pike, A. (2019) '"Deal or no deal?": Governing urban infrastructure funding and financing in the UK city deals', *Urban Studies*, 56(7): 1448–1476.

O'Connor, J. (2020) 'Art and culture after Covid-19', *Wake in Fright: Fearful and Hopeful Things*, [blog] 9 April, Available from: https://wakeinalarm.blog/2020/04/09/art-and-culture-after-covid-19/

O'Connor, J. (2022) 'Art, culture and the foundational economy', Working Paper Reset No 2, Creative People, Products and Places, University of South Australia, [online], Available from: https://resetartsandculture.com/wp-content/uploads/2022/02/CP3-Working-Paper-Art-Culture-and-the-Foundational-Economy-2022.pdf

O'Connor, J. and Shaw, K. (2014) 'What next for the creative city?', *City Culture and Society*, 5: 165–170.

O'Connor, J. and Gu, X. (2020) *Red Creative: Culture and Modernity in China*, Bristol: Intellect.

O'Connor, J., Gu, X. and Lim, M.K. (2020) 'Creative cities, creative classes and the global modern', *City, Culture and Society*, 21: 100344.

Office for National Statistics (2021) 'Household income inequality, UK: Financial year ending 2020', *Census 2021*, [online] 21 January, Available from: https://www.ons.gov.uk/peoplepopulationandcommunity/personalandhouseholdfinances/incomeandwealth/bulletins/householdincomeinequalityfinancial/financialyearending2020

Office for National Statistics (2022) 'Distribution of individual total wealth by characteristic in Great Britain: April 2018 to March 2020', *Census 2021*, [online] 7 January, Available from: https://www.ons.gov.uk/peoplepopulationandcommunity/personalandhouseholdfinances/incomeandwealth/bulletins/distributionofindividualtotalwealthbycharacteristicingreatbritain/april2018tomarch2020

Oliver, H. (2021) 'The 49 coolest neighbourhoods in the world' *Time Out*, [online], Available from: https://www.timeout.com/coolest-neighbourhoods-in-the-world

Oloukoï, C. (2018) 'Precarious gentrification: Dreading the night while "taking back the city" in Johannesburg', in J. Nofre and A. Eldridge (eds) *Exploring Nightlife: Space, Society and Governance*, London: Rowman & Littlefield, pp 19–34.

O'Sullivan, F. (2019) 'Berlin builds an arsenal of ideas to stage a housing revolution', *Citylab*, [online] 21 February, Available from: https://www.citylab.com/equity/2019/02/berlin-germany-housing-rent-how-much-price-landlord-policies/582898/

Owens, L. (2008) 'From tourists to anti-tourists to tourist attractions: The transformation of the Amsterdam squatters' movement', *Social Movement Studies*, 7(1): 43–59.

Owyang, M. and Shell, H. (2016) 'Measuring trends in income inequality', *Federal Reserve Bank of St Louis*, [online] 30 March, Available from: https://www.stlouisfed.org/publications/regional-economist/april-2016/measuring-trends-in-income-inequality#authorbox

Paige, M. (2014) 'Alternative Berlin walking tour & the killer doner kebab', *Escape: The Overseas Escape*, [blog] 8 July, Available from: http://theoverseasescape.com/alternative-berlin-walking-tour-the-killer-doner-kebab/

Palmer, B. (2000) *Cultures of Darkness: Night Travels in the Histories of Transgression*, New York: Monthly Review Press.

Papadopolous, A. (2019) 'The world's best nightlife destinations for 2019', *CEOWORLD Magazine*, [online] 13 June, Available from: https://ceoworld.biz/2019/06/13/the-worlds-best-nightlife-destinations-for-2019/

Park, R. (2013) 'Human ecology', in J. Lin and C. Mele (eds) *The Urban Sociology Reader* (2nd edn), London: Routledge, pp 83–90.

Parker, B. (2008) 'Beyond the class act: Gender and race in the "creative city" discourse', in J.N. Desena (ed) *Gender in an Urban World*, Bingley: Emerald Group Publishing, pp 201–232.

Parnell, S. and Robinson, J. (2012) '(Re)theorizing cities from the global south: Looking beyond neoliberalism', *Urban Geography*, 33(4): 593–617.

Pattaroni L. (2014) 'The fallow lands of the possible: An inquiry into the enacted critic of capitalism in Geneva's squats' in C. Cattaneo, M. Martinez and Squatting Europe Kollective (eds) *The Squatters' Movement in Europe: Everyday Commons and Autonomy as Alternatives to Capitalism*, London: Pluto, pp 60–80.

Pattaroni L. (ed) (2020) *The Domesticated Counterculture: Art, Space and Politics in the 'Gentrified' City*, Geneva: Metispresse.

Patti, D. and Polyák, L. (eds) (2017) *Funding the Cooperative City: Community Finance and the Economy of Civic Spaces*, Vienna: Cooperative City Books.

Pearlman, J. (2011) *Favela: Four Decades of Living on the Edge in Rio de Janeiro*, Oxford: Oxford University Press.

Peck, J. (2005) 'Struggling with the creative class', *International Journal of Urban and Regional Research*, 29(4): 740–770.

Peck, J. (2011) 'Recreative city: Amsterdam, vehicular ideas and the adaptive spaces of creative policy', *International Journal of Urban and Regional Research*, 36(3): 462–485.

Peck, J. (2012) 'Austerity urbanism', *City: Analysis of Urban Trends, Culture, Theory, Policy, Action*, 16(6): 626–655.

Peck, J. (2014) 'Entrepreneurial urbanism: Between uncommon sense and dull compulsion', *Geografska Annaler: Series B, Human Geography*, 96(4): 396–401.

Peck, J. and Tickell, A. (2002) 'Neoliberalizing space', in N. Brenner and N. Theodore (eds) *Spaces of Neo-liberalism: Urban Restructuring in North America and Western Europe*, Oxford: Blackwell, pp 33–57.

Peck, J. and Theodore, N. (2019) 'Still neoliberalism?', *The South Atlantic Quarterly*, 118(2): 245–265.

Peck, J., Brenner, N. and Theodore, N. (2018) 'Actually existing neoliberalism', in D. Cahill, M. Cooper, M. Konings and D. Primrose (eds) *The SAGE Handbook of Neoliberalism*, London: SAGE, pp 3–15.

Perry, G. (2014) *Playing to the Gallery: Helping Contemporary Art in its Struggle to Be Understood*, London: Particular Books.

Petrovics, N. and Seijas, A. (2021) 'Chapter 5: Nighttime governance in times of covid-19', *Global Night-time Recovery Plan*, Vibelab, [online], Available from: https://www.mcgill.ca/centre-montreal/files/centre-montreal/ch5_ nighttime_governance_gnrp.pdf

Phelps, N. and Miao, J. (2019) 'Varieties of urban entrepreneurialism', *Dialogues in Human Geography*, 5(2): 183–200.

Picaud, M. (2019) 'Putting Paris and Berlin on show: Nightlife in the struggles to define cities' international position' in G. Stahl and G. Bottà (eds) *Nocturnes: Popular Music and the Night*, Basingstoke: Palgrave Macmillan, pp 35–48.

Pike, A., O'Brien, P., Strickland, T., Thrower, G. and Tomaney, J. (2019) *Financialising City Statecraft and Infrastructure*, Cheltenham: Edward Elgar.

Piketty, T. and Saez, E. (2003) 'Income inequality in the United States, 1913–1998', *The Quarterly Journal of Economics*, 118(1): 1–39.

Pile, S. (1998) 'What is a city?', in D. Massey, J. Allen and S. Pile (eds) *City Worlds*, New York: Routledge, pp 3–50.

Pinson, G. and Morel Journel, C. (2016) 'The neoliberal city: Theory, evidence, debate', *Territory, Politics, Governance*, 4(2): 137–153.

Piramal Raje, A. (2015) 'Why and how cities succeed', *Mint*, [online] 14 January, Available from: https://www.livemint.com/Politics/3SuJPrCazdq MrCPZPmBGqN/Why-and-how-cities-succeed.html

Pixová, M. (2012) 'Struggle for right to the city: Alternative spaces in post-socialist Prague', PhD thesis, Charles University, Prague, [online], Available from: http://mikatchou.files.wordpress.com/2012/11/dz-pixovc3a1-alte rnative-spaces-in-prague.pdf

Pixová, M. and Sládek, J. (2018) 'Touristification and awakening civil society in post-socialist Prague', in C. Colomb and J. Novy (eds), *Protest and Resistance in the Tourist City*, London: Routledge, pp 73–89.

Prada-Trigo, J. (2017) 'The transition to entrepreneurial governance in a middle-sized Ecuadorian city', *Latin American Perspectives*, 44(6): 124–139.

Pratt, A. (2011) 'The cultural contradictions of the creative city', *City, Culture and Society*, 2: 123–130.

Pratt, A. (2018) 'Gentrification, artists and the cultural economy', in L. Lees and M. Philips (eds) *Handbook of Gentrification Studies*, Cheltenham: Edward Elgar, pp 346–362.

Pratt, A. and Jeffcut, P. (2009) *Creativity, Innovation and the Cultural Economy*, Hoboken: Taylor & Francis.

Pritchard, S. (2018) 'Place guarding: Activist art against gentrification', in C. Courage and A. McKeown (eds) *Creative Placemaking: Research, Theory and Practice*, London: Routledge, pp 140–155.

Proctor, K. (2014) 'From party city to trendy toon: How Newcastle went upmarket', *Chronicle Live*, [online] 13 December, Available from: https://www.chroniclelive.co.uk/news/north-east-news/party-city-trendy-toon---8280468

Pruijt, H. (2004) 'Squatters in the creative city: Rejoinder to Justus Uitermark', *International Journal of Urban and Regional Research*, 28(3): 699–705.

Purcell, M. and Brown, J.C. (2005) 'Against the local trap: Scale and the study of environment and development', *Progress in Development Studies*, 5(4): 279–297.

Quaglieri Domínguez, A. and Scarnato, A. (2017) 'The Barrio Chino as last frontier: The penetration of everyday tourism in the dodgy heart of the Raval', in M. Gravari-Barbas and S. Guinand (eds) *Tourism and Gentrification in Contemporary Metropolises*, London: Routledge, pp 107–133.

Quinn, B. (2010) 'Arts festivals, urban tourism and cultural policy', *Journal of Policy Research in Tourism, Leisure and Events*, 2(3): 264–279.

Raco, M. and Tunny, E. (2010) 'Visibilities and invisibilities in urban development: Small business communities and the London Olympics 2012', *Urban Studies*, 47(10): 2069–2091.

Ramos, R. (2009) 'The new guard: How Latin America's creative class can help the region', *Culture & Religion*, 1, [online] 13 June, Available from: https://bigthink.com/culture-religion/the-new-guard-how-latin-americas-creative-class-can-help-the-region/

Richards, G. (1996) 'Cultural tourism in Europe', *CAB International*, [online], Available from: http://www.atlas-euro.org/pages/pdf/cultural%20tourism%20in%20europe.PDF

Richards, G. and Paolo Russo, A. (2014) 'Alternative and creative tourism', *Association for Tourism and Leisure Education*, [online] September, Available from: https://www.academia.edu/8263324/Alternative_and_Creat ive_Tourism

Rietz–Rakul, E. and Schepens, S. (2010) *Berlin Contemporary Art*, Berlin: Grebennikov Explorise.

Ro, C. (2022) 'How to make movies without a huge carbon footprint', *BBC News*, [online] 17 August, Available from: https://www.bbc.co.uk/ news/business-62051070

Roberts, M. and Eldridge, A. (2009) *Planning the Night-time City*, London: Routledge.

Robinson, F. (1988) *Post-industrial Tyneside: An Economic and Social Survey of Tyneside in the 1980's*, Newcastle: Newcastle Libraries & Information Service.

Robinson, F. (1994) 'Something old, something new? The Great North in the 1990s', in P. Garrahan and P. Stewart (eds) *Urban Change and Renewal: The Paradox of Place*, Aldershot: Avebury, pp 9–20.

Robinson, F. and Gregson, N. (1992) 'The "underclass": A class apart?', *Critical Social Policy*, 12(34): 38–51.

Robinson, R., Martins, A., Solnet, D. and Baum, T. (2019) 'Sustaining precarity: Critically examining tourism and employment', *Journal of Sustainable Tourism*, 27(7): 1008–1025.

Rodríguez, J.P. (2021) 'The politics of neoliberalism in Latin America: Dynamics of resilience and contestation', *Sociology Compass,* 15: 1–13.

Romeiro, P. (2017) '"Manobras no Porto" project (Porto): What can creative activism do for policies and urban place(-making) and the other way around', *City, Culture and Society*, 8: 27–34.

Rossen, I. (2017) 'Olympic gentrification? Hackney Wick, London: from petrol refining to showcasing arts', *The Urban Transcripts Journal*, 1(1), [online] March, Available from: https://journal.urbantranscripts.org/arti cle/from-petrol-refining-to-showcasing-arts-olympic-gentrification-rese arching-urban-transition-in-hackney-wick-london-isabella-rossen/

Rossiaud, J. (2004) 'Le mouvement squat à Genève. Luttes urbaines, expériences communautaires, affirmation locale d'une contre-culture globale', *Equinoxe*, 24: 96–113.

Russell, B. (2019) 'Beyond the local trap: New municipalism and the rise of the fearless cities', *Antipode*, 51(3): 989–1010.

Russo, A.P. and Scarnato, A. (2018) '"Barcelona in common": A new urban regime for the 21st-century tourist city?', *Journal of Urban Affairs*, 40(4): 455–474.

Ryan, L. (2018) 'Ruskin the radical: Why the Victorian thinker is back with a vengeance', *The Guardian*, [online] 30 August, Available from: https:// www.theguardian.com/culture/2018/aug/30/john-ruskin-artists-victor ian-social-critic

Sachs Olsen, C. (2019) *Socially Engaged Art and the Neoliberal City*, London: Routledge.

Salas, E.B. (2022) 'Number of flights performed by the global airline industry from 2004 to 2022', *Statista*, [online] 12 April, Available from: https://www.statista.com/statistics/564769/airline-industry-number-of-flights/

Salazar, J.F. (2015) 'Buen vivir: South America's rethinking of the future we want', *The Conversation*, [online] 24 July, Available from: https://theconversation.com/buen-vivir-south-americas-rethinking-of-the-fut ure-we-want-44507

Salerno, G.-M. (2022) 'Touristification and displacement: The long-standing production of Venice as a tourist attraction', *City: Analysis of Urban Change, Theory, Action*, 26(2–3): 519–541.

Saltmarsh, D. (2011) 'In Geneva, counterculture pushes back', *New York Times*, [online] 22 February, Available from: http://www.nytimes.com/2011/02/23/arts/23iht-swissart23.html

Sanchez Belando, M.V. (2017) 'Building alternatives to the creative turn in Barcelona: The case of the socio-cultural centre Can Batllo', *City, Culture and Society*, 8: 35–42.

Sandoval, M. (2016) 'Fighting precarity with co-operation? Worker co-operatives in the cultural sector', *New Formations*, 88: 51–68.

Sassen, S. (1991) *Global City: New York, London and Tokyo* (2nd edn), Princeton: Princeton University Press.

Saunders, P. (1981) *Social Theory and the Urban Question*, London: Routledge.

Sayer, A. (2015) *Why We Can't Afford the Rich*, Cambridge: Polity Press.

Scherer, J. and Davidson, J. (2011) 'Promoting the "arriviste" city: Producing neoliberal urban identity and communities of consumption during the Edmonton Oiler's 2006 playoff campaign', *International Review for the Sociology of Sport*, 46: 157–180.

Schönwälder, G. (2002) *Linking Civil Society and the State: Urban Popular Movements, the Left, and Local Government in Peru, 1980–1992*, University Park: Penn State University Press.

Schouten, P. (2008) 'Theory talk #20: David Harvey on the geography of capitalism, understanding cities as polities and shifting imperialisms', *Theory Talks*, [online] 9 October, Available from: http://www.theorytalks.org/2008/10/theory-talk-20-david-harvey.html

Scott, A. (2000) *The Cultural Economy of Cities*, London: SAGE.

Scott, A. (2008) *Social Economy of the Metropolis*, Oxford: Oxford University Press.

Scott, A. (2014) 'Beyond the creative city: Cognitive-cultural capitalism and the new urbanism', *Regional Studies*, 48(4): 565–578.

Screti, F. (2022) 'Populism in mediated anti-tourism discourse: A critical analysis of the documentary tourist go home!', *Journal of Tourism and Cultural Change*, 20(5): 617–632.

Seah, C. (2020) 'The gentrification conflict: Death by cappuccino', [blog] 14 March, Available from: https://christelseah.medium.com/the-gentrif ication-conflict-death-by-cappuccino-4c7e93428478

Segovia, C. and Hervé, J. (2022) 'The creative city approach: Origins, construction and prospects in a scenario of transition', *City, Territory and Architecture*, 9(29), [online], Available from: https://doi.org/10.1186/s40 410-022-00178-x

Seminario, M. (2020) 'The creative economy in Latin America', *Center for Strategical & International Studies*, [online] 15 September, Available from: https://www.csis.org/analysis/creative-economy-latin-america

Senate Department for Economics Energy and Public Enterprises (2018) 'Sustainable and city-compatible Berlin tourism plan 2018+', [online] July, Available from: https://about.visitberlin.de/sites/default/files/2018-07/ Berlin%20Tourism%20Plan%202018%2B_summary_EN.pdf

Sequera, J. and Nofre, J. (2018) 'Shaken, not stirred: New debates on touristification and the limits of gentrification', *City: Analysis of Urban Change, Theory, Action*, 22(5–6): 843–855.

Serafini, P. (2020) 'Cultural production beyond extraction? A first approach to extractivism and the cultural and creative industries in Argentina', in K. Oakley and M. Banks (eds) *Cultural Industries and the Environmental Crisis: New Approaches for Policy*, Cham: Springer, pp 51–63.

Serafini, P. and Banks, M. (2020) 'Living precarious lives? Time and temporality in visual arts careers', *Culture Unbound*, 12(2): 351–372.

Serafini, P., Holtaway, J. and Cossu, A. (eds) (2018) *artWORK: Art, Labour and Activism*, London: Rowman & Littlefield.

Seymour, A. (2019) 'Data crunch: UK's four largest pub groups hold 25.5% of the market', *Food Service Equipment Journal*, [online] 24 October, Available from: https://www.foodserviceequipmentjournal.com/data-crunch-uks- four-largest-pub-groups-hold-25-5-of-the-market/

Shaw, K. (2005) 'The place of alternative culture and the politics of its protection in Berlin, Amsterdam and Melbourne', *Planning Theory & Practice*, 6(2): 149–169.

Shaw, K. (2013) 'Independent creative subcultures and why they matter', *International Journal of Cultural Policy*, 19(3): 333–352.

Shaw, K. (2014) 'Melbourne's creative spaces program: Reclaiming the "creative city" (if not quite the rest of it)', *City, Culture and Society*, 5: 139–147.

Shaw, R. (2010) 'Neoliberal subjectivities and the development of the night-time economy in British cities', *Geography Compass*, 4(7): 893–903.

Shaw, R. (2015) '"Alive after five": Constructing the neoliberal night in Newcastle upon Tyne', *Urban Studies*, 52(3): 456–470.

Shaw, R. (2018) *The Nocturnal City*, London: Routledge.

Sheller, M. (2018) *Mobility Justice: The Politics of Movement in an Age of Extremes*, London: Verso.

Shenk, T. (2015) 'Booked #3: What exactly is neoliberalism?', *Dissent*, [online] 2 April, Available from: https://www.dissentmagazine.org/blog/booked-3-what-exactly-is-neoliberalism-wendy-brown-undoing-the-demos

Shi, Q. and Dorling, D. (2020) 'Growing socio-spatial inequality in neo-liberal times? Comparing Beijing and London', *Applied Geography*, 115: 1–13.

Shildrick, T. (2018) *Poverty Propaganda: Exploring the Myths*, Bristol: Policy Press.

Shildrick, T. and MacDonald, R. (2013) 'Poverty talk: How people experiencing poverty deny their poverty and why they blame "the poor"', *Sociological Review*, 61(2): 285–303.

Shin, H. (2020) 'From foreign community to creative town? Creativity and contestation in Itaewon, Seoul', in X. Gu, M.K. Lim and J. O'Connor (eds) *Re-imagining Creative Cities in 21st Century Asia*, Switzerland: Palgrave Macmillan, pp 95–111.

Shin, H.B. (2015) 'Economic transition and speculative urbanisation in China: Gentrification versus dispossession', *Urban Studies*, 53(3): 471–489.

Shin, H.B. (2016) 'Envisioned by the state: Entrepreneurial urbanism and the making of Songdo City, South Korea', *LSE Research Online*, [online] June, Available from: https://core.ac.uk/download/pdf/42486722.pdf

Sholette, G. (2011) *Dark Matter: Art and Politics in the Age of Enterprise Culture*, London: Pluto.

Slater, T. (2021) *Shaking Up the City: Ignorance, Inequality and the Urban Question*, Oakland: University of California Press.

Smit, W. (2021) 'Urbanization in the Global South', *Oxford Research Encyclopedia of Global Public Health*, [online] 26 April, Available from: https://doi.org/10.1093/acrefore/9780190632366.013.251

Smith, N. (1984) *Uneven Developments*, Oxford: Basil Blackwell.

Smith, N. (2002) 'New globalism, new urbanism: Gentrification as global urban strategy', *Antipode*, 34(3): 427–450.

Smith, N. (2008) 'Neoliberalism is dead, dominant, defeatable – then what?', *Human Geography*, 1(2): 1–3.

Solnit, R. (2016) '"Hope is an embrace of the unknown": Rebecca Solnit on living in dark times', *The Guardian*, [online] 15 July, Available from: https://www.theguardian.com/books/2016/jul/15/rebecca-solnit-hope-in-the-dark-new-essay-embrace-unknown

Song, Y., Stead, D. and de Jong, M. (2020) 'New town development and sustainable transition under urban entrepreneurialism in China', *Sustainability*, 12(12): 5179, [online], Available from: https://www.mdpi.com/2071-1050/12/12/5179/htm

Springer, S., Birch, K. and MacLeavy, J. (2016) 'An introduction to neoliberalism', in S. Springer, K. Birch and J. MacLeavy (eds) *The Handbook of Neoliberalism*, London: Routledge, pp 1–14.

Stahl, R.M. (2022) 'Neoliberalism with Scandinavian characteristics: The slow formation of neoliberal common sense in Denmark', *Capital & Class*, 46(1): 95–114.

Standing, G. (2011) *The Precariat: The New Dangerous Class*, London: Bloomsbury Academic.

Startupgeeks (2022) 'Most creative UK towns and cities 2022 – our comprehensive ranking of 118 locations', *Startupgeeks*, [online] 21 January, Available from: https://www.creative.onl/startupsgeek/creative-cities/#summary

Steadman-Jones, G. (1969) 'The meaning of the student revolt', in A. Cockburn and R. Blackburn (eds) *Student Power: Problems, Diagnosis, Action*, Harmondsworth: Penguin Books, pp 25–58.

Steglich, U. (2016) 'Open country for a time', in U. Brezborn and S. Weismann (eds) *KuLe: Art and Life. A House in Berlin Since 1990*, Berlin: Revolver Publishing, pp 31–36.

St John, G. (2000) 'Alternative cultural heterotopia: ConFest as Australia's marginal centre', PhD thesis, La Trobe University, Australia, [online], Available from: https://www.academia.edu/2078666/Alternative_Cultural_Heterotopia_ConFest_as_Australia_s_Marginal_Centre

Storper, M. (2016) 'The neo-liberal city as idea and reality', *Territory, Politics, Governance*, 4(2): 241–263.

Straw, W. (2018) 'Afterword: Night mayors, policy mobilities and the question of night's end', in J. Nofre and A. Eldridge (eds) *Exploring Nightlife: Space, Society and Governance*, London: Rowman & Littlefield, pp 225–232.

Stren, R. and Polese, M. (2000) 'Understanding the new sociocultural dynamics of cities: Comparative urban policy in a global context', in M. Polese and R. Stren (eds) *The Social Sustainability of Cities: Diversity and the Management of Change*, Toronto: University of Toronto Press, pp 3–38.

Su, X. (2015) 'Urban entrepreneurialism and the commodification of heritage in China', *Urban Studies*, 52(15): 2874–2889.

Sussman, A.L. (2017) 'Richard Florida on why the most creative cities are the most "unequal"', *Artsy*, [online] 9 May, Available from: https://www.artsy.net/article/artsy-editorial-creative-cities-unequal

Talbot, D. (2011) 'The juridification of nightlife and alternative culture: Two UK case studies', *International Journal of Cultural Policy*, 17(1): 81–93.

Tamari, T. (2017) 'Nation branding and the creative city, Tokyo', [online], Available from: https://research.gold.ac.uk/id/eprint/22388/1/Nation%20Branding%20and%20the%20Creative%20City[25SEP2016FINAL-%20First%20Draft]%20(1).pdf

Taylor, M. (2006) 'Welcome to Newcastle, the UK's capital of the arts', *The Guardian*, [online], 30 December, Available from: https://www.theguardian.com/uk/2006/dec/30/arts.artsnews

Thomasson, S. (2019) '"Too big for its boots"? Precarity on the Adelaide Fringe', *Contemporary Theatre Review*, 29(1): 39–55.

Thompson, M. (2020) 'What's so new about the new municipalism?', *Progress in Human Geography*, 36(1): 25–43.

Thompson, M., Nowak, V., Southern, A., Davies, J. and Furmedge, P. (2020) 'Re-grounding the city with Polanyi: From urban entrepreneurialism to entrepreneurial municipalism', *Environment and Planning A: Economy and Space*, 52(6): 1171–1194.

Threadgold, S. (2017) *Youth, Class and Everyday Struggles*, London: Routledge.

Thurnell-Read, T. (2011) 'Off the leash and out of control: Masculinities and embodiment in Eastern European stag tourism', *Sociology*, 45(6): 977–991.

Tickner, L. (2008) *Hornsey 1968: The Art School Revolution*, London: Frances Lincoln.

Tilly, C. (2004) *Social Movements, 1768–2004*, Boulder: Paradigm Publishers.

Times Travel (2022) 'Glasgow: art for heart's sake', *The Times*, [online], Available from: https://www.thetimes.co.uk/travel/glasgow-galleries-pub lic-street-art-tours-visit-scotland/?fbclid=IwAR1jK5qysDmrIcggGGqpL Sz8iVPswRM0Hqv3PL3VCHtju8K2PsGkH8ydUfA

Toro, P.A. (2007) 'Toward an international understanding of homelessness', *Journal of Social Issues*, 63(3): 461–481.

Toronto Creative City (nd) 'Toronto UNESCO creative city of media arts', [online], Available from: http://www.torontocreativecity.ca/about/

Toronto Star (2020) 'What are the most pressing problems facing Toronto? Here's what the city's leaders had to say', *Toronto Star*, [online] 14 February, Available from: https://www.thestar.com/business/2020/01/30/what-are-the-most-pressing-problems-facing-toronto-heres-what-the-citys-lead ers-had-to-say.html

Touraine, A. (1971) *The May Movement: Revolt and Reform*, New York: Random House.

Tourism Department Manager's Office for Enterprise and Tourism (2017) 'Barcelona tourism for 2020: A collective strategy for sustainable tourism', *Ajuntament de Barcelona*, [online] March, Available at: https://ajuntament. barcelona.cat/turisme/sites/default/files/barcelona_tourism_for_ 2020_0.pdf

Townshend, T. (2022) *Healthy Cities? Design for Well-being*, London: Lund Humphries.

Tozzi, L. (2016) 'Emanuele Braga of Macao', *Zero*, [online] 15 April, Available from: https://zero-eu.translate.goog/it/persone/macao-intervi sta-a-emanuele-braga/?_x_tr_sl=it&_x_tr_tl=en&_x_tr_hl=en&_x_ tr_pto=sc

Trans Europe Halles (nd) 'About us', *Trans Europe Halles*, [online], Available at: https://teh.net/about-us/

Trondi, N. (2019) 'Why Bogotá, Colombia, Is Latin America's rising creative hotspot', *MUSE by Clio*, [online] 10 September, Available from: https://musebycl.io/creative-cities/why-bogota-colombia-latin-americas-rising-creative-hotspot

Trust for London and WPI Economics (2022) 'London's poverty profile 2020', *Trust for London*, [online], Available from: https://www.trustforlondon.org.uk/publications/lpp2020/#:~:text=In%2Dwork%20poverty%20is%20rising,from%2062%25%20a%20decade%20ago

Twizell, A. (2020) 'History, heritage and creativity of the town: Two new art installations in Middlesbrough', *TeessideLive*, [online] 16 December, Available from: https://www.gazettelive.co.uk/whats-on/arts-culture-news/arts-culture-middlesbrough-partnership-installations-19461755

Tyler, I. (2006) 'Chav scum: The filthy politics of social class in contemporary Britain', *M/C Journal*, 9(5), [online], Available from: https://doi.org/10.5204/mcj.2671

Uitermark, J. (2004) 'The co-optation of squatters in Amsterdam and the emergence of a movement meritocracy: A critical reply to Pruijt', *International Journal of Urban and Regional Research*, 28(3): 687–698.

Uitermark, J. (2011) 'An actually existing just city? The fight for the right to the city in Amsterdam', in N. Brenner, P. Marcuse and M. Mayer (eds) *Cities for People, Not for Profit: Critical Urban Theory and the Right to the City*, London: Routledge, pp 197–214.

UNESCO Creative Cities Network (nda) 'Cape Town', [online], Available from: https://en.unesco.org/creative-cities/cape-town

UNESCO Creative Cities Network (ndb) 'Daker', [online], Available from: https://en.unesco.org/creative-cities/dakar

UNESCO Creative Cities Network (ndc) 'Mexico City', [online], Available from: https://en.unesco.org/creative-cities/mexico-city

United Nations (nd) 'Inequality – bridging the divide', [online], Available from: https://www.un.org/sites/un2.un.org/files/2020/02/un75_inequality.pdf

United Nations (2010) 'Creative economy report 2010', [online], Available from: http://unctad.org/es/Docs/ditctab20103_en.pdf

Vail, J. (2022) *Karl Polanyi and the Paradoxes of the Double Movement*, New York: Routledge.

Vail, J. and Hollands, R. (2013) 'Cultural work and transformative arts: The dilemmas of the Amber collective', *Journal of Cultural Economy*, 5(3): 337–353.

Valli, C. (2015) 'When cultural workers become an urban social movement: Political subjectification and alternative cultural production in the Macao movement, Milan', *Environment and Planning A*, 47: 643–659.

Vellinga, M. (2002) 'Globalization and neoliberalism: Economy and society in Latin America', *Iberoamericana: Nordic Journal of Latin American and Caribbean Studies*, 32(2): 25–43.

Venus Orbits for Justice (2015) 'From squatters to owners: Lessons from OT301', *Venus Orbits for Justice*, [online] 10 May, Available from: http://venusorbitsforjustice.tumblr.com/post/118651345634/from-squatters-to-owners-lessons-from-ot301

von Falkenhausen, S. (2016) 'Preface', in U. Brezborn and S. Weismann (eds) *KuLe: Art and Life. A House in Berlin Since 1990*, Berlin: Revolver Publishing, pp 13–15.

Wacquant, L. (2022) *The Invention of the 'Underclass': A Study in the Politics of Knowledge*, Cambridge: Polity.

Wade, M. (2019) 'The rich in Sydney get a bigger share of the income pie', *The Sydney Morning Herald*, [online] 16 June, Available from: https://www.smh.com.au/business/the-economy/the-rich-in-sydney-get-a-bigger-share-of-the-income-pie-20190614-p51xw7.html#:~:text=Greater%20Sydney%20isn't%20just,the%20nation's%20most%20unequal%20region

Wainwright, O. (2017) '"Everything is gentrification now": But Richard Florida isn't sorry', *The Guardian*, [online] 26 October, Available from: https://www.theguardian.com/cities/2017/oct/26/gentrification-richard-florida-interview-creative-class-new-urban-crisis

Wearing, S., McDonald, M., Taylor, G. and Ronen, T. (2019) 'Neoliberalism and global tourism', in D. Timothy (ed) *Handbook of Globalisation and Tourism*, Cheltenham: Edward Elgar, pp 27–43.

Westergaard, J. (1992) 'About and beyond the "underclass": Some notes on influences of social climate on British sociology today: BSA presidential address, 1992', *Sociology*, 26(4): 575–587.

Whiting, S., Barnett, T. and O'Connor, J. (2022) 'Creative city R.I.P.?', *M/C Journal*, 25(3), [online], Available from: https://doi.org/10.5204/mcj.2901

Wilkinson, R.G. and Pickett, K. (2009) *The Spirit Level: Why More Equal Societies Almost Always Do Better*, London: Alan Lane.

Williams, R. (1958) *Culture and Society*, London: Chatto & Windus.

Williams, R. (1977) *Marxism and Literature*, Oxford: Oxford University Press.

Willis, P., Jones, S., Canaan, J. and Hurd, G. (1990) *Common Culture: Symbolic Work at Play in the Everyday Cultures of the Young*, Milton Keynes: Open University Press.

Wilson, M. (2014) 'The gentrification of our livelihoods', *Stretcher*, [online], Available from: https://www.stretcher.org/features/the_gentrification_of_our_livelihoods/

Wilson, W.J. (2012) *The Truly Disadvantaged: The Inner City, the Underclass, and Public Policy*, Chicago: University of Chicago Press.

Witts, S. (2020) 'Deltic saved from administration by Scandinavian nightlife giant', *The Caterer*, [online] 17 December, Available from: https://www.thecaterer.com/news/deltic-nightclub-bought-administration-rekom-scandinavian

Wolifson, P. (2018) 'Civilising by gentrifying: The contradictions of neoliberal planning for nightlife in Sydney, Australia', in J. Nofre and A. Eldridge (eds) *Exploring Nightlife: Space, Society and Governance,* London: Rowman & Littlefield, pp 35–52.

Wood, A. (1998) 'Making sense of urban entrepreneurialism', *Scottish Geographical Magazine,* 114(2): 120–123.

Wood, A. (2017) 'The 10 most creative cities to live in around the world', *Shillington,* [online] 27 November, Available from: https://blog.shillingt oneducation.com/10-best-creative-cities-live-work-play/

World Atlas (2017) 'UNESCO creative cities In South America', [online], Available from: https://www.worldatlas.com/articles/unesco-creative-cit ies-in-south-america.html

World Atlas (2022a) 'The world's most creative cities', [online], Available from: https://www.worldatlas.com/articles/the-world-s-most-creative-cit ies.html

World Atlas (2022b) 'Cities with the most income inequality', [online], Available from: https://www.worldatlas.com/articles/cities-with-the-most-income-inequality.html

World Tourism Organization (1995) *Collection of Tourism Expenditure Statistics,* Madrid: World Tourism Organization.

World Tourism Organization (2015) 'UNWTO tourism highlights 2015', [online], Available from: https://www.e-unwto.org/doi/pdf/10.18111/9789284416899

Wright, E.O. (1998) 'Introduction', in S. Bowles and H. Gintis, *Recasting Egalitarianism,* London: Verso, pp xi–xiii.

Wright, E.O. (2010) *Envisioning Real Utopias,* London: Verso.

Wright, E.O. (2015) *Classes,* London: Verso.

Wynne, E. (2018) 'Perth's Fringe Festival grows to third biggest in the world in just seven years', *ABC News,* [online] 25 January, Available from: https://www.abc.net.au/news/2018-01-26/perth-fringe-festival-grows-to-be-third-biggest-world/9357046

Yeo, S.J., Ho, K.C. and Heng, C.K. (2016) 'Rethinking spatial planning for urban conviviality and social diversity: A study of nightlife in a Singapore public housing estate neighbourhood', *Town Planning Review,* 87(4): 379–399.

Youngs, I. (2019) 'We are Middlesbrough: From a town of industry to a city of culture?', *BBC News,* [online] 24 May, Available from: https://www. bbc.co.uk/news/entertainment-arts-48363282

Zhang, Z., Liang, Z. and Bao, J. (2021) 'From theme park to cultural tourism town: Disneyization turning of tourism space in China', *Regional Sustainability,* 2(2): 156–163.

Zukin, S. (1995) *The Cultures of Cities,* Oxford: Blackwell.

Index

References to figures appear in *italic* type;
those in **bold** type refer to tables. References to endnotes show
both the page number and the note number (178n3).